THE AGE
OF AUTOMATION

THE AGE OF AUTOMATION

Technical Genius, Social Dilemma

GEORGE M. HALL

PRAEGER

Westport, Connecticut
London

Library of Congress Cataloging-in-Publication Data

Hall, George M.
    The age of automation : technical genius, social dilemma / George
M. Hall.
        p.   cm.
    Includes bibliographical references (p.   ) and index.
    ISBN 0–275–95194–4
    1. Automation.   2. Automation—Social aspects.   I. Title.
T59.5.H27   1995
303.48'33—dc20   94–44175

British Library Cataloguing in Publication Data is available.

Library of Congress Catalog Card Number: 94–44175
ISBN: 0–275–95194–4

First published in 1995

Praeger Publishers, 88 Post Road West, Westport, CT 06881
An imprint of Greenwood Publishing Group, Inc.

Printed in the United States of America

The paper used in this book complies with the
Permanent Paper Standard issued by the National
Information Standards Organization (Z39.48–1984).

10 9 8 7 6 5 4 3 2

Copyright Acknowledgments

The author and publisher gratefully acknowledge the following sources for granting permission to
use copyrighted materials:

Excerpt from Harold L. Wilensky, "The Road from Information to Knowledge," in Alan F. Westin,
editor, *Information Technology in a Democracy* (Cambridge, MA: Harvard University Press, 1971).
Reprinted by permission.

Excerpts from Cornelius E. Gallagher, "Computing Power in Real Time," in Alan F. Westin, editor,
Information Technology in a Democracy (Cambridge, MA: Harvard University Press, 1971), 220,
221. Reprinted by permission.

Excerpt from Jerome Lawrence and Robert E. Lee, *Inherit the Wind* (New York: Random House,
1955), 83. Reprinted by permission.

In memory of my grandparents
Richard and Jenny Finley

Contents

IV. AMELIORATION

Illustrations and Tables

ILLUSTRATIONS

TABLES

Preface

The original idea for this book was to demonstrate that man, at least in developed countries, was increasingly subjecting himself to machine logic at the price of individuality. The superintending purpose was to support some work in computer-assisted education. That still holds, but the research yielded a more serious problem—namely, that automation is beginning to *supplant* human endeavor rather than merely support it. This will likely compound, if not create, major economic and sociological consequences, making any educational solution by itself moot.

Philosophically speaking, this is the Frankenstein issue writ large, only this time in a down-to-earth edition in which the debate focuses on matters of degree and the acceleration of trendlines. A case in point was the recent General Accounting Office report on Medicare claims review procedures. The GAO gave high marks to the computer programs that did most of the work, but it had the opposite opinion of the clerks.

Still, the idea of machines replicating humans seemed absurd. In time, however, the problem became abundantly clear. The machines were taking over piecemeal in economic terms. Colloquially speaking, Frankenstein had submitted to plastic surgery and now outfits himself at Brooks Brothers clothiers. Moreover, the poets have been railing against this potential since the time of Jonathan Swift. By the 1940s, the best technical minds began to foresee the problem and began to write a surprising number of books and seminal papers on the subject. All I could do, then, was try to present the evolving picture a little more clearly and offer a few suggestions.

The research also ran into some problems with definitions and with what material to include. First, the terms *computer science* and *robotics* have become increasingly entangled. Accordingly, this book regards them as two facets of automation. On the other hand, the bulk of the text focuses on computer science because robotics can best be understood as a computer program that controls mechanical movement in lieu of processing information. Second, the term *ethics* is used in a broader context than usual and includes the economic consequences of automation because those consequences will have a major effect on people's lives, not always to the good. Third, it was tempting to include extensive detail on existing systems and programs, but that would have detracted from the thesis—namely, to depict the evolving problem.

Fourth, this book does not say much about the international scope of the problem because automation technology is universal, and sooner or later most, if not all, developed countries will encounter the same dilemmas. For example, when Germany was reunified in 1990, the former West Germany was obliged to bail out the former East Germany. In the process, the old Trabant automobile manufacturing plant was replaced with one that relied almost entirely on automation. As a result, it employed only 10 percent of the former workforce, and most of that was drawn from a labor pool other than former Trabant workers. This left a continuing welfare drain to support the vast balance of the newly unemployed. Meanwhile, halfway around the globe in Singapore, the local government installed a massive fiber optics network that is capable of micromanaging almost all human conduct outside the privacy of homes.

On the positive side, the potential benefits from increased automation appear to be much more extensive than at first presumed, and many new sweeping applications are recognized almost monthly. Hence this technology presents a very mixed set of equations to solve. I hope this book provides some insight.

*   *   *

I wish to acknowledge acquisitions editor Lynn Flint at the Greenwood Publishing Group for recognizing the potential value of the manuscript; Cathryn Lee, administrative editor; Patricia M. Daly, the copy editor; and Dina K. Rubin, the production editor.

THE AGE
OF AUTOMATION

I. Setting

This is one of the machines that started it all—an automated loom built around the year 1700. Look carefully at the conveyor belt of punchcards.

1. Early automated loom

It is similar in concept to a piano roll, except that instead of playing music the instructions contained in the arrangement of those holes direct the loom to weave certain patterns. A subsequent model permitted the owner to substitute or insert additional cards, thus combining computer programming with robotics.

Today, this programming technique survives in the familiar but rapidly fading IBM punchcard and more strongly in some commercial washing machines. In the latter, several rows of punchouts represent different functions of the machine, such as hot water, cold water, spin, and so forth. The act of punching different strings of holes in different sequences programs the machine to handle almost any kind of load. The wooden loom also survives but, ironically, *sans* automation. Its purpose has become an avocation—a temporary retreat from the maddening pace of work. Unfortunately, the same cannot be said for other applications of automation. They permeate nearly every aspect of business, of government, and of everyday living, so much so that this technology now threatens, among other things, to displace an increasing amount of human labor without creating compensating jobs.

The four chapters in this part of the book explain the underlying reasons. The first chapter is an overview. The second delves into the technology and concepts behind automation with the purpose of demonstrating that its most advanced forms are only combinations and permutations of distressingly simple steps. The third chapter reviews the bidding on a very old issue—just how far mankind can create machines that in turn overwhelm society. The fourth returns to here-and-now considerations by delineating the major incentives that impel automation to expand much further beyond its already impressive—and invasive—presence.

1

The Machine at the Door

Men become the tools of their tools.
—Thoreau

Historians often divide the past into eras. Each era is marked by a dominant characteristic, of which the Renaissance and the Reformation are perhaps the most well known. At first glance, the current era seems to warrant the title of the Century of Global War. Yet as devastating as the two world wars in this century have been, that militaristic title would be inaccurate. War is common to all of recorded history. The aspects that mark the wars in this century have been the lethality of weapons, the instantaneousness of communications, and the magnitude of logistics capability, in a word *technology*. However, even that view is inadequate. Technology is a permanent part of civilization and is likely to exert an even stronger influence in centuries to come, be it constructive or destructive.

To qualify as the appellation for an era, a dominant characteristic must be resolved or at least fade in importance by the end of a period of time. Automation, admittedly a facet of technology, admirably fills that bill. The term itself did not appear until 1936, but its roots go back perhaps to ancient times and certainly to 1305. In that year, Ramon Lull completed the final version of his *Ars Magna*, a treatise in which he envisioned mechanization of the structure of knowledge, using wheels and gears to relate various ideas.[1] By 1550, the automation concept took root in the form of mechanized water gardens and fountains, later inspiring George Frederick Handel to compose his *Water Music Suite*. By 1700, these toys of kings had evolved into programmed looms to weave various patterns in cloth. Workers fearful for their jobs smashed most of them, and the few that were spared ended up in museums. A century later,

Joseph Marie Jacquard modified the design by adding variable programming.[2] Some of his machines survived the wrath of the working class, and as a result he is now credited with introducing automation into the world of commerce.

A generation later, Charles Babbage obtained funding from the British government to develop what he called an "analytical engine." His government saw its value as an aid to navigation—no small consideration in what was then the world's foremost maritime power. Shortly afterward, his protégé Ada Augusta—the daughter of the poet Lord Byron—wrote a treatise on how to program it. Drawing an analogy to Jacquard's loom, she said the machine could weave "algebraic patterns."[3] Moreover, Ada recognized that Babbage's machine was the first true computer, implying that it would eventually come to fulfill Ramon Lull's prophecy. She said that

> a new, vast and powerful language is developed through which alone we can adequately express great facts of the natural world, and those unceasing changes of mutual relationships which, visibly or invisibly, consciously or unconsciously, are interminably going on in the agencies of the creation we live amidst.[4]

About thirty years later, Stanley Jervons fashioned an automated logic machine that operated somewhat like a piano, and demonstrated it before the Royal Society in 1874, which technically made it the first working computer. Fifteen years after that, a Census Bureau employee, Herman Hollerith, realized that it would take eleven years to compile by hand the data from the 1890 decennial accounting. Accordingly, he persuaded his superiors to give him a contract to build automated tabulators nearer in design to Jacquard's loom than Babbage's engine. When a pin protruded through a punched hole in a data card, it closed an electrical circuit that turned the dial on a counting gauge one notch. Notwithstanding cost overruns, his machines worked well and reduced the anticipated eleven-year period to seven years, not bad for a first try. Afterward, he quit his job and formed a company to sell improved models to the business community at large, apparently with some success. Today that company is known as IBM.

These early computers relied on electricity for both power and some of the processing, but they lacked electronic innards. One might conclude, therefore, that they weren't really computers, merely heavy-duty tabulators. That may be correct in terms of popular definition, but as a matter of principle, it is wrong. A computer is a special case of automation. Automation is any machine that performs work according to instructions held in memory or at least can read. That work may be physical or calculative. Both types result in physical change in some form. In the robot, the change is in the form of useful work. In the computer, it is in the form of a physical display or recording to be read. In short, automation is a generic concept, not a circuit board.

On the other hand, without the benefit of electronics, most forms of automation are dinosaurs. They need miniaturized electronic equivalents of levers and gears in order to achieve high speed, efficiency, and reliability, all at much lower cost. Not surprisingly, research in the first half of this century sought ways to harness this alternative. Unfortunately, the large vacuum tubes of the era proved too cumbersome. Then in World War II, the need to break the German *enigma* code, combined with down-sizing of many electronic components, gave computer science the impetus it needed. The rest is history, although not everyone at first realized what was happening. In 1945, Thomas Watson, Sr., chairman of IBM, projected the worldwide annual market for electronic computers at five units. He later changed his mind.

At any rate, automation—especially computational applications—has vastly exceeded what its most optimistic practitioners envisioned forty years ago. By using parallel processors and advanced optical-media storage, a computer no larger than a briefcase can store more than fifty pages of information on every person in the United States and execute trillions of instructions per second to analyze that data.[5] This would reduce the seven years that Hollerith's machines took to compile the 1890 census to about ten seconds while generating ten times more information in the process. Or, by using image processing, the contents of the Library of Congress could be compressed into the space of a small house, and a hundred pages from that collection could be transmitted anywhere in the world in the same ten seconds. Elsewhere, programs enable physicians to increase diagnostic proficiency from mediocre to near perfection. It wasn't on a whim that *Time* magazine declared the computer as its "man of the year" in 1983.

Overall, then, automation permeates almost every aspect of government, business, and life in general—directly or indirectly—in a spectrum of applications from payrolls to psychiatric therapy. This proliferation is so extensive that if a vast electromagnetic storm shut down every computer, the U.S. economy would freeze.

To date, this trend has been more beneficial than harmful. Automation has created more jobs than it eliminated while permitting other work to be done that would be impossible with the present labor pool. It has opened the door to the exploration of space and has immeasurably aided medical research. Even the side effects have often been more comical than debilitating—for example, the bank that repeatedly dunned credit card holders because they owed zero cents. Unfortunately, this once favorable paradigm is deteriorating into an invidious if not abhorrent range of problems. The reasons whereof underwrite this book.

Argument. Those reasons can be stated in many ways and in many sequences. The one selected parallels the organization of this book:

1. *Automation has reached a point of critical mass at which on balance it can supplant human capability more than it supports it.* The majority of human activity with economic value, both physical and mental, is either relatively simple or can be subdivided into a sequence of simple steps. Automation can both replicate those steps and execute the sequences faster and cheaper, 24 hours per day, 365 days per year. This substitution is not a matter of building robots but networking bits and pieces of electronic and mechanical labor. Automation also has time on its side. Human nature doesn't seem to have changed much in six thousand years of recorded history; technology has.

2. *This critical mass arose from increasingly efficient permutations and combinations of ordinary processes.* Automation draws on neither magic, nor fantasy, nor flights of imagination, nor science fiction, except in the limited sense that many technological innovations first appear as theoretical ideas in literature. Supposedly, this limitation will assuage mankind's angst because the machine will only do what it is told to do. Unfortunately, it is what the machine *can* be told to do that is the problem.

3. *As such, automation bears little physical resemblance to androids or other electronic Frankensteins, yet the piecemeal diffusion of the implementations generates consequences that are more difficult to counter.* Androids are a popular focal point for science fiction, especially R2-D2 and C-3PO from *Star Wars* and Lieutenant Data from *Star Trek*. Perhaps someday in the distant future, these walkie-talkie Erector Sets® will come off the assembly line, but it would be irrelevant to the thesis.

4. *Automation is impelled by enormous economic forces coupled with many subjective counterparts.* If economic leverage is the fuel of business, a continuous expansion of automation is inevitable and, furthermore, most applications will be practical. This situation also implies that society either cannot or will not pull the plug.

5. *The growing dependence on automation is immersed in a socioeconomic malaise which further impels the expansion of this technology.* The principal aspect of this malaise is the massive and exponentially expanding federal debt, which therefore seeks automation as a more cost-effective means of doing business and providing services.

6. *Automation continues to generate enormous benefits; hence most of the side effects arise from excesses.* It takes four chapters in this book just to survey existing and potential benefits of automation. Almost without exception, every side effect results from these benefits being pushed too far.

7. *Of the consequences, automation-related crime is the least controversial from an ethical viewpoint and generates the highest immediate losses.* Although the roots of crime precede technology by millenniums, the increased *magnitude* of these losses is largely attributable to the opportunities presented by vast impersonal automated networks. The losses amount to between $200 and $300 billion annually, perhaps more.

8. *In the long run, however, the greatest economic cost will occur by a realignment of socioeconomic classes.* Automation is reducing the number of jobs, proportional to the working population, and lowering the net skills required of most of the balance. This is a reversal of previous trends, fueled insidiously by both economic incentives and a socioeconomic malaise. Furthermore, the growing proportion of retirees within the population will eventually tax the working proportion beyond its ability to pay.

9. *Automation has also led to a metastasizing invasion of privacy while at the same time encouraging overdependence on its capabilities at the expense of developing critical reasoning, judgment, and a personal sense of responsibility, against which laws to the contrary have succeeded only in delaying the process.* The right-to-privacy issue has been well publicized for more than twenty years, although the pervasiveness of the electronic databases is commonly underestimated. By contrast, the degradation of personal attributes is just now beginning to surface in the literature.

10. *Fortunately, the bulk of these consequences could be ameliorated by a judicious application of automation technology itself, employing countermeasures to offset, if not abate, the excesses.* Unfortunately, it usually takes a crisis to institute fundamental reform, combined with permanent economic incentives to make that reform stick. That's a tall order but strangely the potential of an economic meltdown stemming from the mounting federal debt offers a narrow window of opportunity to achieve it.

The first step in coming to grips with this admittedly long-winded thesis is to understand the idea of *critical mass*—a common enough term—and the related if more abstract concept of *interior lines*. Together, they make automation tick.

Interior lines and critical mass. The expression *interior lines* originated in military history. It describes the advantage that accrues to a defender when surrounded or nearly so. In this situation, the defender's resources are compressed into a small area; hence he can shift and mass them quickly to meet an attack from any direction. As a result, the attacker typically needs a minimum of a three-to-one superiority in strength to dislodge a defender.[6] Thus interior lines partly explain the Union victory over General Lee's stronger forces at Gettysburg. The Union fought a primarily defensive battle from the heights of Seminary Ridge, but it had the advantage of interior lines. Four score and seven years later, United Nations forces—predominantly U.S.—held out along the Pusan perimeter in Korea against at least ten-to-one odds until MacArthur made his spectacular end run at Inchon.[7]

In more general terms, the concept of interior lines means to arrange resources in close proximity with few obstacles between them in order to concentrate those resources as necessary to meet an objective. Cities grow large because they offer efficient interior lines among people of influence and commerce, especially when the location straddles intersecting lines of commerce. This concept also explains the high dollar value of carbon crystals (i.e., diamonds) wherein the perfect alignment of the atoms lets light waves resonate internally. The result is a spectrum of brilliant and sometimes flawless reflections, an interesting phenomenon because carbon is literally the central element in the generation of all living organisms.

On the abstract side, truth itself is said to possess interior lines. A body of facts should not wage war among themselves. When they do, it usually means that the accompanying explanation is faulty. The best explanations adhere to the interior lines of the Euclidean model of logical deduction in order to link clearly the relevant facts in a tightly woven logical network or theory. Lincoln's *Gettysburg Address* grew famous in part because it expressed the essence of his country and the role of the Civil War in a mere 270 words. Most of the newspapers of the day panned it, but Edward Everett (Edward Everett Hale's uncle), who gave the principal oration, wrote to the President the next day: "I wish I could flatter myself that I came as near the central idea of the occasion in two hours as you did in two minutes."

Navy investigators also picked up on the idea of logical interior lines following the recent Tailhook scandal by immediately recording all testimony in a structured text database. Each new piece of evidence was immediately compared to what was known and especially to what the individual being questioned had said previously. Considering the fact that those questioned were stationed all over the world, often on ships at sea, this was no small accomplishment.[8]

Perhaps the simplest way to visualize interior lines is the old pastime of lining up dominos on edge and then felling them in various patterns or sequences. Most arrangements make the dominos fall in a one-for-one sequence. A few, however, progress along multiple branching paths, causing the rate to increase. Conversely, the entire process can be rendered inefficient by removing a few dominos from the chain or placing some of them further apart. The former improves the interior lines; the latter disrupts them.

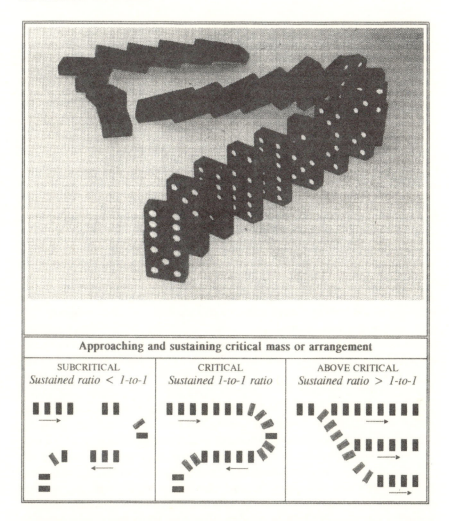

Approaching and sustaining critical mass or arrangement

SUBCRITICAL	CRITICAL	ABOVE CRITICAL
Sustained ratio < 1-to-1	*Sustained 1-to-1 ratio*	*Sustained ratio > 1-to-1*

2. Interior lines and dominos. The concept of interior lines means to place resources in close proximity with the least interference along the routes among them. This lets the user concentrate these resources as needed to meet various objectives. Different arrangements of falling dominos illustrate the principle in action.

The domino idea is more extensive than it may seem. In the summer of 1914, the assassination of Archduke Ferdinand in Sarajevo triggered a chain reaction of events that led to mobilization throughout most of Europe, followed by the outbreak of the first world war. Another chain of events cascaded a larger number of countries into the even more destructive second world war. The psychotic geopolitical hunger of Hitler, Mussolini, and Hideki Tojo was backed by enormous military force that these dictators did not hesitate to use.

In Vietnam, however, the domino theory fell into disrepute. The loss of that country did not lead to a communist takeover of southeast Asia because events, resources, and national propensities were not lined up as they were at the time of the two world wars and because communism by then had decayed into impotency.

Applied to computer systems, interior lines take the form of electronic paths and logical arrays of data. However, because data can be transmitted at nearly the speed of light, physical distance loses its meaning except inside hardware. Thus when the key electronic elements of computers were integrated into a single chip, the interior lines shrank tremendously. This meant that data could be processed with lightning speed at a much lower cost, sparking what is sometimes called the computer revolution.[9] On the other hand, the use of worldwide networks to share masses of data instantaneously demonstrates why physical distance is no longer a barrier.

For a practical illustration, start with hundreds of bibliographic reference papers thrown into a pile helter-skelter. Next, sort them by subtopics. Then place them in a binder with color-coded cross references. Finally, type the essence of the information and data that each source points to, and include a telephone number on each page that will provide more detailed answers to any relevant question, twenty-four hours a day, every day of the year. With each of these steps, the interior lines improve markedly. At a certain point in this progression, even the most lackadaisical individual will begin to take advantage of the system.

The concept of interior lines also leads directly to an understanding of *critical mass*. This term originated in nuclear fission and means "concentrating a sufficient amount of radioactive material to sustain a chain reaction." A chain reaction occurs when the neutrons released from the fission of one atom trigger more than one new fission—like falling dominos arrayed in multiple branches. However, the word *mass* is misleading. Insufficient mass in one arrangement may be more than enough in another. The test explosion near Alamogordo on July 16, 1945, and the bomb dropped on Nagasaki, used an implosion configuration. Implosion works by compressing a subcritical mass of radioactive material. This momentarily reduces the length of the interior lines (the distances between nuclei) sufficient to initiate a chain reaction, like placing dominos that are too far apart closer together. By contrast, the bomb used on Hiroshima was a projectile type that rammed two subcritical masses into one critical configuration. Obviously, it required more total mass than the implosion model, or else the latter would have detonated the moment it was made. Other arrangements also work, but they are used primarily for power generation.[10]

Since that time, the expression *critical mass* has been used analogously to describe a wide variety of phenomena, from "the straw that broke the camel's back," earthquakes, revolutions, epidemics, and perhaps even cancer wherein a single cell among billions suddenly goes berserk and literally consumes its host organism. In these analogous situations, the fact that mass is not converted into energy is irrelevant. Common to all of them is that the interior lines among the constituent elements improve to the point at which each reaction triggers more than one new reaction; hence a great deal of potential energy is suddenly released dynamically. This panorama of explosive events also comes under the heading *catastrophe theory*.[11]

However, the use of the word suddenly to describe critical mass or, more precisely, crucial arrangement, is sometimes inappropriate. For example, cancer does not give the appearance of being explosive, but the damage done is just as bad. In other cases, the repeated two-for-the-price-of-one process may take decades if not centuries. An example of this slow-motion critical mass occurs with compound interest, which is sometimes called "the eighth wonder of the world." Consider a modest one million dollar university-chair endowment invested at 8 percent, including capital growth and dividends. That sum will provide $80,038 per year for a century, at the end of which time the account balance will reach zero. If the endowment is increased by a mere $450, the million dollars will still be there at the end of the hundred years. If it is increased by another $4,050, it will be worth ten million dollars a century later.

Genetics and evolution also demonstrate slow-motion critical mass or, more accurately, crucial arrangement. First, a handful of simple elements combined into peptides, chromosomes, and related constructs. In turn, these constructs combined into viruses and related subcellular organisms, which in turn contributed to the development of cells, which then evolved into complex multiple-cell organisms.[12] On the other hand, no other known arrangement of simple elements—natural or man-made—comes remotely close to yielding the sophistication of *any* organism. The lowly amoeba markedly outclasses the fastest supercomputer in design if not in speed of processing information.

Yet because every biochemical process in every organism comprises permutations and combinations of simple chemical reactions and processes, arrangement (or configuration) per force must play a crucial role. Apparently, a rare few arrangements of various atoms, using carbon as a base, possess especially efficient interior lines to work their productive miracle.[13] Furthermore, the whole scheme of evolution has been mathematically duplicated by a relatively short computer program in which a few key arrangements of numbers and parameters generate an incredible complexity of output, at least symbolically.[14]

The point is that nature itself is automated. It spins and weaves its fabric without any help from mankind and apparently without further intervention on the part of the Creator. Moreover, because genes are said to be programmed, they are being mapped out in increasing detail in the Genome project. Further-more, a year hardly goes by when one or more genes are not linked to some disease, dysfunction, or deformation. In fact, this quest has spawned a new subfield of biology known as *artificial life*, which concentrates on developing computer models to mimic organic phenomena. Thus our ability to program in computer science will continue to yield a better understanding of genetic programming for much the same reason that the existence of closed circulation systems with pumps led Harvey to hypothesize the circulation of the blood.[15]

In other words, mechanical automation replicates its biological forebear and, in a manner of speaking, begins to take on a life of its own. It is doing this by having attained a critical enough mass and an arrangement of its resources that enables it to expand its influence beyond anticipated boundaries. The scientific expression for this is called *reversing entropy*.

Reversal of entropy. Roughly speaking, reversal of entropy means getting more out of a system than is invested in it. Granted, such a feat seems to violate some immutable law of nature, like building a perpetual motion machine that builds additional perpetual motion machines. But reversing entropy is not the same thing as perpetual motion, no more so than the phenomenon of compound interest eventually fattening a small deposit into riches. The scientific understanding of this arose from the study of thermodynamics in the last century. Thermodynamics concerns heat transfer, the equations of which led to three ground rules that are now recognized as having universal application.[16]

• *First Law.* Energy is conserved in all transactions. It can be neither destroyed nor created. However, because mass can be converted to energy and vice versa, this law has been modified to read that the sum of mass and energy is conserved.[17]

• *Second Law.* Energy occurs in two forms, potential and dynamic (or kinetic). The dynamic form does work. The potential form is just that, the potential to do work. Energy is conserved, but the *availability* of energy (its potential form) to do work decreases with time, at least in a *closed* system. A closed system means that no new energy is introduced from or by an external source. The measure of this unavailability is called *entropy*. More entropy means less availability. Another way of describing entropy is that it is the measure of decay, degradation, or self-destruction; in a word, *rot*.

• *Third Law.* On occasion the second law is reversed within a local system. That is, more rather than less potential energy becomes available. This gives the *appearance* of getting something for nothing.[18]

Entropy is sometimes illustrated with a towel. When a towel is used to dry off, it absorbs water until it becomes saturated. When that point is reached, it remains a towel but it is useless. Its "energy" is no longer available and won't be until an external source of heat evaporates some of its water content. Thus a towel which can reverse entropy must, in a manner of speaking, dry itself out faster than it is tasked to absorb water. This may sound ludicrous, but consider the action of a tidal dam. Oceans rise and fall locally because of the gravitational pull of the moon and other factors. A tidal dam retains some of the high water within its walls. As the tide ebbs, the dam discharges water through turbines in order to torque one or more generators. The cost of building and operating these tidal dams—the energy expended—is usually much less than the energy obtained. This is what is meant by a local reversal of entropy. The genetic process reverses entropy far more dramatically than this when unattended it builds a complex sophisticated organism from chemical scraps.

The critic may respond that no new energy is being created in any of these situations. Rather, the systems are merely capable of latching onto energy from their environs and putting it to work in constructive ways. This is absolutely correct, but it has little to do with the point. The point is that in the absence of continual maintenance from external sources, most systems degrade. Their energy content burns up, sometimes literally. Even when a system keeps the residue within its boundaries, the potential to do work dissipates. By contrast, a biological machine invests some of its energy to resupply and maintain itself, at least for its design lifetime. These organisms do not create energy, but they do grab for it tenaciously. Still, nothing more seems to be necessary for nature to create and sustain life. As the French philosopher-physician Julien de la Mettrie put it, "the body is a machine that winds its own springs."

However, except for organisms and metascale phenomena like the evolution of solar systems and planets, this process does not occur in nature very often. Automation can extend the life of a system and reduce the amount of external care and feeding it requires, but to date none of the productions have taken on an *integral* life of their own, bureaucracies excepted. There are no mechanical Frankensteins to consign to the fire or the microwave, as the case may be. On the other hand, the sheer mass of automation is generating an equivalent effect. This technology in the hands of its managers is performing more labor and exerting more control than may be beneficial for a human economy or for personal development.

A columnist for *PC Computing* magazine, Paul Saffo, in recognizing the inevitability of this trend, indicated that he could not determine if he was "exhilarated" or "appalled" by the advances in information handling. He liked what networks had to offer but was bothered by an increasing dependence on distant bureaucracies. It dawned on him that the brief period of anonymity provided by microcomputers had almost come to an end because they merely set the stage for an integrated "global-scale megamachine."[19] This is no idle concern. More than twenty-five million computers worldwide are directly linked to Internet, including tie-ins with at least ten thousand sub-networks.[20]

Thus applied to the argument of this book, automation has reached a point at which it mimics nature's process of genetics and is reversing entropy within the scope of its influence. It returns more than it costs in an ever-widening array of sophisticated applications, although it took almost two centuries to achieve this level of sophistication measured from the advent of Jacquard's loom. The loom eventually gave rise to an assortment of business machines during the first half of this century.

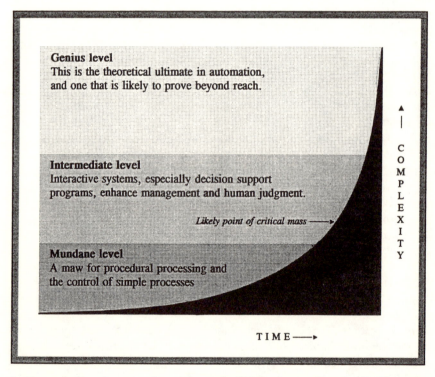

Genius level
This is the theoretical ultimate in automation, and one that is likely to prove beyond reach.

Intermediate level
Interactive systems, especially decision support programs, enhance management and human judgment.

Likely point of critical mass ———➤

Mundane level
A maw for procedural processing and the control of simple processes

C O M P L E X I T Y

T I M E ——➤

3. The evolution of automation. Automation evolved over three levels. The mundane level replicates menial tasks and took the longest time to surmount because of technological obstacles. The intermediate level progressed more rapidly, drawing on combinations of menial applications. Fortunately, the genius level is beyond automation's reach. Unfortunately, that is immaterial in the economic scheme of things.

For the most part, these machines processed routine procedures on a repetitive basis, thus eliminating only the most mundane forms of mental labor. The introduction of electronic computers and electronic control of physical automation elevated the level of tasks performed beyond this, but still well within the range of straightforward procedural logic.

Then as hardware and software gained in sophistication, the applications became interactive and could support higher level mental tasks, including control of lesser tasks. This stage is still evolving, and the frontier now looks to the high end of human intelligence—the province of genius and creativity. More than likely, the curve will prove too steep to scale. Yet while this unscalable height spares the creative genius, it also provides him or her with untoward influence, if not control, over the masses.[21] When Sir Isaac Newton became president of the Royal Society in 1703 (reelected every year for life), there were no scientific periodicals. Instead, copies of letters were circulated by way of his office. Being at the focal point of the interior lines of his day, he sometimes used that office to squelch criticism of himself and to sabotage any papers that might show him in a lesser light than the general public perceived.[22] Aldous Huxley would later say of Newton that "as a man he was a failure, but as a monster he was superb."[23]

Thus the inherent power and capability of automation could easily be abused because a few individuals would be able to control massive databases. This is what is meant by a virtual Frankenstein, a point thrashed out in chapter 3. Of necessity, that discussion is preceded by a primer on automation. While reading that didactic chapter, keep in mind that the most sophisticated applications of automation are only permutations and combinations of ordinary processes, much the same as the whole of genetics, evolution, and physiology arises from sequences of ordinary chemical reactions. In practical terms, these mechanics include the following:

• *Processing efficiency.* Computers are now capable of processing information and answers for virtually all requirements with known or established procedures, at a cost of a millionth of what it would take human labor to grind out by hand.

• *Virtual androids.* Although the popular concept of a robot is a mechanical clone of a human being, the commercial focus is on replicating specialized human functions by machines and then controlling them with some form of network. When the nature of a task makes this impractical, an alternative can often be found that does lend itself to automation.

• *Networks in combination with databases.* Any number of databases can be linked as if they were elements of a single system, notwithstanding physical separation measured in thousands of miles. In theory, everything that mankind knows, including comprehensive data on every individual, can be linked into one network.

• *Image processing*. Image processing stores electronic replicas of documents and all other kinds of paperwork. This will increase the amount of information on tap in automated media from roughly 2 percent (plus another 3 percent in microfilm and variants) to perhaps 50 percent or more, retrievable instantly anywhere in the world by any number of users.

• *Decision support programs*. These programs apply interactive logic to banks of data that have been linked in one or more ways. They do not differ fundamentally from ordinary processing, but the speed, the mass of data, and the ability to interact with human judgment often result in substituting solid analysis for guesswork. Humans can keep a firm grip on these programs, but the more important ones are apt to gravitate to the control of fewer and fewer people unless a concerted effort is made to preclude this.

Complexity of the problems. Although the organization of this book is straightforward, the resolution of the more difficult issues associated with automation are just the opposite. The three following cases briefly illustrate the entanglements:

• *International crime*. International crime is accelerating due to the ease with which proceeds can be laundered through international bank accounts. This practice erases audit trails or relies on a lack of reciprocity agreements. The theoretical solution is an international consortium to monitor all financial transactions, but that would reveal legitimate proprietary information and open the door for an abusive invasion of privacy on personal accounts.

• *Competitiveness*. American business is growing more competitive by emphasizing quality control and reduction of costs. The primary means of lowering costs is labor reduction, and the mainstay of that tactic is to substitute automation for labor. In the early 1980s, Roger B. Smith, then Chairman of the General Motors Corporation, said "every time the cost of labor goes up a dollar an hour, a thousand more robots become economical."[24] But workforce shrinkage means that government tax receipts will fall just as the demand for compensatory entitlements increases. This could lead to an "economic ecology" policy that requires government approval for layoffs or, alternatively confiscatory taxation that negates competitive edge, which of course would further reduce tax receipts.

• *Discrimination via databases.* This practice is exemplified, if that is the correct word, by Courtscan Services. Headquartered in Greenwich, Connecticut, this company offers a proprietary database-access service for doctors on litigation records of prospective patients, and it plans to expand that service to employers with respect to job applicants, to landlords with respect to prospective renters, and so forth.[25] The information sold is clearly public knowledge, but the practice strikes many professionals as morally abhorrent and in all probability will restrict access to health care for some individuals. Doctors in private practice are not legally obliged to accept new patients and may refuse to continue seeing existing patients. Thus should legislation be passed that restricts access to public information? Or should doctors and other professionals be compelled to accept all patients up to some government-regulated minimum workload? Similar questions also apply to Employer's Information Service, located in Gretna, Louisiana. This firm (and several others) provides on-the-job injury-claim information to employers, who can use that information to screen out applicants who have made such claims.[26] Other firms keep tabs on people who have been arrested, regardless of disposition, and on those who have previously legally contested the actions of previous landlords.

2

Primer on Automation

There are no astonishing ways of doing astonishing things.
All astonishing things are done with ordinary materials.
—Benjamin Haydon

In a sense, all machines can be classified as automation. By definition, the operation of a machine replicates some aspect of human activity without *continuous* human oversight except in a few cases as a source of power. Alternatively, machines can perform operations that are beyond the ability of mankind, of which flying is the best-known application. However, as technology progresses, the informal entry level for an apparatus to qualify as automation rises. A washing machine is now considered automatic only if it can be programmed to meet varying requirements of the user. That wasn't true fifty years ago. The key feature, then, is programming, an idea that hasn't changed since Jacquard advanced the design of the automated loom to permit reprogramming by the owner. Furthermore, the programming aspect of an automated machine or a computer itself can be (and has been) built with Tinkertoys®, or with ball bearings rolling down chutes with branches and various size drop holes, or as mentioned in Chapter 1 by a modification to a piano roll player. The reason is that all processing reduces to permutations and combinations of a handful of inanely simple steps.

Granted, this reductionism wars against personal feelings, but even the greatest physicist of all time came to appreciate it. When Sir Isaac Newton first read Euclid's *Elements*, he penciled the margin that the derivations were painfully obvious and rather childish. Yet his attitude changed radically when he wrote the immortal *Principia*, in which he adopted the Euclidean model of deduction fulsomely and afterward chastised himself for not following it even more closely than he did. Then early in this century, Alfred North Whitehead and Bertrand Russell, in their *Principia Mathematica*, proved that the whole of mathematics can be derived from a handful of axiomatic assumptions. Some years later, Alan Turing demonstrated that a simple, one-size-fits-all computer (now called a "Turing machine") could be used to solve any problem if the logic to solve it was known, provided that the machine had sufficient memory and time was of no consequence.[1] Finally, one need only recall the genetic process and how a handful of simple elements combine in various ways to generate the indisputably rich variety of life in plain evidence everywhere on this planet.

To be sure, the study of progression from simple to complex can sometimes be a chore, but there are few other ways to understand the ramifications of automation and its power to do good as well as wreak havoc. Accordingly, this chapter briefly reviews the six main aspects of automation: (a) basics of processing, (b) forms of automation, (c) networks and communications, (d) data content and structure, (e) image processing, and (f) software and programming. These aspects overlap considerably, and the efficiency of each depends on interior lines. As technology progresses from clumsy to streamlined, it does so by improving these lines, not by modifying principles.

Basics of processing. Although the programming mechanism in early automated looms survives in some commercial laundry machines, the most well-known application today is the piano roll player. The owner mounts a scroll of stiff paper with rectangular slits cut in it in various patterns. Powered either by foot pumping or electricity, this scroll passes over a rotating cylinder. The piano then plays various notes corresponding to the pins that momentarily pass through the slits in the scroll.

This is programmed automation. The program equates with the *arrangement* of the slits on the scroll, which therefore can be considered as input. The output consists of sound waves. The processing is the act of pins protruding through the slits as they pass over the cylinder, which therefore makes them symbols for what a human would otherwise do. That is, the act of pressing a key is symbolized by a hole in a sheet of paper, which then activates a machine to press the corresponding key.

Interestingly, this humble apparatus lacks only three elemental features of a computer: (a) the ability to add (which it can do half-heartedly by striking two or more keys at the same time), (b) the ability to make comparisons (which it does in a limited way when it determines if a pin can protrude through the paper), and (c) the ability to jump to another part of the scroll (which it could do if the scroll were instead manufactured as a disk with additional holes that directed the platter to spin to a different sector similar to programmable compact disk players).

Restated, automated processing is built from a mere six elements. The first two—input and output—are obvious necessities. Without them, nothing would get done. Yet with nothing else between, you would still have an automated storage box (i.e., a database). As for symbols, we all have names (and Social Security numbers). Books have titles (and ISBN numbers). And photographs are symbolic of actual persons or objects. It is natural, therefore, to carry this scheme of things into automation. The neat part of it is that symbolism can be effected by a series of switches or equivalent that have only two positions: off or on, raised or level, polarized or unpolarized, magnetized or not magnetized, a hole in a card or none.

Thus every letter, mark, or digit can be equated with a number, and that number can be represented by a set (commonly called a *byte*) of these switches (commonly called *bits*). Bytes, like dollars, typically have eight bits. Because each bit can be turned off or on (or the equivalent in mechanical systems) for a total of 256 different combinations, one byte can be set to represent any one of 256 different characters.[2] An encyclopedia with thirty million words, with an average length of six characters each, could thus be represented by about 215 million bytes, allowing for spaces and punctuation marks. That may seem like a lot of memory but it will all fit on a single optical disk. Note, too, that both information (commonly called *data* in computer systems) and the instructions on what to do with that data (the *program*) can thus be represented (i.e., symbolized).

Electronic processing, instead of passing pins through openings in scrolls of paper, directs streams of electrons through tiny circuits. This can and sometimes does result in the playing of notes, but far more often it is used to create new data, or move the arm of a machine, or slowly drive a programmer insane when a mistake cannot be found. So this leaves the three *processing* procedures: (a) to add data, (b) to compare data, and (c) to jump or branch either to another part of the instructions, or to other data, or both. All processing—beyond symbolization, input, and output—uses combinations and permutations of these three processing procedures:

• *Adding.* Computers do not subtract; they can only add. To subtract, they convert the subtrahend to a different form (called *taking the complement*), next add the two numbers, and then modify the result. Thus while a human might say 11 minus 7 equals 4, a computer takes the compliment of 7 (which it does by reversing all of its bits, not by subtracting) and adds that to 11.[3] In the everyday paper-and-pencil base-10 system, this would convert the 7 to a 3. The sum of the addends 3 and 11 equals 14. Knock off the 1, and *voila*, the answer is 4. Multiplication is then easily accommodated because it is merely a sequence of additions, while inversely division is a sequence of subtractions. Dividing 100 by 25 means how many times 25 can be subtracted from 100 before the difference reaches zero. Thus the simple ability to add can be harnessed to perform quantitative calculations.[4]

• *Comparing*. All automated decisions are based on two or more options. The option chosen depends on comparisons made among quantities or strings of characters (which are represented by numbers). The only question the computer can ask is if they are equal and, if not, which one is larger. It usually does this by routing two voltages representing the quantities through an electronic circuit. You could also do it with a balance scale. More complex comparisons are broken down into a sequence of these simple one-to-one comparisons. And when a decision requires subjective judgment that cannot be quantified, the computer pauses to display the intermediate results of its processing. Sometimes this is accompanied by calculations of probability as to which option is most likely to work best.

• *Jumping or branching*. If instructions are to be followed from beginning to end without interruption or side trips, then branching is not required. If all or part of them are to be repeated, then either the input mechanism must be capable of jumping back, or the instructions must be placed on a loop. The latter method was practical for looms but is impractical in most other instances. Furthermore, when different conditions require different processing, then the automated machine or computer must be instructed to jump to the appropriate section of the program. A complex problem may require millions, perhaps billions, of these branchings, but each one is executed in essentially the same way. One may drive from Portland, Maine, and reach any number of accessible locations on the continent, in any sequence, simply by way of different sequences of branching at thousands of road junctures.

The reason why most if not all complex problems can be subdivided into these simple steps requires speculation. That it happens has been amply demonstrated: in physics, in genetics, in mathematics, and in many other fields. One possible explanation is that the brain itself can manifest thought only by way of processing with simple neurons, synapses, and a few other biochemical components. A second explanation harkens back to the statistical concept of degrees of freedom. Roughly speaking, this means that as the number of independent factors operating in a system increases, the more difficult it is to control or resolve that problem. Conversely, if the elements are all the same (cellular automata), it simplifies the process of combining them into complex structures or analyses. One can imagine the hell to pay if the English alphabet had a hundred rather than twenty-six letters (sixteen of which account for 90 percent of usage).

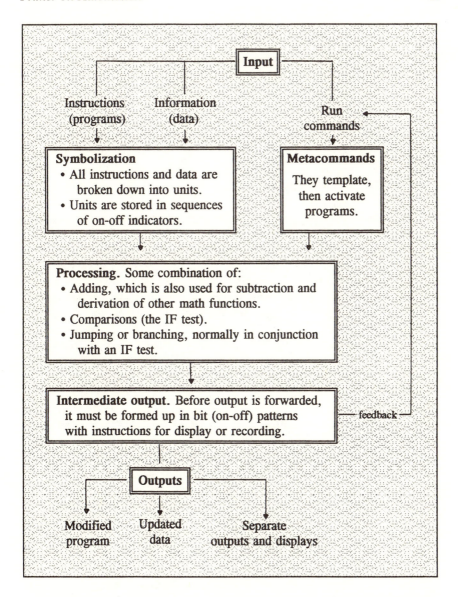

4. Elements of processing. The trite input-processing-output paradigm of automation remains valid to this day, but it is a gross oversimplification. It doesn't take feedback and interactive input into account, or the many different forms that input and output can have. This chart barely covers the possible scenarios.

At that, it is tough enough to generate order. Given the countless quintillions of subatomic particles operating in the physical universe, it is nothing short of miraculous that gravity adheres to simple equations and that the genetic process works flawlessly most of the time. A single fertilized egg will generate hundreds of billions of cells, of which no more than 1 percent—at worse—will ever experience trouble from internal causes, and only a few of those will devolve into serious problems. Automation seeks to replicate this near perfection, and sometimes when a system grows very large individuals are perceived as disruptions to it. Passengers waiting for an overdue bus in London grew irate when it finally came and then passed without stopping. One of them wrote the-powers-that-be to complain. The official answer, so the story goes, was that if the bus had stopped to pick them up, it would have been even more late at its terminal destination.

This discussion on programming presumes a platform of some kind to carry out the processing. As mentioned, almost anything will do (including a modified piano), provided that it can send objects or energy through gates of some type that can compare, add, and cause control to jump to other data or other instructions. A modern processing chip shoehorns millions of these gates into a very small nutshell. Although the specific design can have a major influence on processing speed, the main boost in efficiency comes from miniaturizing the circuitry and then putting more of it in less space. This compresses—implodes—the interior lines, which in turn permits the processing steps to be executed in less time. Some computers have ten, a hundred, or even a thousand of these chips mounted in parallel arrays to increase processing speed vastly.

Forms of automation. In its role as a prototype cell, the loom was the protozoan of automation. The protozoa is a one-celled organism that has both botanical and zoological characteristics and from which the two main branches of living things are thought to have evolved. Similarly, the loom was an alloy of robotics and computer processing. Ironically, these main branches of automation are beginning to merge again. The result is that automation can be subdivided into three forms: (a) physical robotics, which is the most easily understood form, (b) electronic substitution, to include computers, and (c) psychical mimicking, in which the *illusion* of human presence or phenomena is created in sufficient measure to evoke a response as if a person were there. As such, the concept of robotics apart from computers has become blurred.

Physical robotics are everywhere—for example, automatic washing machines, many assembly lines, automated mail carts in large office buildings, pool chlorinators with sensors, heat-seeking missiles, programmed drones, and space probes. By contrast, electronic-substitution robotics bypass replication of human movement and instead concentrate on functions. For example, while robotic assembly lines for manufacturing electronic equipment are common, robotic technicians are a long way off. Yet as the labor cost of repair increases, it is cheaper to build this equipment in modular form with an additional chip to identify which module or modules have gone bad. The owner simply swaps a bad module for a good one. The replacement module is usually more expensive than a specific part, but the virtual elimination of the labor charge more than compensates.[5]

Laser scanners for UPC codes are another example. While this technology has not replaced checkout clerks in stores, it has more than doubled their productivity, thus displacing labor *in part*. Many prosthetic devices also come under this heading, including the equipment which permits the famed physicist Stephen Hawking to continue his work notwithstanding the advanced stage of amyotrophic lateral sclerosis (Lou Gehrig's disease). He sometimes opens a talk with the line "now you will have the experience of talking with a computer." And the computer itself substitutes for hundreds of manual labor tasks, including amanuenses in the form of pen readers, word processors, grammar checkers, and reference citation formatters.

The third category—psychical mimicking—relies as much on the power of suggestion as it does on computers. The applications range from the sublime to the ridiculous. Of the latter, one can buy a bathroom scale that keeps track of weighings and announces "Attaboy, you lost a whole pound last week" or words to that effect. Honest.[6] On the sublime side, psychiatrists and psychologists have demonstrated that interactive therapy recorded on a common floppy disk proved as effective in dealing with chronic (but not psychotic) depression as conventional therapy.[7] Given the prevalence of mental problems and the high cost of intense personal therapy, this alternative has true merit. Between these polemics, recorded voices are sometimes used in fully automated subway systems to alleviate fears arising from the absence of human operators on the trains.

Networks and communications. Networks are the means by which three or more people, or machines, communicate with each other. From the earliest days until about 150 years ago, communicants relied on messengers traveling over roads and sea lanes, or alternatively on signals relayed along a string of hilltops (e.g., the heliograph). Modern networks substitute pipelines, cable, and microwave radiation, but the concept hasn't changed much. Nature also relies on networks, although they are not always thought of in those terms. The central nervous system of an organism is a communications network; the circulatory system is a mechanical one. Weather—especially wind patterns—is another circulatory network and, all things considered, it *is* programmed. Science just hasn't fully broken the code yet.

For obvious reasons, networks illustrate interior lines better than any other aspect of automation. Signals travel at nearly the speed of light, and high-capacity lines can send hundreds of thousands of impulses per second, fast enough to satisfy the vast majority of users. The problem is linking stations that were not designed with that idea in mind. Many, if not most, systems evolved piecemeal. But the increasing consolidation of corporations and the assumption of more and more responsibilities by governments mandates revamping them to work together. The most well-known applications, if not the most extensive, are police information nets.

Networks exercise at least three degrees of relationship among their stations (or nodes): (a) linkage, (b) interface, and (c) integration.[8] The first level—linkage—suffices when independent stations need only talk to each other occasionally. The third level—integration—is appropriate when the stations no longer have a reason to remain independent and must act as if they were integral parts of one system. The intermediate level—interfacing—covers situations such as coordination among the separate but interdependent airline reservation systems.

Linkage seldom presents overwhelming difficulties. Unfortunately, interfacing and integration still do, both for technical and semipolitical reasons. By analogy, consider what happens when a group of international representatives meet to discuss a problem. At least four types of obstacles intervene. First, they may not speak the same language. The automation equivalent is incompatibility among operating systems. Next, and after securing competent translators, the participants may find that they cannot come to grips with each other's manner of expression. One may prefer the ironclad written agreement; another, a spineless oral understanding; still a third, an agreement in principle. The equivalent in automation is usually called *format*.

Presuming that these differences are negotiated, the problem of meaning then arises. The expression *basic necessities* has a much richer content for an American than a Somali. The equivalent in automation goes by many names, but for the moment *logical incompatibility* will suffice. Finally, after all of this oleum is resolved, there remains the great obstacle of willingness to carry out an agreement—the politics of it all. The history of international relations and war suggests that this is the most challenging obstacle, and so it has been with automation. Turf battles have stymied more than one attempt at integration or resulted in bad blood—witness the aftermath of General Motor's purchase of Ross Perot's Electronic Data Systems (EDS). In part, EDS had been tasked to integrate GM's vast computer systems.[9]

On the other hand, it must be recognized that when political operatives attempt to sabotage an integration project, they will usually attack it on the grounds of technical inadequacy. More often than not, their complaints are valid. The differences among the component systems can be so massive that an integration would be no more efficient than a Rube Goldberg cartoon. About the only way to make of this kind project work would be complete rebuilding, and that runs into the twin problems of high expense and the preference of most executives to avoid radical change. Hence, the networking and communications aspects of automation, especially in computer applications, are the most troublesome.

The trade categorized these incompatibilities under seven headings, exclusive of purely logical incompatibilities and turf battles, in the process of developing an agreement to standardize manufacture.[10] In practical terms, however, these technical disconnects are more easily understood under the aforementioned levels. Hardware and operating system incompatibilities come first, including communication links. Operating systems are unique to each manufacturer of computers. Although they carry out the same functions, they are not interchangeable by any stretch of the imagination (except for IBM-compatible PCs). The analogy would be an attempt to use a 110-volt appliance on a 220-volt power source. A transformer is required.

The next level—format incompatibility—is easier to reconcile, like finding the correct voltage but having the wrong size plug. In most cases, the incompatibility can be overcome by a software utility program or by a relatively simple hardware circuit, roughly analogous to an adapter plug. Other format problems present greater challenges, especially the ubiquitous Social Security number. It contains nine digits, which means that it can accommodate one billion (minus one) different numbers. However, because the total population of the United States, living and dead, born since the system went into effect is approaching a half-billion, and because blocks of numbers are allocated to different regions for issuance, the system is running out of numbers. The simple solution would be to add a digit or to convert at least one of the digits to an alphabetical character. Unfortunately, changing hundreds of thousands of programs that rely on the existing format would cost billions of dollars. Hence the decision was made to recycle the numbers—technological if not theological reincarnation.[11]

Aside from turf battles, this leaves logical incompatibilities, and here the analogies are plentiful. In the film *Cool Hand Luke*, the character played by Paul Newman escapes from a road-gang prison for the third time, only to find the warden close behind him. Standing in the door frame of an abandoned building, he cries out "What we have here is a failure to communicate." Hearing this, the warden rectifies the error by shooting him. This illustrates the vast differences in meaning among various observers. Applied to automation, these differences include degrees of accuracy, valid entries and what they mean, timeliness, and even the basic meaning of two data fields that carry similar names and would at first seem to have identical meanings. For example, number of exemptions and number of deductions may be identical in number for the same person, but they don't mean the same thing legally.[12]

Notwithstanding this formidable array of disconnects, the general rule is that any computer, its database or its software can be made to communicate with any other, limited only by logical incompatibilities beyond the reach of procedural reconciliation. The reason is that all programming instructions and data break down to simple patterns of zeros and ones, or the equivalent. Any and all compatibilities can thus be overcome by *emulations*. This means that either the message can be transformed to emulate what the receiving station is able to understand, or the receiving station can emulate the operating character-istics of the sending station. This extends even to translating spoken languages by way of voice recognition software.

So far so good, at least until the problems of cost, time, and reliability intrude. A famous cartoon has the commanding general of a army post issue a bulletin that Halley's comet will be visible at such and such a time, a phenom-enon that occurs only once every seventy-six years. After four endorsements down the chain of command, the message reads that Colonel Halley will be inspecting the company area tonight, something he does once every seventy-six years. Restated, then, the number and degree of incompatibilities between two or more systems determine whether networking is economically feasible. The significance of this can be better understood by reference to databases. Al-though software can be shared within a network, most networks are used over-whelmingly to transmit messages and data or (what is essentially the same) to read in one location data that is stored in another.

The next point is the emergence of ultra-high-capacity transmission trunk lines. The prototype was recently authorized by Congress in the High Perfor-mance Computing Act of 1991. Spearheaded by Albert Gore (at the time a Senator), this act established and funded the National Research and Education Network to the tune of $2.9 billion. It will link a dozen or so research centers and be capable of transmitting a billion bits of information per second. This equates to sending the entire *Encyclopaedia Britannica* in just under two sec-onds. In turn, this network will be linked to approximately 1,300 sites in li-braries, universities, and other research centers, although the rate of transmis-sion to these satellites will not be as high.[13]

Finally, the mushrooming of Internet with all of its electronic tentacles has been nothing but awesome, although the system is already inundated with abuses, such as rabid opinion- and hate-mongering as well as unwelcome ad-vertising.

Data content and structure. Two schools of thought address the question of data collection and storage. The first claims that priority should be given to data. The more data that is collected and linked, the more reliable and simpler analysis will be. The other school advocates minimum collection of data and maximum use of statistical inference. The usual reason proffered is that data collection is expensive and difficult to maintain. In truth, the two approaches are useful for different requirements. Sound accurate data is the *sine qua non* of the Social Security Administration. By contrast, inferential analysis for weather prediction is the best that can be done at the moment. And in practice, the majority of systems, both computer and physical automation, rely on data more than inference. Even those programs that make projections and interpolations tend to draw heavily on data extracted from various databases (often called *roll-ups*). Thus because massive databases already exist, the task is to link them together. The efficiency of this depends on the way the data is arranged.

There are two ways to go about it: (a) for the convenience of a single user, and (b) for the convenience of many users.[14] The first usually (but not always) arranges its data *hierarchically*. Airline reservations are a good example. The first tier of records covers all routes between cities. The second tier encompasses all scheduled flights between each pair of cities. The third tier contains records for each seat on each flight. The actual databases are more complex than this, and each airline runs its own database, sometimes by leasing time on a larger airline's computer system. Nevertheless, the concept and its rational is clear. An individual must first designate the route he or she wants to fly. Then the time (i.e., the flight) is selected and finally a seat is selected (if available at the fare category chosen).

The other approach—the one intended for use by many users—is called *relational*, a misnomer because it is each user's programmer that does the relating. The idea is to group data in logically related sets *but without any embedded linkage*.[15] The difference can be shown by reference to a school system. The hierarchical approach requires several different systems, each with its own database: one for student records, one for scheduling, one for analysis of program and course offerings, and so forth. The relational approach requires separate *programs* for each requirement, but they would all be tethered to the same database and would not require modification when new data fields were added (unless they wanted to use that data). It achieves this, for example, by creating separate files for students, faculty, programs, courses, and facilities. Each program then relates the various data as necessary. If additional semipermanent specialized records were needed, they would be generated from the primary database. These adjunct files are called *views*. All updates to data, however, are made only to original files. In turn, the system automatically updates any views.

At first glance, the relational approach appears to violate the principle of interior lines. For single-user systems it does, but most large systems have multiple users, and software development is expensive. Changing many programs every time the underlying data structure is modified is even more expensive, not to mention the aggravating process of compromise among the users affected. Thus relational databases are a trade-off, and usually a good one. If the *initial* programming for each user is more difficult, the easier maintenance more than compensates. Would you rather buy system A for $50,000 if you knew it would need upgrading every month at $10,000 a clip, or would you prefer system B at $100,000 if it could be upgraded for pennies?

Assuming that a relational design is more favorable except when the situation begs for a specialized alternative, the next question asks how much data to include. The superficial answer is that the efficiency of a system is directly proportional to the amount of data included, analogous to the maximum range of an airplane being a function of the fuel it carries. Yet if the amount of fuel is negligible, the plane will barely get off the ground before it has to return or land at another airfield so nearby that it would be faster and cheaper to drive. At the other extreme, too heavy a load of fuel would consume its own excess just carrying it until it was needed, resulting in a reduction of the range—the point of diminishing returns. Similarly, too little data may prove useless, while too much data can create an administrative burden that is not worth the cost.

5. The interstate highway system as an exemplar of integration. Interstate highways comprise less than 5 percent of the nation's roads, but they carry about 90 percent of commercial interstate traffic. If cities are considered as separate systems, this clearly demonstrates the efficacy of a good integration.

Additional questions arise when separate databases are consolidated, especially on the distribution for processing and storage of data. The options range from complete centralization of data and programming in one computer, with all other computers working primarily as so-called dumb terminals (no processing, just read-only access); to complete decentralization, wherein the network serves primarily to let each station read data stored at other stations. The advantages and disadvantages of these polemics, and options between them, depend on costs, frequency of access, and other factors, many of which change with time after a network is installed.

One thing is clear. It is becoming cheaper to centralize at least key data in one place or under the control of one unit in a distributed system. The reason is that hardware and communication costs are falling, while the labor cost of reconciling conflicting data is soaring. As such, this path of least resistance often motivates the development of massive databases, be they singular in fact or by linkage. This makes the most of logical interior lines, again bearing in mind that the speed of transmission makes physical distance meaningless. If the component databases happen to be in a relational format, the consolidation becomes all the easier—and so too does potential abuse.

Image processing. Image processing warrants its own section because it is beginning to overshadow digital databases. Conventional data is stored in digital format—strings of on-or-off bits representing characters and numbers. By contrast, an image record is an electronic photograph, essentially a variation of a wirephoto. The image record is stored in a string of bits, but here the entire picture is considered to be a single piece of data, even if it is a million bits long.[16] If you look closely at a newspaper photograph, you will see that it consists of rows of dots (called *pixels* or *pels*, for picture elements). The dots are single-size black specks, with the illusion of shades of gray achieved by putting more or fewer of them per unit of space. In other media, the same effect is achieved by making the dots larger or smaller. In still other cases, the dots can be printed in different shades of a single color. For color documents, each apparent dot is the effect of combining different shades of three dots, one for each of the primary colors.

The reason for this different process is that there is no digital substitute—that is, character data—to record photographs or most forms of handwriting.[17] It is true that typed or printed data can be converted to digital form by optical character recognition, and it will take up a lot less storage space on the disk. However, this kind of conversion is troublesome, time consuming, and error prone. Hence whenever the information in the document will not be processed per se, but only referred to, it is simpler and cheaper to image it. Furthermore, documents of all types can be stored in a singular electronic "folder."[18]

The significance is in volume, cost savings, and the ability to achieve the old management dream of a paperless office. As mentioned, only 2 percent of the information used in business and government is recorded in digital automated form, with another 3 percent on microfilm and microfiche. Imaging increases that to a theoretical 95 percent or more, excluding only those documents that by law cannot be imaged (primarily money and most negotiable instruments). In practice, the actual number imaged will never reach that figure, but the vast quantities that are being imaged free up millions of square feet of storage space and eliminate the need for file clerks and the personnel to maintain that space.

In short, once paperwork is reduced to an image, all the limitations imposed by the handling of physical objects are nearly eliminated. The ideal is thus to bypass the creation of paperwork in the first place, a process which already exists in electronic banking and deposits. Instead of checks being written, digital data is sent directly to the receiving institution by wire. Similarly, the Internal Revenue Service advocates electronic submission of returns and is experimenting with direct dial filing from touch-tone phones, at least for very simple returns.[19]

Also, consider the evolution of the humble traffic ticket. The original process was to write the ticket on paper, forward it to a traffic court, and hand the motorist a carbon or pressure sensitive copy. With image processing, this advanced to having the original imaged upon receipt by the traffic court. The next step is to have the officer write the ticket on a hand-held machine, which would then image it immediately and transmit that image to the traffic court. The offender would be given a thermal printout as a receipt. The final stage (this is already practiced in Germany) is to eliminate the officer and instead use radar cameras, computer networks, and the mails to ticket offenders. This last step may be impractical in some situations, but it goes to show just how far automation can replace human endeavor.

So much for mundane image processing, which is often called *raster imaging*. The other half of this technology is called *vector imaging*. This technology *creates* rather than *records* images, and it can do this in both still and dynamic form. The still form is often used in conjunction with commercial raster imaging. Text data can be formatted into an image and that document can be printed. Insurance companies use this technique to generate hardcopy policies for policyholders who want one, but they need not maintain their own paper copies. Instead, the software generates the image on screen whenever there is a need to review it. Other examples include graphs that are generated by various productivity software packages, especially spreadsheets.

Still, it is the dynamic form of vectoring that captures the imagination, and this is called *virtual reality*. Virtual reality generates dynamic images from data, or at least from a template image, which is then modified by programming as if it were drawn on a rubber sheet. Animated films are now made this way, including one scene in *Indiana Jones and the Last Crusade*. In that scene, a German officer, seeking the Holy Grail, drinks from the wrong chalice and as a consequence ages and crumbles into dust in a matter of ten seconds. The ultimate is three-dimensional holography, which can be seen in the visitor section of the computer center in Epcot Center in Disney World near Orlando, Florida. The December 1988 issue of *National Geographic* also featured holographs printed on its unique silver cover.

However, this technology is not free from potential problems: (a) the legal standing of image records when used as evidence in court, (b) copyright issues, and (c) psychological acceptance. The legal-standing issue in part stems from the potential for alteration of documents, intentional or unintentional, during scanning or after recording. Because maintaining back-up paper copies would largely defeat the cost-saving advantage of the technology, the image record itself must be as good as its paper sire. Fortunately, that is proving to be the case, as evidenced by a few courts switching over to it.[20] More than one judge has a terminal sitting on his or her bench. The copyright issue is more complex but does not normally apply to the bulk of commercial applications. It does apply to the imaging of books and related material used in libraries and computer-assisted instruction (more on this in Chapter 8). This leaves the psychological acceptance issue, the resolution of which is probably more a function of time than anything else, supported by generation of hardcopy whenever it remains a sticking point.

Software and decision support programs. When *you* write instructions for an automated machine, it is called programming. When someone else does, it is called software. Recall, then, the essence of programming (or software): (a) it consists of a set of instructions that tells a machine or a computer what to do (in a language that it can understand), (b) these instructions are permutations and combinations of six basic procedures (symbolization, input, output, adding, comparing, and jumping), and (c) the instructions themselves are reduced to sets of on-off switches or their equivalents. The principal exception occurs when analogue (continuous range) data or processing is substituted for digital data (e.g., a thermostat).

The key to useful programs is breaking down logical requirements into those chains of on-off switches or indicators, and the ideal is to have automation do as much of this spade work as possible. Accordingly, software development environments exist at four levels. The first—machine language—was initially the only one available (e.g., the punchcards on the loom). Its use today is limited to items like commercial washing machines. The familiar IBM punchcard is not the same thing, because these cards can be used to record programming at any language level. The next level up is called *assembler*. This substitutes names (called *mnemonics*) for specific low-level instructions. It is still popular because it makes the most efficient use of the central processing unit in computers and the controlling mechanisms for robotics. In practice, however, the uses are concentrated on software that operates computers themselves or on developing software that in turn supports higher level programming.[21]

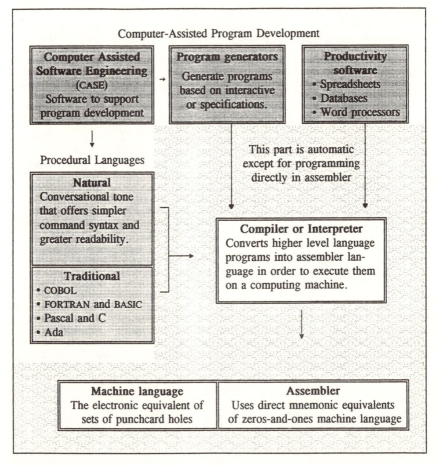

Computer-Assisted Program Development

| Computer Assisted Software Engineering (CASE) Software to support program development | → | Program generators Generate programs based on interactive or specifications. | Productivity software • Spreadsheets • Databases • Word processors |

Procedural Languages

This part is automatic except for programming directly in assembler

Natural
Conversational tone that offers simpler command syntax and greater readability.

Compiler or Interpreter
Converts higher level language programs into assembler language in order to execute them on a computing machine.

Traditional
• COBOL
• FORTRAN and BASIC
• Pascal and C
• Ada

| Machine language The electronic equivalent of sets of punchcard holes | Assembler Uses direct mnemonic equivalents of zeros-and-ones machine language |

6. Levels of programming. Although all levels of programming reduce to the most simplistic machine language before execution, the idea behind the higher levels is to simplify the work that a programmer must do in order to develop more reliable systems in less time at less cost.

The third level, known as third-generation or procedural language, includes the well-known languages COBOL, FORTRAN, BASIC, and Pascal. These languages use semi-readable English (in English-speaking countries) but mandate strict adherence to prescribed formats.[22] The advantage with these languages is that it takes only 10 percent of the time to do the same work using assembler. To this day, they remain the most popular languages to this day, with more than eighty *billion* lines of COBOL alone in extant.

However, procedural languages are difficult to work with and are being gradually supplanted by even higher level languages. These newer languages can *do* nothing new, but they are easier to use and hence less costly, somewhat like driving a car with an automatic transmission on a desert highway compared to maneuvering a truck with a twelve-speed transmission on the hills of San Francisco. These higher level languages come in a variety of forms and are often subdivided into fourth-, fifth-, and even sixth-generation phyla. In some cases the forms overlap in one package:

• *Natural languages.* These differ the least from third-generation languages, substituting more conversational English for cryptic commands.

• *Productivity software.* Examples include spreadsheets and word processors. They perform most so-called housekeeping tasks automatically, leaving the user free to concentrate on practical requirements.

• *Program generators.* This software, which goes by many names, interactively prompts for goal-oriented instructions or specifications and then translates the input into procedural language essential for computer implementation—an electronic middleman.

• *Computer assisted software engineering (CASE).* This is software which supports the development and management of larger programming requirements—for example, by keeping track of various modules or partially automating the testing of them.

Now let us look at production of information. It comes in three flavors: (a) plain-vanilla management information reports, (b) Neapolitan executive information systems, and (c) hot-fudge-sundae decision support programs. The dividing lines are not clear, but management information reports typically consist of printouts of selected data accompanied by various statistical summations. These printouts are the source of endless jokes, and the power plant at the Pentagon uses them for 25 percent of its winter heating fuel. Executive information systems (EIS) put an end to most of the jokes. Instead of printing endless reams of paper, executives are provided with terminals. They can access data as necessary and apply various formulas and programs against that data to determine trends, weigh options, and so forth. Some versions of EIS are designed for computer illiterates, while others require moderate programming skill.

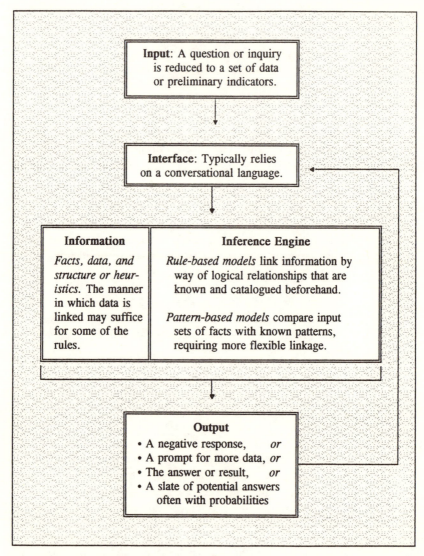

Input: A question or inquiry is reduced to a set of data or preliminary indicators.

Interface: Typically relies on a conversational language.

Information	**Inference Engine**
Facts, data, and structure or heuristics. The manner in which data is linked may suffice for some of the rules.	*Rule-based models* link information by way of logical relationships that are known and catalogued beforehand. *Pattern-based models* compare input sets of facts with known patterns, requiring more flexible linkage.

Output
- A negative response,   *or*
- A prompt for more data, *or*
- The answer or result,   *or*
- A slate of potential answers often with probabilities

7. Anatomy of a decision support program. A decision support program automates as much spade work as possible prerequisite to answering a question. There is no magic to it, but when time is short a good program often means the difference between solid analysis and mere guesswork.

Decision support programs crown the hierarchy. They start with the idea of an executive information system and then highly automate the process of using it. For that reason, they are also called expert systems.[23] Regardless of the nomenclature, though, they are all applications of so-called artificial intelligence. Artificial intelligence relies on logical interior lines to superintend information relevant to major or complex problems. One type stresses looking for the proverbial needle in a haystack (finding a relevant reference among millions). Another seeks patterns in seemingly random data (diagnosis). A third does the opposite and finds exceptions in what appears to be orderly (detection of fraud). Still others interpret, predict, design, plan, monitor, debug, repair, instruct, or control.

In most cases, these decision support programs adhere to one of two models: (a) a rule-based model, or (b) a pattern-based model. A rule-based model is useful when all or most of the information regarding a requirement or problem is known and therefore can be highly structured for immediate use by others—a cookbook of sorts. The pattern-based model, by contrast (as the name implies) compares images, photographs, and the like. In 1929, Clyde Tombaugh discovered the location of the hypothesized ninth planet (Pluto) by a manual predecessor of this technique.[24] However, the pattern-based model is now expanding into detecting and comparing logical patterns of facts and relational dynamics among objects that are the hallmark of the science of chaos. In a sense, this is how the fictional Sherlock Holmes worked, and most archaeologists for that matter. Out of the mass of what they observe, certain items become clues that relate to known patterns. This hypothesized pattern can then be used to analyze further the situation or problem. In some models, the program can modify itself based on these experiences. An example of this is a computer chess game that alters its moves after analyzing your strategy.

3

The Frankenstein Issue

What hath God wrought?
—Heard after Alexander Graham
Bell demonstrated his telephone

The preceding chapter emphasized that the most sophisticated and complex applications of automation are nothing more than permutations and combinations of inanely simple elements. If the same is true for the biological mechanisms of the brain, at least in physiological terms, then it must be asked if technology can create an electronic Frankenstein—not just one, but thousands, perhaps millions. The surprising thing about this issue is how far back in history it goes and the seriousness with which some modern scholars have considered it. The list includes Nobel laureate Erwin Schrödinger and mathematicians John von Neumann and Norbert Wiener.

These roots trace back to the year 1000 B.C., in Psalm 139. In the Revised Standard Version, line 16 reads "Thy eyes beheld my *unformed substance*; in thy book were written, every one of them, the days that were formed for me, when as yet there was none of them" (emphasis added). The italicized expression in transliterated Hebrew is *golem* (גלמי), and in this context implied the teleological design of man that his genetic chemistry was programmed to attain. Today, science seeks to unravel that mystery, but in the intervening three thousand years, that line, combined with folklore from other ancient lands, laid the groundwork for no less than six major variations on the Frankenstein idea: (a) an image which takes on lifelike attributes, (b) possession or control of a human by a spirit, (c) creation of a biological monster, (d) creation of a mechanical monster, (e) a mortal who attains the knowledge of the gods (sometimes called having one foot in the godhead), and (f) the belief that man is already a robot and needs to be scientifically controlled.

Granted, these variations are the stuff of literature, and a ton of fiction does not an ounce of science make. However, the reader should not dismiss them out of hand on that account. Serious literature is in part an attempt to understand and record truth before more objective tools and methods become available. For example, a number of psychiatric dysfunctions are named after characters in Greek mythology (e.g., narcissism and the Oedipus complex). More importantly, even when an idea lacks a whit of objective validity, it can still impel human conduct. When applied to automation, this suggestive influence is a profound point. In 1950, Alan Turing wrote that when an individual can no longer distinguish between a stimulus or reaction as coming from another human being or from a machine, any discussion on the difference between the two becomes moot.[1]

Six themes. Each of the six themes has an objective counterpart recognized by science, and each ties in or leads to various issues in automation, some more so than others:

• *Golem.* For obvious reasons, this seems to be the original theme and means "the giving of life or power to an image." It is somewhat related to the concept of a ghost, but the latter is normally associated with a former mortal, of which the ghost of Hamlet's father is the best known in literature. A golem, by contrast, is either an independent spirit or one that becomes mortal. The most well-known literary example is the ancient Greek myth of Pygmalion, wherein a sculptor falls in love with the image of a woman from one of his statues. Aphrodite answers his prayers and gives life to that image. This plot found its way into many stories, of which George Bernard Shaw's 1912 play of the same name is the best known and from which the Broadway musical *My Fair Lady* was derived.

The objective counterpart to this is psychological in nature, as when a child is convinced that a favorite stuffed animal is very much a living being or when the ethos of a nation becomes personified in an imaginary human being or animal—for example, Uncle Sam (the United States, of course), John Bull (Great Britain), or a bear (Russia). These spirits may not exist in the ontological sense of that word, but they can abide as a powerful idea in human minds and thus become a force that can affect history. And certainly most creations of mankind start with a vision to which materials are fitted or otherwise refined until they conform to the conceptual template. Finally, Trevor Pinch and Harry Collins used the term *golem* in their recent book *The Golem: What Everyone Should Know About Science.* The argument was that too many people were giving too much credit to the ability of science to solve problems or resolve issues objectively.

As mentioned, the application in automation is called *virtual reality*, in which a visible image is created and by the power of suggestion is considered to have real attributes. This technology is a true blessing when it comes to training pilots before they are allowed to fly living passengers.

• *Lucifer.* This is a common name bestowed on the devil of scriptural origin, who is reputed to have the ability to possess or control an individual. It is a powerful theme and is central to Milton's *Paradise Lost* and Goethe's *Faust*, although in the latter story (which has seen many popular offspring, e.g., *Damn Yankees*) the pending possession is by way of ownership rather than occupancy. With the publication of *The Exorcist* in 1973 (based on a case history observed by more than thirty psychiatrists), the subject of demonic possession has almost edged its way into the mainstream of curiosity.[2] Whatever the truth may be, the intense reality of the case elevates the explanation above mass hysteria.

Modern psychiatry calls this phenomenon by many names, especially compulsion, obsession, and *idée fixe*. When so afflicted, an individual no longer has full rational control over his or her behavior. Virtually every week the papers report a mass murder somewhere in the United States, committed by an individual who seems possessed by his or her emotions. In a more positive vein, the process of maturation in part entails gaining control over one's impulses, a major theme in Spinoza's *Ethics* and brought out in W. Somerset Maugham's *Of Human Bondage* (the title was drawn from *Ethics*). True enough, these objective explanations do not entail an external spirit, but given the often destructive force of these impulses, that is a moot point and as such is the counterpart to Turing's thesis. To repeat, when an individual can no longer discern the difference between a machine and another human being, and then carries out the instructions provided by that machine, the poor devil might as well be possessed by one.

• *Frankenstein and androids.* These two strongly related themes entail the giving of life to inorganic or man-made biological material, and both trace their roots to the aforementioned line in Psalm 139. By 1500, the scriptural theme of bestowing life to an image evolved to breathing life into an effigy. Adherents of the Jewish faith sometimes placed a charm of letters spelling out the Hebrew name for God into a figure in the belief it would protect them against pogroms.[3] About the same time, Rabbi Judah Bezulel of Prague created a persona that was the forerunner of fictional monsters of this genre.

Three hundred years later, Mary Wollstonecraft Godwin, at the age of nineteen and just before she married her lover—the poet Percy Bysshe Shelley—wrote the seminal *Frankenstein, or the Modern Prometheus*. Published shortly after they were married, the story of how the book came to be written has itself been made into at least three different films.[4] The critical moment occurred when Percy Shelley's friend Lord Byron challenged him, Mary, and his doctor to write a ghost story. In part, Mary's story took note that a number of "scientists" had tried to regenerate life in cadavers and animal limbs using static electricity. At any rate, many plays on this theme were produced during the nineteenth century, and by 1910 the first film appeared. It was followed by several others, most notably the German production of *Der Golem* in 1920. In 1931, Hollywood made the film *Frankenstein*, which has been followed by countless others.

The scientific counterpart of this theme replays hundreds of times a day. An individual whose heart fillibrates or even stops is often restored to life by way of a strong electric shock. We also see this theme vaguely in biogenetic engineering and so-called test-tube babies. In 1993, a pregnant drug addict was killed while attempting to rob a legless man in his apartment. Doctors in an Oakland, California hospital kept her body "alive" for fifteen weeks until the baby could be delivered by Caesarean section.[5]

Needless to say, many observers, including some staunch right-to-life advocates, were repelled by the procedure, perhaps because the next step would be to use cadavers, or mechanical wombs, to bypass a medically inadvisable internal pregnancy. On Christmas day, 1993, a fifty-nine-year-old woman in Great Britain gave birth to twins, the zygote of whom had been artificially inseminated by way of a donor's egg. Dr. John Marks, the former chairman of the British Medical Association's ethics committee, said publicly that it was "getting close to the Frankenstein syndrome." (A year later, a sixty-two-year-old woman in Italy gave birth using the same technique.) The step after that could be gene selection in an attempt to create a master race. That is truly frightening, but eugenics by way of amniocentesis, sonograms, and selective abortion has become more or less policy in China.

The more immediate counterpart in automation is equally strong. By the late 1940s, scientists and other serious thinkers began to ponder the issue. Could man make a machine—organic or inorganic mattering little—that would subsequently destroy him? In 1948, Norbert Wiener noted in his book on cybernetics that he expected automation to become capable of unlimited good and evil.[6] Next, Isaac Asimov, concerned about the potential tragedy, wrote *I, Robot* (1950), a piece of science fiction in which an android is programmed with a set of ethics to avoid turning on his former masters. Then in the last year of his life, Wiener penned a second and truly profound book titled *God and Golem, Inc.* (MIT Press, 1964), becoming the first bona fide scientist to tackle the Frankenstein issue head on.

Over the next thirty years, this theme picked up so much momentum that today scholarly anthologies on the ethics of automation typically include an article or two that ponder questions like how an android or decision support program should take an oath in court to tell the truth.[7]

The theme in literature	Counterpart in automation
External spirit *Golem*—a spirit independent of mortals or which becomes one—for example, the ancient Greek myth of *Pygmalion*.	Virtual reality, where an individual begins to mistake the operation of a system for a real event or human response.
External possession or control The devil (or Satan, or Lucifer) as portrayed in Milton's *Paradise Lost*, Goethe's *Faust*, and Dante's *Inferno*.	Occurs when individuals become too dependent on computer output without questioning its validity.
Mechanical automata Examples include R2D2 and C-3PO from *Star Wars* and Lt. Data from *Star Trek*. Many others adorn science fiction.	Automation uses robots to perform specific tasks, often linked together sequentially in assembly lines.
Biological automata Mary Shelley's story of *Frankenstein* is so well entrenched that most similar stories borrow the name.	One long-term goal in automation is to build computers with biological material in an attempt to replicate the brain.
Promethean knowledge *Prometheus* shared the knowledge of gods with mortals and was chained to a rock for thirty years as punishment.	Comprehensive databases combined with decision support programs can put nearly all knowledge at one's fingertips.
Human automata *Brave New World* and *Nineteen Eighty-four* depict man reduced to de facto automata, regulated by a dictatorship.	Massive government databases coupled with electronic surveillance supposedly justified by national security.

8. Variations on an old idea. Six separate themes, one dating back three thousand years, contribute to the idea of man creating a monster that could destroy him. The age of automation seems to be synthesizing all of them in down-to-earth terms.

• *Prometheus.* This theme derives from another ancient Greek myth, wherein man suffers the consequences of learning too much. According to some analysts, the idea traces back further to the legend of Adam and Eve being driven from the Garden of Eden. Some modern writers see this as egotism but, if so, that is only the mechanism by which a genuine surfeit of knowledge can lead to self-destruction. Granted, it is impossible to ascertain what constitutes excessive knowledge, but history offers many examples of

powerful minds grown intolerant, which then presaged the fall of their possess-
ors. Woodrow Wilson's intransigence on the peace treaty and League of Nations after World War I contributed to the stroke that made him an invalid,
while General Douglas MacArthur, the only American to serve as a general
officer in both world wars and the Korean conflict, was summarily relieved of
command for trying to push his country into a war its leaders did not want.
Even when individuals of this caliber possess a genuine humility, they risk
assassination at the hand of a crazed killer (most notably Lincoln and Gandhi).

The tie-in with automation is obvious and is the theme of this book. For
starters, recall the full title of Mary Shelley's book—*Frankenstein, or the Modern Prometheus*. Frankenstein was the name of the creator, not the creation,
and in the end the creator dies from exhaustion in an attempt to destroy his
creation (followed by the monster's self-immolation). Furthermore, Shelley's
plot more or less drew on four of the six major themes. The Promethean and
biological-automata aspects are obvious. As for demons, the character of Vic-
tor Frankenstein surmises that he is possessed by one, which he later manifests
in the form of his creation and calls it by that epithet (which qualified it as a
golem). As Mary wrote in a later preface,

> every thing must have a beginning . . . and that beginning must be
> linked to something that went before. The Hindoos [sic] give the world
> an elephant to support it, but they make the elephant stand upon a tor-
> toise. Invention, it must be humbly admitted, does not consist in creating
> out of a void, but out of chaos; the materials must, in the first place, be
> afforded: it can give form to dark, shapeless substances, but cannot
> bring into being the substance itself. . . . Invention consists in the
> capacity of seizing on the capabilities of a subject, and in the power of
> molding and fashioning ideas suggested to it.[8]

As for one of the two themes that Mary Shelley left out, the daughter of Lord
Byron, whose suggestion led to the tale, made up for it. That was Ada Augusta's attempt to assure her readers that Charles Babbage's analytical engines
could never do more than they were programmed to do.[9]

• *Human automata.* This theme holds that mankind is something of an
anomaly in the process of evolution and must be controlled using scientific
methods in order to bring him in harmony with the rest of the universe. By far
the most well-known literary works on this theme are *Nineteen Eighty-four* and
Brave New World, and there is ample serious nonfiction writing that either
predates or is contemporaneous with both of them. Perhaps the most influential
of the latter was Arthur Koestler's *The Ghost in the Machine*. The scientific
counterpart is seen in the strong, if not dominant trend, in modern psychiatry
to rely on psychoactive drugs to control behavior in lieu of more humanistic

therapy. The euphemism is "the organic approach." Franz Alexander, who was Freud's first student, said,

> the role of the devil now has been taken over by brain chemistry. No longer a devil but a *deus ex machina*, a disturbed brain chemistry rather than the person's own life experiences, is responsible for mental illness. Whatever the cause of faulty brain chemistry may be, the new conviction is that the disturbed mind can now be cured by drugs and that the patient himself as a person no longer needs to understand the source of his troubles and master them by self-knowledge.[10]

The counterpart in automation is the growing tendency to micromanage individual and organizational behavior by way of massed databases, sometimes by attempting to predict behavior based on known correlations. This is not chemistry per se, but the effect on the psyche can be just as strong. Furthermore, it is on this theme that most published criticisms of automation concentrate, usually under the heading of invasion of privacy.

Mind versus matter. Literature, as pervasive as it may be, is not the only font of the Frankenstein issue. Science itself contributes by way of its foremost tenet—namely monism. This is the belief that mind and matter are inseparable aspects of the same thing. In many ways, nature itself seems to support this view. For example, many viruses, when magnified by electron-microscopy, give the appearance of machinery. The T-2 and T-4 bacteriophages in particular bear an uncanny resemblance to the lunar landing module. Now considering that complex cells in part evolved by simple, undifferentiated cells swallowing such constructs, the phenomenon suggests that man is some sort of biological machine. As Marvin Minsky put it, "the brain is a computer made out of meat" (quoted in Martin Gardner's forward to Roger Penrose's *The Emperor's New Mind*). Penrose's book, however, argues to the contrary. Drawing on nearly the whole of physics, he amply demonstrates that nothing in physics can measure up to the sophistication of the human mind. Therefore, even if the monist premise is correct, no machine will ever supplant or surpass humanity.

Other physicists have taken a different view, notably Erwin Schrödinger. He argued that no matter how sophisticated the human mind was, its brain consisted of permutations and combinations of physical mass and the laws which govern it. Regardless of any psychical attributes, every human act must be manifested or carried out by the laws of physics and chemistry, and the brain itself must act as a receptor of physical or electromagnetic stimuli. In effect, he argued that a human being was a robot that just hadn't realized it.[11] Any ghost within was merely a decoration. Schrödinger did admit that genes could weave a fabric that was more like a Raphael tapestry than repetitive wallpaper, but he could have countered this with the fact that an automated loom can be programmed to reproduce any pattern, no matter how intricate. Moreover, science tends to back up Schrödinger's main thesis in that every known process in organic chemistry has been reduced to some combination of inorganic reactions.

The one sticking point in monism was that organisms learn while inorganic compounds do not. Norbert Wiener demolished that obstacle with his seminal *Cybernetics or Control and Communications in the Animal and the Machine*, first published in 1948. He studied the organic process and began to replicate it with machines. John von Neumann compiled a similar treatise in his last few months of life—*The Computer and the Brain* (Yale University Press, 1958). Today it is not uncommon to write software that "learns" from its reactions with its environment and reprograms itself accordingly.

How, then, does one go about resolving this issue? That is clearly beyond the scope of this book, and perhaps it can never be resolved because it must be an axiom of any unified understanding of mankind and science. Seventy years ago, Kurt Gödel demonstrated that no theory—regardless of its reach, irrespective of its profundity, and despite any elegance in its logical sinews—can prove its own axioms. Axioms are logical bones, the utility of which depends on how well the flesh and blood of derived theorems hang on them—that is, how well they *consistently* explain a body of facts without contradicting other theories (unless the theorist is prepared to challenge them too). Fortunately, the idea of pure monism must eventually collapse. It is impossible to explain a joke with a set of equations. Unfortunately, the debate is largely irrelevant.

Minding what matters. Irrelevant? Yes, and for many reasons. First, man is quite capable of blowing himself and the earth out of existence without any help from golems, courtesy of thermonuclear power. Second, he is equally capable of genocide and other unspeakable crimes, to the point at which the imagined tragedies perpetuated by fictional monsters are child's play compared to the sins of history and the excesses of technology. Third, presume that a machine *could* be built that was able to perceive and create art, to write a book on its own initiative, and to evince intrinsic emotions and everything else that is commonly regarded as distinctly human. In the larger perspective, it would not amount to a hill of beans.

The manifestation of human attributes must be carried out in biological or mechanical terms in some order or sequence. Automation can replicate almost every one of those steps and manage them in an ever-widening sphere under the control of a few individuals while reducing the need for human labor whenever the mechanics prove cheaper. Furthermore, this "progress" opens few new doors to employ the skills of the dispossessed. Aldous Huxley foresaw this in *Brave New World*, and later Woody Allen humorously capitalized on the theme in his film *Sleeper*. Finally, the power of suggestion combined with man's tendency to obey authority may yet pay too much homage to decision support programs, especially as they grow more sophisticated.

These programs come closest to human thinking and as mentioned trace their roots to the beginning of the fourteenth century. By 1729, Jonathan Swift felt obliged to satirize this endeavor in *Gulliver's Travels*. The character of

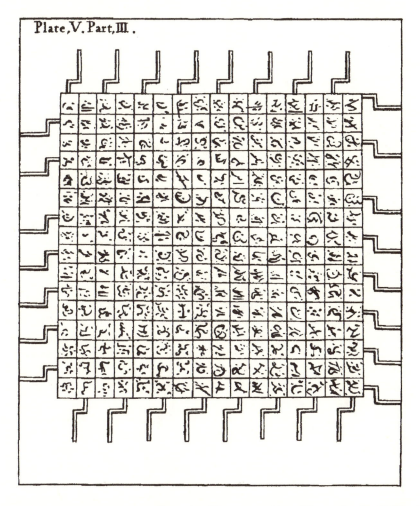

9. Swift's tongue-in-cheek artificial intelligence machine. The satire in *Gulliver's Travels* poked fun at man's early attempts to replicate human intelligence, but if Swift were alive today, he might be more inclined to satirize the potential abuses rather than the idea itself. Incidentally, this was the only illustration in his manuscript beyond the maps of imaginary places that Gulliver visited.

Gulliver, on his imaginary voyage to Balnibarbi, finds a university at which the professors have inscribed words (in their symbolic language) on the faces of blocks mounted on axles. On signal, clerks turn the axles at random speeds. Upon another signal, they stop. The faculty then records the words appearing face up as sentences for a book, and the whole process is repeated as many times as necessary.

This satire is no longer appropriate. Machines may not write books from scratch, but word processors, spell-checkers, and grammar analyzers aid immeasurably in the process. Text for newsmagazines and *The Wall Street Journal* is assembled electronically and sent over networks to printing plants located through the country, where robotics take over and print the paper copies. For man has slowly realized that not only economic productivity but much of his thinking can be broken down into small steps, and those steps can be regimented like a parading gaggle of geese.[12]

Aiding and abetting this crush of automation is the increasing division of labor into specialized fields of work. This simplifies the application of physical robotics, and worse it means that workers must be carefully managed in order to manufacture products or provide services. This, in turn, requires more paperwork and accounting, which itself requires specialization and more management and more paper. Even if the economy concentrated on manufacture, it would still be information oriented.

Add to this the progress of technology in general, which means that fewer people can maintain what they own or use. This expands the service industry base even further, which generates even more paperwork and accounting. It should therefore be no surprise that automation matured just in time to preserve profits while dealing with these mounting requirements. It should also be no surprise that many individual workers—with their payrolls, their emotions, and their host of other problems—are increasingly viewed as an expensive luxury if not an anachronism in some circles, notwithstanding lip service to the contrary. An individual may find it hard to love a machine; corporate man does not. More on this in the next chapter.

Finally, let us admit that yesterday's miracle is today's ho-hum. With the advent of (a) biogenetic engineering, (b) state-of-the-art research in computer science, and (c) the exponential increase in knowledge, man seems to have placed one foot in the godhead and is determined that its mate follow suit. Recall that the earth and its civilization took four billion years, more or less, to arrive at their present state. If that time is represented by a line a mile long, you would need a microscope to perceive the last one hundred and fifty years (equal to about two one-thousandths of an inch). In that minuscule period, knowledge has leaped from imagined Frankensteins to the threshold of piecemeal but nevertheless insidious technological equivalency. It doesn't take much imagination to project what might evolve at the end of another speck of time.

Thus mankind's creations may devour his economy while the intrusion into individual privacy by way of expanding databases and abuses perpetrated therefrom nibbles away at his soul. Furthermore, this situation has nothing to do with imagination, with literature, or with fantasy. It is that machine on your desktop—all ninety million of them. Restated, and reminiscent of the cartoon character *Pogo's* most famous utterance, we are discovering that the ultimate adversary "is us." The next chapter outlines why this new antagonist is on such a roll.

4

Impetus and the Encompassing Malaise

Reality asserts its own logic and
overcomes legal arrangements.
—Hans Morganthau

The impetus of political revolution is discontent grown malignant. It heats to a flash point—critical mass—whereupon a single event—sometimes a pamphlet or ninety-five theses nailed to a door—ignites it. Substituting need for malcontent, technological revolutions sometimes follow suit, witness Fulton's steamboat and Bell's telephone. So far, automation has not experienced that level of drama beyond the academic discussions of the Frankenstein issue, but it is impelled by an unusually large number of incentives.

These incentives are both economic and subjective in nature. The economic side includes both cost and marketplace considerations, plus the growing emphasis on quality control. The subjective side is equally pervasive, and most of it reinforces the economic pressures. The degree of force exerted by some of these incentives is debatable (not to mention whether they will continue with the same intensity). On the other hand, there is no refuting their sheer mass, especially in the absence of significant counterincentives.

Furthermore, the decline in defense spending, which has been the source of much development in automation, has many vendors scrambling to find private markets for their expertise, for example, developing handwriting character recognition for the Postal Service. Other applications include state-of-the-art pilot trainer cockpit modules that replicate movement of aircraft, and ways to blow up asteroids that might crash into the earth.

All of these incentives are enmeshed in what might be considered a socioeconomic malaise, headed by an enormous federal debt that continues to grow unchecked and therefore ordains an economic catastrophe in some form. In the interim, the need to provide more services for less cost further encourages new applications for automation.

Cost economics. This type of incentive aims at reducing the cost of manufactured goods or services without a commensurate reduction in selling price or market share. However, competition often compels cost reduction in order to lower prices just to keep that share. In either case, the focus is on economic surgery. In the formative stage of automation technology, this may not have been the main impetus. That technology was too busy catching up with needs. For every job cut, at least one new job was created. Furthermore, a few management information departments (or their equivalent) in the largest corporations now have budgets that exceed the billion dollar mark.[1] Yet this situation is changing. Automation no longer exudes mystique. Rather, executives increasingly see it as a scalpel.

The most common operation is a laborectomy—the elimination of jobs. Laborectomies have two protocols. The first is direct substitution by specialized robotics, typically by dividing manual labor into small increments and then replacing those increments with machines. The robotic baggage handling system at the new Denver airport may be an Edsel of sorts, but the Edsel did not bring the automobile industry to its knees, and the next attempt at automated airport luggage handling will likely succeed. The second protocol is an overhaul of the way business is conducted by realigning labor requirements in order to replace some of the workforce with electronics. As an alternative, management can farm out lower skilled jobs to lower cost contract labor, or it can increase the proportion of lower-pay-and-benefits part-time labor.

The second most common procedure is reduction of operating costs. This form is less drastic, but the savings mount up and the opportunities are more numerous. Examples range from increased reliance on electronic mail, to elimination of storage space by way of image processing, to finely tuned inventory control in order to reduce the costs of storage and pilferage. Superficially, this approach preserves jobs, yet most operating costs depend on the labor of suppliers and vendors. When the demand is reduced, so too is the total labor requirement.

A third procedure seeks to reduce fraud and embezzlement. These losses are not always thought of as costs, but they are. Losses of any kind reduce profit margins. Alternatively, higher prices must be charged to compensate, which makes products and services less competitive. To date, as detailed in chapters 6 and 10, automation has led to a vast increase in the magnitude of these crimes because larger amounts of money are being processed at a greater distance, so to speak, from human oversight. In combination with the human tendency to accept what a computer reports, it takes longer to identify the losses. By the time identification is made, tracking down the culprits is difficult at best.

On the other hand, automation itself can be harnessed to throttle these losses by extending the interior lines of data networks. When the Internal Revenue Service required that all claimed dependents be identified with a Social Security number, seven million children disappeared. It wasn't genocide, though; they never existed in the first place. Filers knew that the IRS could compare any numbers entered with the actual Social Security database and hence immediately detect a fraudulent claim.

Finally, as costs are reduced by the aforementioned approaches, the need for management, especially middle management, shrinks. Senior executives in large corporations and institutions may inflate their their salaries, but that is small stuff compared to the high cost of the management bulge in the middle. More to the point, the tasks at this level often comprise little more than paper shuffling and data gathering. Electronic automation, especially as databases are enlarged and reconciliation of conflicting data becomes less onerous, reduces the need for this kind of oversight. Furthermore, upper levels of management can directly evaluate worker performance, although this micromanagement can sometimes backfire by loss of initiative on the part of the lower level supervisors that are retained.

What proportion of these savings is real and how much is accounting technique? General MacArthur told the story of a cavalry patrol crossing the desert in search of a water hole. They met up with an Indian scout, who informed them that the water hole was only ten miles ahead. After riding that distance they found no water, but another scout promptly informed them that his colleague was mistaken; the water hole was ten miles from the spot on which they now stood. When this scene played out a third time, the first sergeant said "Thank God, Captain, we're holding our own."

And so it is with cost accounting. Claimed savings are often illusory. An analysis may point to them, but the bottom line on actual costs refuses to budge. Although this accounting legerdemain may have been prevalent in the past, it is less so today (witness the emerging history of image processing). In one stroke, it gave organizations the ability to reduce both staff and operating costs, often at a pace that amortizes the capital costs by way of bona fide savings within a period of three years or less—and that's without counting any gains in marketplace leverage. Hence, virtually every large bank, insurance company, institution, and government agency has adopted this technology, or at least is on the verge of it. Moreover, the business opportunities are so numerous that most vendors have voluntarily agreed to open-architecture design. This means avoiding proprietary designs that more or less force clients to continue buying from the same vendor.[2]

10. When empty space speaks volumes. The former records area of an insurance company in transition from paper recordkeeping to image processing. What formerly consumed acres of space now settles for a desk and terminal. It is a step toward Hamlet's infinite kingdom in a nutshell. Unfortunately, there is less room for existing employees in such confines.

In short—and this is not always readily apparent—cognizance of automation's leverage now permeates entire organizations, not just MIS departments. In previous decades, executives were seasoned on a regimen of hard work and individual judgment. They had limited toleration for automation except for mundane transactional tasks, and they seldom took any time to understand the technology. By contrast, an increasing number of today's executives were required to buy a computer as part of their undergraduate schooling, and most had to come to grips with applied computer science in their M.B.A. programs. Furthermore, as automation begins to support broader ranges of decision making, as terminals proliferate on desks at every level, and as software grows more user friendly, the attitudes of even the foot-draggers will change.

Marketplace economics and quality control. If cutting costs is the province of management bean counters, expanding market share and developing new or at least more reliable products is the quest of business leadership. The former has limits, below which any further cutting is likely to reduce quality and eventually lead to a loss of market share or increased liabilities. No so the marketplace. In the professional sense of the word, that is where all the fun is. If the game can be won without cutthroat tactics, simply by building a better and cheaper mousetrap, all the better. From this vantage point, automation is viewed more as a weapon than as a tool of management or, as scholars would put it, as an instrument of strategic leverage. Not every corporation or agency is up to it, of course, but there always seems to be enough to start the applications on an inexorable roll. Once these prototypes prove themselves, the competition has little choice but to follow suit. As for new products and services, the opportunities are extensive. Examples—some of which have been operating for years—include the following:

• *Pinpoint marketing.* Mass mailings aimed at sales are rarely cost efficient. For any given product or service, only a small fraction of the population is ready and willing to buy it, and some of those will do so without prompting. Enter selective mailing, or what is sometimes referred to as trading in the shotgun for a rifle. This technique assesses records of previous purchases or other data that correlate with the product. The brochures and flyers are then sent only to those with the higher correlation factors. This greatly reduces postage and printing costs, more than offsetting the often negligible cost of scanning databases. Sometimes vendors use their own databases—for example, American Express.[3] At other times they purchase mass marketing data compiled by other companies.

• *Instant response and fewer lost orders.* The extent to which order and client information is put on electronic media (presuming it is done well) is the extent to which paper records do not get lost and the speed with which customer representatives can respond instantly to inquiries. Although the impact on market share in specific cases may be too subjective to measure, the technology has a marked impact on customer loyalty when considered on a cumulative basis. That never hurts.

• *Prediction of unavoidable mechanical failure.* All mechanical devices need maintenance and are bound to break down sooner or later. Preventive maintenance can reduce the number of these incidents but not eliminate them. Nor would scheduled preventive overhauls solve the problem; the cost is usually too high. On the other hand, breakdowns can often be predicted based on a decision support program analysis of routine maintenance needs. The Otis Elevator Company uses this technique to keep its customers happy.[4] Repair of elevators that takes longer than overnight engenders discontent among building tenants. Those tenants remember the delays when it comes time to renew the lease, especially in cities with a glut of office space selling under par.

• *Product ingenuity.* There is no limit here. For instance, marketing-oriented technologists clearly see the day when three-dimensional holographic television—as well as theme parks and virtual sex, for that matter (perhaps in combination)—will be commonplace, even if takes twenty years to get the cost down.[5] Then, too, every year some automobile manufacturer develops a new computer-aided accessory for its cars. Elsewhere, the evidence suggests that computer-aided instruction for public schools has turned the viability corner. The list goes on and on.

• *Quality control.* In the past few years, American industry has recognized that shoddy goods' turn customers to foreign manufacture even if the products are more expensive. Consequently, American industries have striven to make amends, as discussed at length in *Business Week*.[6] Automation plays a role in this, but it is not nearly as important as the personal interest of chief executive officers. On the other hand, some analysts report that commitment to quality control is fading. It has not always led to increased profits, reduced costs, or improved market share.[7] Here is where automation offers a more cost-effective substitute, although it can displace labor.

• *Training and development.* The era of *pervasive* decision support programs is still a few years in the future. In the interim, various models have gained acceptance as a tool for training and development at every skill level, from just above common laborer to high level management. The idea goes back to the Link pilot trainers in World War II and perhaps earlier. In other words, while many (if not most) senior executives are reluctant to accept machine logic to support actual decision making, they have come to recognize its economic value in training. Mistakes made in the classroom often prevent similar and more costly mistakes on the job.

All of this leads to the potential impetus within the professional consulting market—the need keeps growing in direct proportion to the rising price tags of professionals (hence their unavailability to an increasing segment of the population). The question is how automation can substitute for professionals with years of formal schooling and intense experience. Would you have your appendix removed while your gurney rode the rails of an assembly-line operating room? Probably not, but Robodoc can perform the drilling part of hip replacements and do a better job than doctors.[8] The answer to the question, then, is that automation would not substitute for professionalism but only improve the interior lines to render it more effective, more available, and less costly.

The potential is especially strong within the medical profession. By some estimates, 60 to 70 percent of office calls are medically unnecessary. But it is not easy to triage every case in advance, while the rising cost and decline in insurance coverage (and very high deductibles for those who have it) discourage even the attempt.[9] In other words, a national health care system would only fuel these costs, even with some form of rationing, simply because it would increase these diagnostic office visits. Significant copayments—assuming some form of waiver for the indigent—might reduce the misuse, but the problem would remain. The need, therefore, is for better communications access between patients and physicians or clinic that goes far beyond what now transpires over the telephone. This is discussed at more length in the next chapter and again in Chapter 8.

Subjective impetus. Of the subjective incentives, perhaps the strongest is the scientific quest itself. This has grown especially influential with the elimination of geographic frontiers. Every high mountain has been climbed, including Mount Everest more than 400 times, twice solo without the aid of supplementary oxygen.[10] In other words, the remaining frontiers are almost all scientific in nature, witness the increasing number of articles in this regard appearing in *National Geographic* magazine.

Automation can be construed as a field of science, and indeed the expression *computer science* is bandied about freely and has been a field of specialization in Ph.D. programs for decades. More often than not, however, automation is regarded as technology to support research in other scientific fields and perhaps as a model for investigating the automation aspects of nature, especially genetics. Still, this constitutes a powerful incentive, and if the results do not have immediate commercial value, the techniques developed usually find their way into other applications.

The technology of automation also feeds on human impatience. Supposedly, most people can be divided into type A and type B behavior. Type A's are impatient and the source of most workaholics. By contrast, type B's are patient, calm, and serene. Although there are many intermediate conditions, the theory posits that individuals tend to crowd the polemics rather than fill out a normal distribution curve between them. Perhaps so, but at least one experiment suggests that everyone is potentially type A; it just takes a stronger dose of aggravation to trigger that behavior. Both types were placed in a computer lab and tasked ostensibly to edit a document with what to them was a familiar word processor. However, the real purpose of the experiment was to measure their reactions as the software was intentionally modified to produce increasingly long delays between commands and response. Eventually every participant became infuriated.[11] Smart vendors can capitalize on this impatience by finding more ways to use automation to reduce delays in any kind of situation.

Concern for the environment constitutes another subjective impetus. At the elementary level, computers and automated sensors are used to control emissions, especially in cars. More advanced applications include models to assess long-term ecological damage and the costs of abating it. Somewhat related to this are activist campaigns intended to persuade laboratories to cease using animals for research and rely instead on computer models. Medical science is a long way from that point, but it is spurring development of such models.

Still another major impetus are the needs of the military. The Department of Defense remains the world's largest single user of automation, and much attention is now focused on "smart" programs to make more efficient use of resources, especially in the often split-second decision making associated with tactics and, for that matter, on vastly complex operations such as the Strategic Defense Initiative ("Star Wars"). A good example occurs in anti-submarine warfare, wherein changing from passive to active sonar at the wrong moment can mean disaster.[12] Another, more extensive example applies to military weaponry in general. The supposedly subjective debate on the best mix of the elements of war—sea, land, or air, and what type of each—lends itself to more objective analysis than popularly assumed.[13] Finally, the government, especially the Department of Defense, now requires that most bids on major contracts be submitted in automated form.[14]

By far, however, the strongest impetus is the drum beating for ever more sweeping integrated databases. For example, the National Center for Disease Control recently proposed a nationwide database to track birth defects for the purpose of research and for possible aid to victims.[15] This is a door opener. The same logic can be applied to every contagious disease and serious dysfunction. Sooner or later these specific registries would be integrated on the grounds of more effective research on individuals afflicted with two or more of these problems. In turn, this would lead to justification for including all individuals in order to compare the afflicted with "normal" individuals.

Another example is the recent recommendation of the U.S. Commission on Interstate Child Support, proposing a national computer network and harness the mechanics of tax and tax-withholding forms to track down deadbeat fathers and force them to meet their child support obligations.[16] The Commission estimated that only a third of the assessed $15 billion per year is being paid, which severely threatens the welfare of more than eleven million children. On October 19, 1992, the outgoing Secretary of Health and Human Services, Louis Sullivan, announced that his department was proceeding with a plan to create a national computer system for all Medicare and Medicaid billings and that he had the authority to do so without benefit of any additional legislation.[17] The reasoning was that a system of this kind would cut billions from administrative overhead.

Still another project is the proposed national database of convicted child abusers. Legislation on this issue made it through the Senate Judiciary Committee (chaired by Senator Joseph Biden) in 1992 but failed passage when it was tacked onto a crime bill that included the so-called Brady Bill gun-control measure (subsequently passed in 1994).[18] A television program on the problem in general—*Scared Silent: Exposing and Ending Child Abuse*—was aired on all four networks in early September 1992. It was hosted by Oprah Winfrey, who was also the prime mover behind the legislative proposal.[19]

On the commercial side, consider the Lotus Development Corporation marketing information database, known as *Marketplace: Households*. This company compiled detailed marketing-related data on virtually every consumer purchasing unit in the country (on optical disks by regions) and planned to market them piecemeal or in sets at the purchaser's option. Public outcry put the project on the back burner, but neither the disks nor the means of updating them were destroyed, and corporations continue to use them and similar databases (more on this in Chapter 6).[20]

Yet another example of potential invasion of privacy is the Metromail real estate ownership database on 81 million households representing 151 million individuals, including virtually all homes worth more than $40,000. This database covers every state except Kansas (because of restrictive state laws there) and relies on a wide net of consultants to obtain updated information from original sources. Metromail sells this information to lending institutions intent on soliciting refinancing business for home mortgages.[21]

Elsewhere, some well-known writers outside the government have proposed various forms of national data banks. For example, the famed psychiatrist and author, M. Scott Peck, advocated a national register of all individuals whom psychiatrists label as "evil." This proposal is clearly stated in his *People of the Lie*.[22] Peck admitted the need for precautions to prevent abuse, but since when have psychiatrists been sanctioned to be the arbiters of character and ethics? Worse, the typical cases he described in that book are arguably not what the general population would commonly regard as evil.

When one considers the extent to which doctors, including psychiatrists, have defrauded Medicare and other insurers, the prospect of such a database is truly reminiscent of Hitler's gestapo, yet public reaction to proposals of this kind has been essentially nil.[23] This is especially disturbing when one considers the immense popularity of Peck's earlier book *The Road Less Traveled*, which a survey reported in a December 1991 issue of *Parade* magazine identified as one of the three most influential books read in modern times. The other two were the Bible and Ayn Rand's *Atlas Shrugged*.

Finally—and this is a black mark on a major slice of corporate America—employees are sometimes regarded as an expensive, troublesome, poorly motivated, and often illiterate resource; while unions, which now represent only a small fraction of the workforce, are often held in such disrepute by senior management that their opinions are largely unprintable. Additionally, many corporations are getting rid of older employees systematically, probably to cut the costs of higher wages and pension obligations. At least one company openly offers incentives for employees to leave after a mere three years.[24]

Furthermore, this situation has been exacerbated by the Americans With Disabilities Act of 1991. According to some interpretations, the fact of having been a former alcoholic, no matter how many relapses have occurred, is no bar to employment. Addiction has been declared to be a disability rather than a defect in character.[25] This means that no inquiries can be made on this score during interviews, although exceptions can be made when public safety is obviously involved (e.g., operators of passenger conveyances). Similarly, individuals with AIDS must not be excluded, notwithstanding that a few of them on the payroll of a small company would bring ruination to its health care benefits plan.

There are three methods of dealing with such employees or potential employees, all of them unfavorable (if not illegal) but realistic for any company that depends on profits to survive. One is to determine the applicant's history by surreptitious checking of other databases. The second is to use computer-based micromanagement of employee performance, which (if imposed equally on all employees) is bound to weed out a lot of troublemaking that seems correlated with these newly defined "disabilities." The third is to harness automation in order to reduce the number of employees.

Wise employers recognize that chronic discontent among employees often stems from bad or insensitive management practices. It is a truism that when properly motivated, employees are a corporation's best resource. Unfortunately, wise employers are scarce. Furthermore, in times of high unemployment, cheap foreign labor, and merged corporations, the job market belongs to the employers. Even when management is enlightened, it must sometimes cut costs drastically in order to survive.

Socioeconomic malaise. Undoubtedly, some members of every generation presume their own era is the worst in history and that "the good old days" are a thing of the past. There is some objective evidence that they are now correct. Fordham University researcher Marc Miringoff reported that the Index of Social Indicators recently fell to its lowest point in many decades.[26] This index is drawn from a large number of government data sources. George Will used more direct terms by titling one of his columns "America's Slide Into the Sewer."[27] The late Allan Bloom put the case in academic terms in his popular book *The Closing of the American Mind*.

By far the single biggest item on the malaise agenda is the national debt and the anxiety it engenders as it seemingly grows out of control. This debt has already passed the five trillion dollar mark (including the funds borrowed from eight federal trust funds in excess of the "official" annual deficits), and it continues to increase at a rate between $200 and $300 billion a year. No matter how much the 1993 tax increase reduced annual deficits, each remaining deficit will increase the debt further, which will thus continue to increase annual interest costs, thus further increasing the amount to be borrowed annually. Sooner or later, the mathematics of the situation must lead to economic collapse; no nation can borrow to infinity. The mechanics of how the collapse will occur are, of course, speculation, but a number of economists have written popular books on the subject, and at least two of them made it to *The New York Times* best seller list.[28]

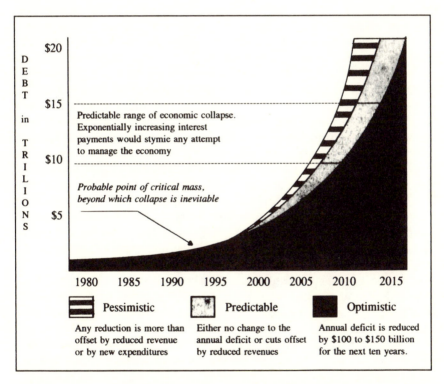

Pessimistic	Any reduction is more than offset by reduced revenue or by new expenditures
Predictable	Either no change to the annual deficit or cuts offset by reduced revenues
Optimistic	Annual deficit is reduced by $100 to $150 billion for the next ten years.

11. Critical mass and the national debt. Annual deficits continue unabated, incurring ever larger interest payments and causing the cumulative debt to mushroom even faster. The precise rate of growth is immaterial because it passed the point of critical mass several years ago and is now metastasizing at an exponential rate. Collapse is all but inevitable; a nation cannot borrow to infinity. Think of it as an economic cancer consuming its host.

However, one point is clear. The current per-family national debt share of $75,000 is misleading. At least 60 percent of the families and other consumer units in the United States do not have the savings or income to pay off any of this debt. This means that the de facto share for the 40 percent (or less) of the families that have any significant disposable income is roughly $188,000 and rising fast.[29] Restated, every family or consumer unit with an income of $25,000 or more will eventually have its future mortgaged for $250,000, and that's after paying taxes. Obviously, few families can pay that kind of mortgage, and therefore the economy will have no choice but to collapse eventually.

Furthermore, the Bipartisan Commission on Entitlement and Tax Reform, chaired by Senator J. Robert Kerrey (a Medal of Honor recipient), openly admits that within fifteen years taxes must be raised 85 percent just to maintain *present* spending and to avoid any increase to the current level of deficit financing.[30] Unfortunately, the federal tax load on the highest incomes is now approximately 41 percent (39.6% plus the 1.45% Medicare tax), which means that the upper rate would be increased to 76 percent. Furthermore, this increase does not include state taxes (which must also increase, perhaps to an upper level rate of 15 percent), and it does nothing to stem the continued increase to the debt. So it doesn't take too much analysis to realize that even a tax rate of 100 percent will eventually prove insufficient. Note also that even the most conservative government estimates of the annual deficit project it to mushroom again beginning in fiscal year 1999 in light of existing entitlement legislation and that many new entitlement programs—especially some form of national health insurance—are itching for enactment.

To this must be added the growing trade deficit and the mounting cost of welfare. One child in seven is on the rolls of Aid to Families with Dependent Children, and one in ten persons buys food stamps (more are eligible but have not applied). More significantly, at least for the long haul, the growth of the retired population at the expense of the proportionally shrinking workforce, must eventually bring chaos to the Social Security system. And that's just the federal debt. Most states, especially California, are also in deep economic trouble. They look to the federal government to bail them out, with what heaven only knows.

Next on the list is rampant crime. The National Research Council Committee on Law and Justice (an arm of the National Academy of Sciences) reported that the rate of crime is nearing its historic peak reached during the Great Depression. Moreover, the United States has the highest rate of violent crime among developed nations. This rate translates into 10,900,000 victims annually.[31] Another survey determined that as many as one person in seven was physically or sexually abused as a child. That survey—*The Day America Told the Truth*—also painted a grim picture of the American ethos in general.[32]

Then, too, there is the matter of an all-time low in academic achievement coupled with an all-time high in functional illiteracy, at a time when the economy demands a more highly educated workforce.[33] Without that, corporations will naturally turn to a more intense use of automation as a substitute.

Table 1. The exponentially increasing federal debt
(dollar amounts in millions)

Year	Annual deficit	Federal debt	Available income above $30,000/yr	Amount to fund deficit & amortize the debt	Percent of available income
1995	$424,000	$5,724,000	$1,676,470	$839,842	50.1%
1996	$436,720	$6,160,720	$1,693,235	$884,290	52.1%
1997	$449,822	$6,610,541	$1,710,167	$930,070	54.1%
1998	$463,316	$7,073,857	$1,727,269	$977,224	56.1%
1999	$477,216	$7,551,073	$1,744,542	$1,025,793	58.1%
2000	$491,532	$8,042,605	$1,761,987	$1,075,818	61.1%
2001	$506,278	$8,548,883	$1,779,607	$1,127,345	63.1%
2002	$521,467	$9,070,350	$1,797,403	$1,180,417	65.1%
2003	$537,111	$9,607,460	$1,815,377	$1,235,082	68.1%
2004	$553,234	$10,160,680	$1,833,531	$1,291,386	70.1%
2005	$569,821	$10,730,500	$1,851,866	$1,349,380	72.1%
2006	$586,915	$11,317,420	$1,870,385	$1,409,113	75.1%
2007	$604,523	$11,921,940	$1,889,089	$1,470,638	77.1%
2008	$622,658	$12,544,600	$1,907,979	$1,534,009	80.1%
2009	$641,338	$13,185,930	$1,927,059	$1,599,282	83.0%
2010	$660,578	$13,846,510	$1,946,330	$1,666,512	85.6%

Notes:

1. This table is based on a run of program *Collapse* described in the section on software at the back of this book (using the most favorable parameters).

2. The data incorporate the unfunded borrowing from all eight major U.S. trust funds.

3. The interest rate is set at 6 percent.

4. The annual deficit and the increase to taxable income is set to increase 3 percent per year.

5. Keep in mind that 85 to 90 percent federal taxation marks the saturation point because of state and local taxes.

The list goes on *ad nauseam*: drugs, sexual promiscuity, high divorce rates, political and corporate corruption, massive greed among many professionals and brokers, fraudulent claims for insurance benefits, $127 billion annually in unpaid income tax liability (exclusive of criminal operations), a lack of health care insurance for forty million Americans, decaying physical infrastructure, sprawling urban slums, politically correct thinking carried to asinine extremes, and at least 41,000 regulations governing the common hamburger that nevertheless leave most of them tasting awful.[34]

One may argue on the magnitude of each item as well as on the extent of its effect. One may also argue about the exact size of the iceberg with which the *Titanic* had its final encounter. Norman Mailer once said that if the nineteenth century suffered from a kind of socioeconomic tuberculosis, this century has virulent cancer, metastasizing to every nook and cranny of the national ethos.[35] Granted, automation may not be responsible for this malaise, or only indirectly and then only in part, but the effects are forcing governments and businesses to buy into it at an accelerated pace. That, in turn, intensifies the malaise. Perhaps the only hope lies in the potential of a severe and prolonged national crisis that will force the United States to shake off the naive assumptions that led to this unfortunate situation. As Abba Eban, the former Israeli ambassador to the United States, put it, "my experience teaches me that men and nations behave wisely, once they have exhausted all other alternatives."[36]

II. Opportunities and Applications

As mentioned in Part I, image processing has all but revolutionized the way corporations and governments conduct business. This technology vastly increases the amount of information maintained in electronic form from a mere 2 percent to perhaps 50 percent or more.

12. An image processing operation

In the process, it is eliminating the need for tens of millions of square feet of record storage space. A variation of this processing is used not to store images but to create them, analogous to animated films, this time with three-dimensional holographic dynamic images so eerily lifelike that it is called virtual reality. This is not to say that conventional computer processing and robotics have become passé. For the foreseeable future, the bulk of the automation dollar will still find its way to that side of the house, and that offers great potential, especially in the form of decision support programs and massive databases. To say the least, then, the opportunities and new applications for automation are bound to spur its own further development.

This part of the book subdivides this potential into four chapters, corresponding to commercial applications, government applications (insofar as their magnitude makes them nearly unique), research opportunities, and health care and education. The purpose is to illustrate the positive aspects of automation before examining the ethical ramifications of its excesses in the third and fourth parts of the book.

One minor point—in practice, specific applications and techniques in each of these categories often overlap into the others, especially the commercial variety. However, each category has its own distinct theme in terms of intent, respectively: profit, large-scale management, searching, and nurture.

5

Commercial Applications

Business is more agreeable than pleasure; it
interests the whole mind, the aggregate nature
of man more continuously, and more deeply.
—Walter Bagehot

Commercial applications are the bread and butter of automation. They are widespread and strongly motivated by economic incentives, be it on the part of the manufacturer or the user or both. In dollar volume, they probably account for 80 percent of automation usage, and even higher for robotics considered alone. As such, each new application quickly loses it fascination and fades into the woodwork of day-to-day routine. However, their mere existence fuels the creation of even more sophisticated models. No one seriously challenges this trend. The issue is just how explosive this growth will continue to be. The answer is not as speculative as it might seem. All six generic applications discussed in this chapter have taken root and show little sign of let-up. If anything, most of them are opening up new or at least expanded markets for related products.

First, portability and automated input now dominate retail sales. Second, training developers have invested heavily in decision support programs, which in turn inspire "graduates" to use them in actual work. Third, files and records management is on the verge of making image processing a household word. Fourth, electronic funds transfer permeates business and government. Fifth, the professional consulting market now uses automation heavily because the potential economic gains are enormous. And sixth, the concept of the home workstation is the endpoint of the evolving information superhighway and cyberspace.

Portability and automated input. In 1869, Louisa May Alcott wrote *Little Women*, an autobiographical novel intended for children that brought her financial independence. Today the vendors are writing one called "Little Robots." The idea is to compress as much automation into as small a space as possible in order to extend this technology and its marketplace into every nook and cranny in existence. In some cases, this also benefits individuals. The best known are the "smart" surgical implants to take over physiological control functions when a human organ fails (e.g., pacemakers).

Courtesy of Zeos International, Ltd., Minneapolis, MN

13. An impressive frontrunner of computer miniaturization. Palmtop computers that accept miniature memory cards suggest that automation is expanding from the desktop and taking up residence in hip-pockets. Furthermore, twenty years from now—perhaps sooner—a machine of this size will rival today's mainframe.

On the commercial side, the most popular applications are the familiar magnetic strip for data on the back of credit and bank cards, and the ubiquitous Uniform Product Code (UPC). Further, many computers are now built to accept memory cards and other peripherals about the same size as a credit card under the acronym PCMCIA (Personal Computer Memory Card International Association), not to mention computers that fit in the palm of the hand. There is no practical limit to the crucial information that can be recorded on those cards, which in turn can be used to activate, use, or otherwise manage other automated devices or programs.

Zeos makes a small computer that accepts these cards. It weighs only 1.3 pounds and sells for under $400 (under the Prolinear label). Hewlett-Packard makes an even smaller computer that easily fits in a pocket—the HP200—although it does not have a normal-size keyboard. Another product, marketed by Apple Computers, is a "personal digital assistant" called the Newton (which now has several competitors). This small palmtop device is both a computer and modem that links easily with a wide variety of sources of information and is perhaps a forerunner of the home workstation. A fourth product is Sony's portable multimedia CD library machine.

The implication of this miniaturization is that the computer will extend from the desktop to the individual, and as a result an exponentially increasing number of individuals will be corralled by automation. This metastasis of electronic information will peek up at you from your pocket to the point that you may not be able to leave home without it.

Training and development. Training at all levels increasingly relies on automation. It provides intense, one-on-one instruction that can be parsed out in small modules and integrated with on-the-job experience. Computer-assisted instruction is also used extensively in formal training programs, particularly when it is essential to learn by making serious mistakes without inflicting actual damage. Pilot and air controller training are obvious examples. To be sure, these applications have been in use for decades. What *is* new is the extent to which virtual reality and decision support programs can be added to the scenarios. No one has accurately determined the price tag on inadequate training, and perhaps it would be impossible to do so. Still, the one thing certain is that the more realistic and intense the training—especially when the participants sense or feel that they are dealing with reality—the fewer losses that will occur on the job.

The same benefit is even more applicable for management positions and the command equivalents in the military. The higher one climbs the executive ladder, the more costly the mistakes, sometimes in lives. In these situations, however, virtual reality is less important than decision support programming. Not every executive dilemma can be addressed with this technique, but there are more opportunities than commonly perceived.[1] This even extends to a program designed to train SWAT teams how to react in hostage taking situations.[2] Members of these teams have more than once had their "common sense" notions corrected. For example, when a hostage-taker demands food, it is better to send in victuals that must be prepared rather than fast food. The act of preparing food may create a more positive bond between terrorists and hostage.

Many of these systems have emigrated into actual operations (though not the hostage-situation model) and include a variation that focuses on group decision making. Anyone with experience on committees knows how exasperating they can be. Either a few dominant individuals foreclose the opinions of their less forceful colleagues, or decisions are reached by compromises that satisfy no one. By force of personality, a few chairmen may be able to overcome these tendencies and bring out the best in a committee, but for the most part it takes an external influence to do this. Networked interactive systems are beginning to make inroads here, some of them pioneered by the Ventana Corporation located in Tucson, Arizona.[3]

Files and records management. Although computer stocks began to decline in the later 1980s, a cover story of *Forbes* magazine (November 26, 1990) advised holding onto them; image processing would turn things around. The reason is that business and government—almost all organizations for that matter—are inundated with paperwork with no end in sight. This paperwork is the inorganic equivalent of obesity, and the conventional or digital side of the computer house has done little to reduce it. If anything, it created more paperwork of its own. Microfilming reduced some of the space problems but not much else. Image processing is a different story. It eliminates the physical medium except for a jukebox-like repository for optical memory disks, from which any number of visual copies can be retrieved instantly from any location in a network.

At first, computer manufacturers shunned this line of business. They reasoned that this technology was beneath the dignity of automated processing; it was merely electronic microfilming. As a result, the pioneering work was done as much by entrepreneurs as by established vendors, and it was one of the former that put image processing on the map. That company is FileNet, based in Costa Mesa, California. Meanwhile, two end users had been experimenting with it and thus played pivotal roles. One was USAA, an insurance and diversified financial services company headquartered in San Antonio, Texas. Their main building is one of the few in the United States with its own ZIP code, which hints at the volume of paperwork. The other was the Internal Revenue Service, the paperwork of which is easily the Himalaya of recordkeeping.

USAA has been featured in *Harvard Business Review* and *Business Week* as a paradigm of sound corporate practices, but it remains largely unknown outside the insurance industry because with few exceptions its clientele are limited to military and former military officers and their dependents.[4] Its chairman (at the time), Robert F. McDermott, was a retired brigadier general and former dean of the Air Force Academy. He had advocated a paperless office for more than twenty years, but early experiments with microfilm, which was the only viable option at the time, did not pan out. The efficiency of the existing operation was already razor sharp, and the medium did not provide for instant retrieval. Fortunately, experiments with image processing were more successful. Then when USAA requested bids for a full-fledged system, IBM decided the time had come to move this technology into the commercial mainstream. Its bid was successful, and image processing hasn't been the same since.

The IRS presents a similar story, except that the volume of documents, the variety of sizes, the relentless stream of new input and the need to keep records on tap for as long as seventy-five years dwarfs all other organizations. The massive volume of documentation needs no further comment. The requirement to maintain it for long periods of time is less evident. Among the reasons are that systemic fraud usually covers a period of many years, while the perfectly legal (and mandatory) practice of postponing taxes on gains from the sale of primary residences can extend for decades upon decades.[5] Furthermore, the approximately 19,000 auditors can barely make a dent on the estimated $127 billion dollars per year of fraud and unpaid taxes, in part because each audit requires access to paperwork. Image processing will obviously improve productivity due to instant retrievability of all related documents. The eventual price tag for this image system is estimated at $23 billion, but the resulting system will be more than recompensed by the elimination of immense storage and retrieval requirements.[6]

Other large users of electronic records and document management include the Library of Congress, the Department of Defense, the Patent Office, and nearly every major bank, insurance company, manufacturer, and service corporation in the world. Furthermore, as the cost of this technology shrinks, ever smaller organizations are able to buy into it, almost forcing the hold-outs to lower their resistance. This growth in applications has spread faster than wildfire, a metaphor that differs from actual conflagrations only by figuratively burning paper.

Moreover, imaging is now integrated with conventional processing. For example, engineering drawings (blueprints) have been produced using computer-assisted drafting for more than a decade. Today, existing hand-drawn blueprints can be imaged and then converted to a format suitable for digital processing and reworking. In other cases, imaged documents can be indexed within the context of decision support programs. When an attorney or a jurist needs to research an obscure legal point or seek precedence thereon, he or she need only go to an imaged-documents index and start searching, accomplishing in minutes what it would have otherwise taken hours, if not days, to do by traditional methods.

Electronic funds transfer and mail. When data is retrieved over a network, the intent is often to update that data. As such, there is no transfer of ownership, and the prime copy usually remains where it was found. Transfers, by contrast, shift ownership or its equivalent, and this is where automation continues to have a field day, bypassing the Postal Service. The technology is roughly the same as data sharing, but the incentives are much stronger. This all pertains to a realization of what money is. Physically, money is paper or coinage, but its value is not based on its physical content or the process which shaped or printed it. Rather, money is just a medium of exchange or what might be thought of as a floating accounting system. It can just as easily be logged and maintained in bitstreams and databases as on paper that fits neatly into wallets.

This electronic transfer of funds is so well entrenched that the use of physical currency has become an anomaly for all but petty cash expenditures and the underground economy, where the intent is to avoid leaving an audit trail. Common applications include payrolls and benefits, stock market transactions, most internal government and corporate funding, and credit or debit cards. By 1986, the volume of traffic had reached $300 billion *daily* in the United States, and double that amount internationally.[7] Today, the daily electronic-transaction rate is reaching for the trillion-dollar mark. Additionally, transaction data is commonly fed into other databases (e.g., input into credit bureaus). Then, too, every time someone buys a bag of french fries at a McDonald's restaurant, that data goes into a local database, summary data from which is sent periodically to the corporate headquarters near Chicago.

The proof of this is that the largest bill in circulation today is $100, whereas it used to be a $10,000 note, at a time when it took only a nickel or a dime to acquire what it takes a dollar to buy today. Moreover, fifties and century notes remain uncommon. Even the use of checks is declining as companies persuade customers to let them debit their bank accounts directly. In short, handling currency is just as troublesome as paperwork but the need to account for it remains. The advantages for billers and buyers alike are increased interest on accounts, vast reduction in postage, and usually more accurate accounting.

For example, assume that there are eighty million households with an average of four monthly utility bills. If utility companies debited bank accounts once a month with a preset average amount based on each account holder's usage (with semiannual or annual reconciliation), it would save these companies about $1.1 billion in postage, and customers would save a like amount.[8]

The resulting float would earn more interest, save another few billion in office overhead in preparing bills and processing payment envelopes, and reduce the number of meter readers to less than a fifth of the present workforce. Even with part of the savings passed on to customers as incentives, the balance would be significant indeed.

Closely associated with electronic funds transfer is electronic mail. This operation also saves time and postage by way of the lower cost of faxing or its equivalent, and for that reason few companies or mail-order firms lack a fax number. Further, as the cost of first-class postage rises and because the Postal Service has a monopoly on this class of physical-media correspondence, it's a safe bet that electronic mail will continue to mushroom and household fax machines may become as popular as VCRs.

A variation on electronic mail is electronic travel. This is not the same thing as being "beamed in" à la *Star Trek*, but the effect is similar. Tele-conferences may be old hat, but images as well as voices are interactive. More importantly, this technology reduces costs and the hassle of travel. In addition, three-dimensional holographic imagery will likely propel this usage further despite its eeriness. Granted, some critics believe that this technology will never pan out in the marketplace because, so they say, there is no substitute for human contact.[9] For sales and momentous decision making, this is probably true, but most meetings and conferences are more mundane than that.

Another variation is the program to tailor newspapers to individual needs and deliver them electronically. The MIT Media Laboratory is conducting research on behalf of an international consortium that includes Gannett Company, Knight-Ridder, Inc., Times-Mirror Company, Tribune Company, Hearst Corporation, and IBM.[10]

Still another variation on this "brings the mountain to Mohammed." This is *electronic commuting*. Using networks, some nine million employees work in their homes at tasks far more legitimate than stuffing envelopes. This approach draws on the ability of computers—called workstations—to operate as if they were units of a single computer and extends that reach to the operators themselves. When the nature of the work lends itself to this model, the advantages include savings on office and parking space, a reduction in commuting, flexible scheduling, and the ability of parents of young children to continue working without shuttling their offspring to a day-care center. To make the point even more clear, the chief executive officer of AT&T (Robert Allen) works at home via computer two hours every day. Furthermore, it isn't necessary for all work to be done on a computer; nor is it necessary to spend the entire work week at the home station.

Professional consultation. When you dispense advice for free, you are regarded as a gadfly. When you charge for it, you are a professional. Therein lies the single biggest pot of gold for automation's itchy fingers. To be sure, the attempt to use automation for professional advice was at one time considered a sham, except in the limited sense of using networks to transmit information. Doctors have used the telephone to consult with patients and colleagues for more than a century. Additionally—and this is hardly automation—how-to volumes in health care, law, and financial matters cram bookstore shelves. At least forty million parents bought a copy of Dr. Benjamin Spock's *The Common Sense Book of Baby and Child Care*. These and other books demonstrated that consumers of professional services were not blank tablets on which advice was to be inscribed or prescribed. They were active participants. Provided that consumers understood the limits of their professional knowledge, the more the better. Successful patients, litigants, and investors almost always contribute to their own well-being,

Two events brought automation into the picture. The first event comprised decision support programs to aid medical diagnosis. Perhaps the most well-known is *Mycin* (not to be confused with antibiotics ending in "mycin"), developed in the early 1970s at Stanford University as an aid to train doctors. This prototype and its many offspring were expensive to produce, but in the hands of competent physicians they have proven to be extraordinarily accurate.[11] These programs achieve this reputation by confronting doctors with the essence of vast amounts of knowledge and similar cases applied to the information available on a specific patient's condition, prompting the doctor to consider the probabilities and options before proceeding. Competent physicians are challenged by these programs; the incompetent are threatened.

The second event has been the plethora of low-priced self-help software programs, typically selling for under $100. The best known among them are the income tax preparers. They prompt for data and then, depending on options selected, produce filled-in forms ready for mailing. They can also be used as what-if decision support programs when there are options, the choice of which may affect subsequent annual reporting.[12] Other software includes preparation of legal forms and even preliminary medical advice, although the liabilities of the publisher on the latter are still risky. In short, there is a lot of money to be made as long as the software publishers do not attempt to *supplant* necessary professional judgment. The details are as follows:

• *Financial advisement.* The great problem with making personal decisions on investment and financial planning is the difficulty of considering all the factors that might affect future income, especially in dealing with probabilities and other uncertainties. Automation pulverizes these bones of contention, limited only by the amount of supporting information one is willing to pay for, be it on a disk or from a network service system (e.g., *Prodigy*). Such programs counterbalance the effects of mortgages, savings, tax consequences, interest, dividends, estimated Social Security benefits, likely budgets, and any of hundreds of other factors, all by interactive questions that require only simple numerical input.

• *Legal services.* This differs from financial services primarily by using an interactive front-end program to help the user (a) understand his or her own situation in legal context, (b) learn what the options are to resolve that situation, and (c) weigh the advantages and disadvantages of pursuing each of those options. It would not be a course in law. On the contrary, the vast majority of legal problems that individuals and families are likely to encounter fall into relatively few categories. As for the esoteric situations, the programs could at least guide the user to recognize the situation before contacting an attorney. If all this sounds far fetched, the reader is advised to visit the Maricopa County Superior Court in Phoenix, Arizona, where the *QuickCourt* computer generates various legal documents and court papers for the indigent who cannot afford lawyers.[13]

• *Health care services.* It is too early to tell if medically oriented programs will remain primarily tools for providers or if they will gravitate to consumer use to offset the unconscionable rising costs of health care. In either event, however, the user would be confronted with all reasonable potential diagnoses to rule out in order of probability, combined with the latest information on similar cases, successful and unsuccessful therapies, and appropriate pharmaceutical data. In time, use of these programs could even reduce malpractice suits (more on this in Chapter 8).

The home-based workstation. The concept of a home-based workstation combines the telephone, which is common to more than 90 percent of households, with the home computer (which often sits in a closet). But this is not the same thing as a business workstation intended for electronic commuting. Rather, it is intended to overcome the limitations of home computers or at least the complexities of harnessing them to consumer requirements, while harnessing the obvious potential of the evolving information superhighway and cyberspace.

The home computer market did not meet expectations for the distressingly simple reason that in most homes there is little *need* for them. Educational software is popular but not exactly dominant. Furthermore, most claims of user friendliness are exaggerated for the majority of the population. The buying public may be fascinated with technology, but that fascination withers in the face of continuous difficulty. Various polls indicate that 25 percent of the adult population will not use computers unless they have to. An even higher percentage are intimidated by them.

The needs of families that *do* lend themselves to automation tend to require input and output with sources external to the home. This includes paying bills, taxes, mortgages, and keeping track of funds; getting through to a doctor or a related professional on the telephone; obtaining legal advice at a reasonable cost; and streamlining the process of telephone shopping, especially given the inundation of mail-order catalogs. These and many other items share a common theme: a transaction in some form with a company, agency, or professional; or, more accurately, improvement of efficiency and reduction of cost for these transactions.

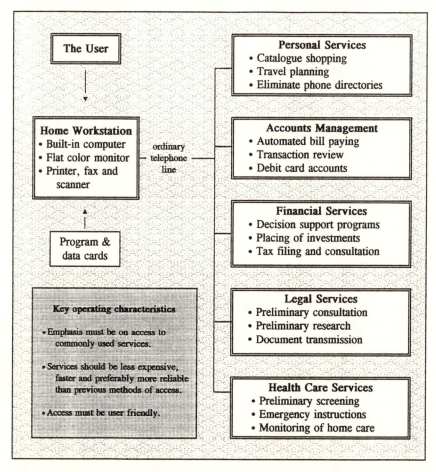

14. Home workstation concept. The home computer market did not live up to early expectations; there is little need for them and, except for games, they are not all that easy to use. However, when miniaturized and linked by telephone to a wide range of services, it would be a different ballgame.

Enter the home workstation once the supporting network of participants is in place in sufficient measure to make the system economically viable, and once the purchase price or monthly lease for the consumer is low enough or is offset by financial incentives. That point is just around the corner. The logical prototype, called *City Net*, began operations in Cupertino, California (in the heart of "Silicon Valley"), in October 1993, albeit accessible by ordinary computers equipped with modems. The home workstation envisioned here would be primarily telephone based with a built-in computer (a physical prototype of which was introduced by Philips in 1993). The deluxe model might include the following:

• A central processing unit with a modem for telephone line communications,

• A flat color screen at least twelve inches across that could be positioned vertically or horizontally and was sensitive to input by a stylus pen,

• A small printer that used ordinary paper that could also serve as a scanner/fax,

• A keyboard or at least an expansion of the touch-tone phone number pad, to be used for simple user responses to interactive prompts (even if the screen itself is interactive), and

• The ability to accept, read, and update information or programs recorded on credit-card-size media.

These units would obviously replace video phones, and they might supplant the present home computer market for many light-use consumers, but that is not the primary intent. The intent is to enhance the interior lines between consumers and a wide range of services, both professional and commercial. In poverty-stricken and high-crime areas, these devices could be set up in local storefronts with sufficient security during open hours and removed afterward. Another option would be portable models, complete with cellular phone, for use while traveling. A prototype briefcase edition was shown at the COMDEX show in November 1992, priced at under $3,000. Now let us look at how these units would work for the range of services just described:

• *Catalog shopping.* Printing and mailing out catalogs is an expensive proposition, whereas a user could simply push-dial L.L. Bean, JC Penney, or another retailer. He or she would enter one-digit numbers by keystroke in response to prompts until the available items were displayed. This display would include detailed information on cue. Workstation memory would hold this information from different outlets to let the user make comparisons without taking notes. Orders could then be placed by automatic debit to bank accounts. A variation on this would include travel services, complete with itinerary planning. Even the maps might be downloaded electronically to chip-type cards that would fit into portable machines, the prototypes of which are already on the market.

• *Billing*. The major advantage is that the consumer could instantly check the status of all accounts and debit arrangements, including a record of transactions over the past so-many years. Credit cards will likely decline in usage, supplanted by proliferating debit cards (which look almost exactly like credit cards). More and more users are paying the balance in full each month, which makes credit cards unprofitable to banks except by charging usurious interest rates to customers who choose otherwise.

• *Financial services*. This option would link the finance programs mentioned previously to brokers, banks, and so forth in order to make investments and their equivalent. A variation on this could be used for preparation and electronic submission of income tax returns.

• *Legal services*. The primary advantage is convenience, and most of the usage would probably be straightforward business conversation. The one major difference between this and telephone calls is that documents could be transmitted back and forth instantly (even if only viewed on the monitors), especially if the *QuickCourt* program is a harbinger.

• *Health care services*. This would offer the same advantages as legal services, with the addition of entering medically related data from instruments that may be in use for home care patients or from that recorded on credit-card-size medical history chips.

No technological hurdles confront the home workstation concept, and yet another prototype exists in the form of a barcode reader linked with a special telephone that automates ordering from catalogs.[14] However, other obstacles can and will intrude. First, psychological resistance on the part of both professionals and consumers is strong. Only time can ameliorate that condition. Second, the potential for fraud, and certainly for increased invasion of privacy, is severe. To protect against fraud, all transactions could be delayed for twenty-four or forty-eight hours to give each user an opportunity to check a current transactions sheet. Further, transactions exceeding a certain level, either individually or in sum within a specified period of time, would require personal verification. Finally, every external access to the databases could be listed. Still, there is no such thing as a fool-proof scheme.

On the other hand, if the love of money is the root of all evil, the scent of profit is the genesis of all enterprise. As happened with commercial image processing, the concept of home workstations will undoubtedly entice the necessary financial investment.

6

Government and Law Enforcement Applications

Government is Genghis Khan with telegraphs
—Tolstoy

The government is the largest class user of automation, often due to necessity. As mentioned, the decisive impetus for electronic computers was the need to break Axis codes during World War II, and the exploration of space would be impossible without automation. The government has the funds and, contrary to popular opinion, is willing to experiment with new ideas. It is also the largest user of commercial-type applications, and thus much of the previous chapter also applies to government usage. However, this chapter focuses on four different requirements, the magnitude of which bears little resemblance to most commercial counterparts:

• *Data and information.* The pressing requirement is to weave a seamless logical blanket among a large number of overlapping and redundant databases.

• *Mass micromanagement.* As the government takes on more and more responsibilities and as the population increases, the need to manage more programs in more detail demands this.

• *Reduction of fraud.* The fraud perpetrated on, within, or with the connivance or indifference of the government dwarfs all that occurs in the private arena. The tab runs to the hundreds of billions of dollars annually.

• *Macrolevel decision support programs.* Technically, these would operate little differently from commercial variations, but the stakes are in the trillions of dollars and the time is measured in decades.

To be sure, the government is guilty of massive waste in this area, and some automation projects give stupidity a bad name.[1] Yet time is on the side of automation, and on occasion the results are nothing short of remarkable. Distribution of more than forty million Social Security payments monthly goes off almost flawlessly. Moreover, while the Internal Revenue Service has made major mistakes in the past, it seems determined to make its image processing system a success. The bidding process for that system took a year in order to iron out potential problems and bottlenecks, and would-be vendors had to submit computer models demonstrating how their proposed approaches would work, both in terms of operating mechanics and costs.[2]

The examples provided in this chapter are only a sample, and one is hypothetical, which means that although current technology could do the job, there are no formal proposals to develop it—yet. Also keep in mind that some of these applications reek of "big brotherism" to a degree that makes them repugnant. The author does not advocate adoption, but as long as the government continues to advocate paternalism and micromanagement, these applications are bound to appear in some form sooner or later, and doubtlessly many vendors will compete eagerly for the business.

Hypothetical national register. The federal government, all state governments, and most county jurisdictions maintain automated databases. The problem is the disparity and inconsistencies within this data and the lack of sufficient programmed linkage—interior lines—to harness this automation to meet requirements. If these databases could be integrated, the resulting system would virtually eliminate inconsistent data, save vast sums of money, and lend itself to more effective programming. Still, recall the point made in Chapter 2 that it is sometimes easier to build a new system from scratch than attempt to integrate existing units. Thus if this approach were followed, the resulting system would constitute a national registry.

The underlying concept is simple enough. A core database would probably be maintained at the one agency that already has the authority to keep records on every U.S. citizen—the Social Security Administration (SSA). Within one year of birth, every child must have a Social Security number in order for the parents or guardians to claim him or her as a deduction on income tax returns. Hence current SSA data could be expanded and then divided into three parts: (a) common or core data available by network to many federal agencies, (b) supplementary common data available on a need-to-know-basis as flagged in each record for each agency with core access, and (c) data used by the SSA accessible to other agencies only by court order or its equivalent. Each federal agency would then maintain its own supplementary files and records, perhaps shared with other agencies in a few instances. However, inputs and updates to the core data would be processed only by the SSA, even if knowledge of the changes originated in another agency.

Lower level jurisdictions would have access to the core data on the same basis as federal agencies, but only for individuals resident or domiciled in their respective jurisdictions, or formerly so if there is a bona fide need to maintain *and update* such records. Each state would maintain a single primary copy of those records to which it had access, and these would be updated automatically by the SSA. Alternatively, depending on network technology, every state could have direct access to its share of the records in the national registry. Each state could then distribute this core data to its own agencies as it saw fit.

As mentioned, the advantages of this set-up would arise mainly from vastly improved interior lines because this system would use dedicated network trunk lines with such high capacity that every station tied into the SSA core database would operate as if it were an integral part of that system. The mechanics of how it might work in specific applications are implied in subsequent sections, but one application is obvious. The decennial census would be compiled in a matter of hours at negligible expense rather than the $2.6 billion it cost in 1990. Even those individuals to be interviewed in depth could be selected randomly in a matter of minutes from the core database. The utility for law enforcement is also obvious.

Admittedly, this concept is bound to (and should) encounter vehement opposition. Yet it would only more efficiently link existing databases to accomplish purposes in the public interest that are formally entrenched in Congressional authorizations, few of which have ever been successfully challenged on constitutional grounds. Thus the key issue is whether the potential for abuse and crime would suffice to prevent the registry from being developed in the first place and, if so, whether the challenge would only amount to a delay.[3] (The author conceived of this model strictly as a means of discussing the ethics of automation with students. Most of them were horrified by the idea but were equally convinced that it was inevitable.)

To restate the issue, then, would this integrated database transform the potential for piecemeal fraud and abuse into a singular, massive reality sufficient to inspire a political revolt? This book is not the vehicle to resolve that issue. However, as discussed in Chapter 4, the immense pressures to create new mega-huge databases or to achieve the same goal by various integrations suggests that a national registry is just a matter of time. Indeed, it already exists in the form of an electronic trinity: (a) the SSA, (b) the IRS, and (c) the interfaces among various marketing, credit reporting, consumer reporting, and tracer-of-lost-persons databases.

To make matters worse, the U.S. Commission on Immigration Reform, chaired by former U.S. Representative Barbara Jordon, recently (July 1994) recommended a computerized registry of all U.S. citizens and registered aliens. This proposed registry was to use Social Security numbers. Although some

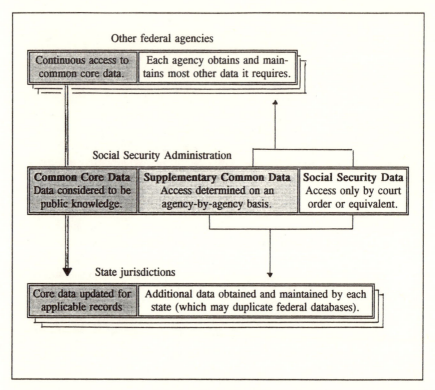

15. Hypothetical model for a national register. The Social Security Administration would maintain core data for all citizens plus additional data intended for its own use. Other federal agencies would tap into that core data by way of high-capacity networks, while states would receive copies of the core data for individuals over which they had jurisdiction.

groups voiced their opposition (especially Hispanic associations), such recommendations are bound to be heard sooner or later, and that will take care of the final push needed to create the hypothesized national registry.

If that isn't enough, consider that early in 1992, two enterprising men, Jim Laux and Graham Bloy, garnered $250,000 in seed money to create a proprietary database to assist in the search for lost or missing persons. A fee of $19.50 is charged for each search, and no request is accepted unless the user is on the database (or added to it).[4] By the end of 1993, this database contained data on 90 to 95 percent of the U.S. population. In reaching that goal, the founders indicated that they had experienced little difficulty buying copies of databases from various agencies, whether governmental or commercial.

Mass micromanagement. Whether it is wise or not, the federal government is increasingly immersed in mass micromanagement. The United States has a population of 265,000,000 and growing. More than 100,000,000 are entitled to specific periodic benefits, either as a direct beneficiary or as an immediate family member. The food stamp program alone supports approximately 29,000,000 people. The earned income tax credit subsidizes individuals (married or single) with dependent children and incomes under $25,000 (in 1994). For income under approximately $20,000, this benefit in effect eliminates income tax, subsidizes the Social Security (FICA) tax, and leaves some left over for spending money.[5] Low-income individuals and families on Social Security benefit from a separate tax credit program, and beginning in 1994, a childless person (or family) between the ages of twenty-five and sixty-five earning less than $9,000 per year is also entitled to a smaller earned income tax credit. Additionally, many families in this income range are eligible for Medicaid, Aid to Families with Dependent Children (AFDC), public housing assistance, and various other welfare programs. Furthermore, virtually all other individuals are potential recipients, primarily from Social Security and Medicare. If or, more accurately, *when* a single-payer national health insurance plan is enacted, everybody will become an immediate beneficiary.

Unfortunately, there is no way to manage these programs without extensive automation support, primarily in the form of computer systems, but there are two ways to go about it. The first is to automate existing systems in essentially their present form. The second is to realign the way business is conducted, or at least the way it is paid for in order to take advantage of the instantaneous interior lines that automation provides. In this regard, health care is a prime example. As columnist Robert Samuelson pointed out, the United States already has socialized health care—witness Medicare, Medicaid, health care plans for federal workers (active and retired), military hospitals, Veterans Administration facilities, and tax deductions for excess medical expenses.[6] Further, private insurance carriers, especially Blue Cross and Blue Shield plans, process most of the Medicare claims under contract. Finally, costs billed to private insurers are heavily inflated to compensate for underpayment by government plans.

In more detail, health care consumes 14 percent of the gross domestic product yet leaves roughly 40,000,000 Americans uninsured. Many others are afraid to use their insurance lest their policies be canceled or the rates raised to prohibitive levels. The editor-in-chief of American Medical Association publications, Dr. George D. Lundberg, calculated that health care costs will reach 1.6 trillion dollars by 1997 and trigger a meltdown.[7] At that point, it is almost certain that the federal government will step in and take over, be it de facto or de jure. Unfortunately, government-run programs and enterprises do not inspire much confidence. Washington would have to manage more than 600,000 active physicians, combined with 35,000,000 hospitalizations and 650,000,000 office visits per year, not to mention billions of prescriptions. If dentistry and long-term nursing and custodial care are included, the bill would begin to approach the entire trillion dollars now spent annually on health care, *plus* the additional cost of services that would be made available to individuals presently without insurance.[8]

Even with streamlined automated support, management of health care may prove intractable, if for no other reason than public insistence on no rationing. And that is just the beginning. If health care is declared a right to be enforced and managed by the government, the logical extension is to declare food and housing as a right. If you think rent control in New York City is an administrative nightmare, that public housing projects are the incubators of virulent crime and drug dealing in the United States, and that the food stamp and other welfare programs are expanding out of sight, just wait until Uncle Sam elects to become the nation's employer and general provider. In short, automation is the only way to reduce these impossible tasks to the status of being merely chaotic and, in the end, self-destructive.

Reduction of fraud and embezzlement. In 1880, Anthony Comstock published a book with the quaint title *Frauds Exposed, or How the People are Deceived and Robbed, and Youth Corrupted; Being a Full Exposure of Various Schemes Operated Through the Mails and Unearthed by the Author in Seven Years' Service as Special Agent of the Post Office Department, and Secretary and Chief Agent of the New York Society for the Suppression of Vice.* In the intervening years, book titles have shrunk considerably, but the magnitude of the theft has shot up astronomically. For every dollar drawn at gunpoint from banks and other financial institutions, another fifty are lifted by fraud and embezzlement. When the latter expands to include the federal government and its many programs, the ratio exceeds 1,000-to-1.[9] Worse, even when the culprits are tagged, the risk of imprisonment is low. The Department of Justice declined to prosecute 55 percent of the bank fraud cases referred to it by the Federal Bureau of Investigation; 85 percent of those under $100,000.[10] In other words, the government considers the theft of $100,000 to be little more than petty larceny.

The exact extent of fraud perpetrated on the government has never been accurately measured, but it's a safe bet that the total exceeds at least two hundred billion and perhaps three hundred billion dollars annually. As mentioned, the IRS alone estimates that $127 billion in income tax liability goes unpaid per annum.[11] Various estimates of health care fraud exceed $50 billion per year.[12] Other large catch-basins of fraud include welfare, unemployment compensation, and defense procurement contracts. Those numbers add up. Moreover, this data applies only to the national level and excludes other big-ticket items such as the savings-and-loan crisis. Nor do they include what is some-times called "soft fraud" (e.g., pork barreling, Medicare billings for unnecessary services, and student loan deadbeats).

Fortunately, automation can be employed to reduce this fraud, and has been for some time. It only takes integration of databases. The IRS again offers a good example. Auditors face an uphill battle in attempting to reduce the massive annual ticket for unpaid or underpaid income taxes, and some of their effort must be spent on a Congressionally mandated sample examination of returns. Accordingly, various computer tools must be used to deter fraud and, when that fails, to detect and prosecute it. Comparisons of forms W-2, 1099, and similar with 1040 forms—combined with requiring Social Security numbers for all claimed dependents—deter some of the wrongdoing.

But to catch a thief requires analysis of all returns to identify those that indicate a high probability of fraud. Statistically, patterns of data in the returns of honest filers will differ from those that are less than honest. The decision support program for individual returns is called the *Discriminant Function System* and is described in at least one IRS publication.[13] Insurance companies commonly use similar programs to detect fraudulent claims. This system doesn't catch every case, and sometimes it misidentifies legitimate returns. For example, a return reporting a gross income of $30,000 and deducting $25,000 for mortgage interest looks suspicious, but one or both income earners may have lost their jobs during the year and paid the interest out of savings rather than lose their home.

The process is more complex than described here, and any return flagged by the program is reviewed before a decision is made to proceed with an audit. However, given the continuing magnitude of this fraud, it seems imperative that these programs be improved and expanded. One way would be to integrate them with the image processing system in development in order to compare data reported over a period of many years (if that isn't already being done). Another approach would compare returns with a wider net of transactions recorded in various banks and other financial institutions. As it is, all transactions over $10,000 are reported to the IRS (and cash transactions over $3000 to the FBI). Finally, these audits could be used to prosecute criminals in general on the grounds that illegal earnings are just as taxable as the legal variety. That is how Alphonse Capone was finally sent to prison, and it may be the only practical route to nab many others. It is easier to prove underpayment of income taxes than to get a conviction on other indictments, *once the data is in hand*.

As for dealing with Medicare fraud, the former Inspector General at the Department of Health and Human Services, Richard P. Kusserow, developed several effective techniques, but like the IRS he and his staff are limited by the funding they receive.[14] There isn't enough money and staffing to prosecute the entire spectrum of fraud. Yet with pattern-identification-type decision support programs bounced against an integrated system of billing, that batting average could be increased dramatically.

However, when it comes to internal fraud and related failures of federal stewardship, a different approach is needed. The crimes vary from intentional delivery of faulty goods and services, to the Housing and Urban Development scandal in 1992, to outright embezzlement. Given this smorgasbord of theft, it would be naive to expect the government to police itself effectively across the board. Arguably, any such scrutiny must be at the initiative of a public interest group. They could use the Freedom of Information Act and some fairly sophisticated decision support programs to detect wrongdoing and then publicize the findings relentlessly. Government officials are adept at concealing wrongdoing in a ream of data.

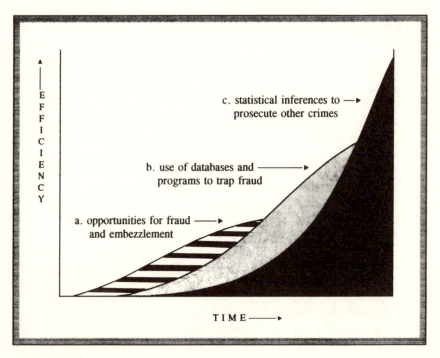

16. The antifraud catch-up game. Automated financial systems beg to be defrauded and embezzled; it is impossible to keep track of all the electronic flow of funds with green-shade audits. Extensive databases and sophisticated decision support programs would change that.

Interestingly, *Fortune* magazine in 1973 compiled a corporate-type annual financial report on the U.S. Government.[15] That issue was published long before the debt ballooned to its present level and fraud became so rampant. Yet neither that magazine nor any other widespread publication has since repeated this eye opener. Perhaps it is time for a reputable publisher to do so.

Macro level decision support programs. As emphasized in Chapter 2, a decision support program does nothing that cannot be done with (a) paper and pencil, (b) a comprehensive knowledge of mathematics and statistics, (c) instant access to all relevant information no matter where located, and (d) unlimited time. Paper and pencil are easy to come by. When any of the other three items is questionable, a program of this kind could be a useful substitute—perhaps not for deciding whether to fly or drive on your next vacation but, say, for decisions involving countless billions of dollars for commitments that in some cases can stretch out a century or more. The government is still funding pensions for a few widows of Civil War veterans.[16]

The magnitude of government spending programs is so large that few minds can comprehend it, much less consider the long-range implications of various options and financial levers. This is why decision support programs rate serious consideration. A few examples follow, noting that while it might take millions of dollars to build a good program, that cost is negligible compared to the funds at stake. Further, once a program is developed, it can often serve as a template to build similar programs at a fraction of the original cost.

The first application could be procurement of Department of Defense weapons systems. These expensive armaments are sometimes a function of pork barreling, service parochialism, or just plain greed, but when objectivity does edge its mangled foot in the door, a host of factors must be considered. These factors include acquisition cost, operating and maintenance costs, training costs, effects on other weapons systems (both those in existence and planned), and sunk costs. To be sure, no sound decision on any system can be based on quantitative analysis alone. The systems analysis excesses of the McNamara era in the Pentagon demonstrated that, and the nature of future risks is always problematic. Another fulsome issue is whether to buy fewer but more technologically advanced weapons, or more but simpler implements of war. Still, this kind of software can quickly display the long-term quantitative consequences of each option. In that way, the partially subjective final decisions can at least be as objective as known facts and reasonable projections permit.

Next consider the Social Security program. This is a much more expensive and longer term situation. Even without the Medicare part, Social Security is the largest single item in the federal budget and one which must eventually collapse without massive increases in taxation. As the average age of the population increases, there will be proportionally fewer tax-paying workers to foot the bill for more and more benefit-receiving retirees. This situation is compounded by the current use of excess Social Security taxes in part to fund the annual deficit. When this money is needed, the government will not be able to pay it back without additional tax increases, thus threatening the stability of Social Security earlier than the projected crunch indicates. Moreover, the expenses of the elderly often increase at a rate greater than the general cost of living, primarily due to health care and living assistance requirements in the last years of life. One already hears the rumblings for much higher increases than set by the cost-of-living index.

Obviously, any revision of the Social Security tax and benefit rules would have enormous consequences for at least the next fifty years and would set the stage for subsequent decisions for a much longer period of time. As it stands, benefits are heavily weighted in favor of the poor. An individual paying the maximum tax—twice that of a wage earner in the middle of the range—will receive roughly 24 percent in additional benefits. Furthermore, in many cases 85 percent of the entire benefit will be taxed, probably at the 28 percent rate (or possibly higher), thus negating even the marginal increase.[17] Then, too, so-called minimum benefits and Supplemental Social Security skew the redistribution even more in favor of the poor. In short, Social Security is rapidly evolving into a welfare program, one that will demand an ever-increasing share of the federal budget. No decision support program can remedy this problem, but at least the technology could help determine the least objectionable course of action.

Similarly, the funding of health care, regardless of the plan adopted, will run into major problems and may prove even more intractable. The demands will encompass the entire population except perhaps the extremely wealthy. Poverty has no monopoly on illness and disease. The great problem, of course, is that although medical technology has extended life expectancy, it has done so only by an enormous increase in health care needs during those extended years. *For the sake of illustration only,* if health care expenditures were cut by 20 percent, and if those cuts were directed entirely at the most seriously ill sector of the retired population, life expectancy would drop by only six months to a year, most of which is now spent in misery and pain. Yet to implement a policy like that would be as bad as anything advocated by the Third Reich. One compromise is to fund only palliative care for the terminally ill (as occurs in most other countries with national health insurance).

Regardless of the outcome, health care planners—all planners, for that matter—face dilemmas. Clearly there is a need for better analytical tools to grasp the full consequences of any decision. When the available funding is less than total requirements, some items must be cut. Unfortunately, it would be almost futile to use decision support programs to monitor selected items if the budget in general continues to be managed on whims and rough estimates. Unless the consequences of different funding priorities are seen as an entity, few items would receive fair and equivalent consideration. Furthermore, different spending priorities would require different taxes and other financial management policies. Finally, future expenditures and revenues will rarely adhere to projections, thus requiring continual adjustment to policy. This is vaguely analogous to parimutuel betting in the mathematical sense, but it is not gambling. It is a matter of economic survival.

Two other points. First, decision support programs need not be concerned with every cent. Random inaccuracies will usually wash out in forecast calculations. Hence projections and probabilities for each set of options could be generated in minutes. As mentioned, a computer with parallel processing chips can execute more than a trillion instructions a second. That is, in one second a single computer can calculate what it would take a lifetime for an accountant to do with an adding machine. And the computers are improving. If and when the mounting deficit triggers economic collapse in some form, policymakers *may* sober up and accept the fact that the government cannot fund everything it would like to do. Unfortunately, the recent pessimistic findings of the Congressional Bipartisan Commission on Entitlement and Tax Reform suggest that it will take just such a collapse to achieve reform.[18] (More on this in chapter 11.) At any rate, once the point of collapse is reached, decision support programs would become essential, if not to find the best option then at least to demonstrate why the answer sometimes must be no.

* * *

The day after the page proofs for this book were completed, Knight-Ridder Newspapers circulated a widely reprinted story (written by Frank Greve) about the Internal Revenue Service (IRS) database. According to Coleta Brueck (the senior document processing official of the IRS), the IRS wants to expand this database so extensively that *it* will be able to prepare tax returns for most individuals. Ostensibly, the rationale is to reduce the annual $127 billion bill for tax fraud and cheating. The primary means of doing this would be to access even more state-level and corporate databases containing relevant data. Hence, a variation of the hypothesized national register described earlier in this chapter already exists and may shortly contain far more information than estimated by the author.

7

Research Opportunities

Every great advance in science has issued
from a new audacity of imagination
—John Dewey

General research and analysis requirements helped propel the early development of computers, if not robotics, and that impetus now drives research in automation itself, especially for the design of chips and networks. However, research is rarely cost effective in the immediate sense. Depending on the science, as much as 90 percent of the investment in research eventually proves to have been a waste or yields marginal utility at best. As such and notwithstanding the long-term dividends from the small balance, the effort is often the first to be cut in a budget crunch.

This is nothing new. The new aspect is the capability afforded by parallel processors and the virtual reality side of image processing. This capability can economically tackle problems that resist conventional analysis. Moreover, the commercial spinoffs, such as holographic television, should accelerate the development of these analytical tools.

The common theme of these recalcitrant problems is the number of independent factors. Because of the ensuing mathematical complexity, research models often compromise by using simplified functions. Unfortunately, as in the study of weather and ecology, these compromises can negate accuracy. Accordingly, this situation gave rise to the science of chaos, which is the study of nonlinear phenomena analogous to a bumper car ride at an amusement park.[1] In practice, therefore, chaos seeks to find order among phenomena that give the appearance of lacking it, but perhaps the better approach is to create visual three-dimensional holographic models. This would allow researchers to perceive how nonlinear systems operate as entities. Each factor, which is sometimes called a *parameter*, could be controlled by its own processor chip in a parallel array of them, and the resulting vectors could be integrated into a three-dimensional dynamic display. The factors could be set to any pattern of values, and the operation could be accelerated or slowed down as necessary in order to perceive significant changes. The balance of this chapter examines some potential applications for this technique.[2]

Physics and ecology. Originally, subatomic physics was a pleasant scenario of neutrons, protons, and electrons, plus a few odd remnants that didn't seem to have much utility. Then came discovery of the particle zoo. Few of these creatures endure for more than a few microseconds (and usually much less), but they in fact exist and some have been linked to the various fields of force that keep the physical universe ticking with a considerable sense of order. In turn, science posited that all these particles—permanent and transient—were constructs of fundamental building blocks. Murray Gell-Mann named these creatures "quarks," after a line in *Finnegan's Wake*.[3] Unfortunately, six of these so-called quarks have been identified so far, and none have any perseverance. Thus quarks are not the likely answer, except as some kind of intermediary construct, like batter on its way to becoming a pancake. Otherwise, one could build a house with bricks that disintegrated before they were mortared into place.

Whatever the answer may be, its resolution depends on coming to grips with what is called "the three-body problem." Equations are adequate for describing the interactions between any two bodies or sets of particles that operate as if they were a singular system (e.g., atoms and molecules). Any number of elements larger than two runs into the physics equivalent of a ménage-à-trois. Calculations become entangled and defy true resolution. For example, three items have three subsets of relationships: A & B, A & C, and B & C. You can solve interactions for any one subset easily. However, the minute you do, the other two subsets destabilize, mathematically speaking. Then when you turn your attention to another subset, the same problem crops up with the others.

Computer programming can deal with this by what is sometimes called recursive processing, but when the number of players increases from three to a thousand or more, even computers are overwhelmed. It should be obvious, therefore, that subatomic physics cannot be fully explored until a three-dimensional model is developed in which each particle or subsystem is controlled by its own processor and each significant interaction is processed as a standard two-body problem within an integrated display.[4] That display can be frozen at any point, with measurements taken and scaled as appropriate.

The same approach may be necessary for research on the genesis and evolution of the universe, which is called cosmology. The particles under consideration change in magnitude from ultra-Lilliputian to ultra-Brobdingnagian, yet mathematically the resolution encounters the same three-body problem that plagues atomic and nuclear physics. About the only difference is that if the subatomic model must be run in slow motion, the cosmological counterpart must be accelerated, except possibly for the first few minutes after the so-called big bang. Even the most generous funding will not wait a billion years to see some results.

So much for theoretical applications. Physics and its kin, engineering, also face practical problems. Of them, energy production is the most pressing, especially in light of the frequent negative side-effects on weather and ecology. Given that more energy can be made *available* than expended to get at it, without relying on fossil fuels, a major goal is to create technology that will do this for cleaner forms. Thus wind generators and solar heating capture otherwise unused energy and convert it into more usable forms, often at a cost less than that derived by conventional fuels. Three-dimensional holographic programs could be used to refine this experimentation with different approaches at a negligible research and development cost. Even more significant is the ability to evaluate the effects on weather and ecology if the research models can be extended to that sphere of interest.

Weather and ecology intertwine, of course, sometimes in dramatic ways. For example, when the former Soviet Union diverted water from the Sea of Aral for irrigation, the lake receded, which affected the weather, which destroyed the increased crop production but without restoring the former water level. Other problems include global warming, the greenhouse effect, acid rain, destruction of forests and wetlands, dwindling natural resources, and encroaching deserts. Because the worst effects are slow to make themselves known and are concentrated in less developed countries, these threats are not always taken seriously by the leaders of developed nations. Clearly, there is a need for accurate, dynamic graphical models that might persuade these leaders that more must be done.

The problem is again the number of variables involved and the unruly manner in which each acts. To date, and relying on vast arrays of equations and algorithms, researchers worldwide (especially at the National Center for Atmospheric Research) have been able to create general circulation models with sufficient consistency to have at least some influence on policymakers.[5] Another fascinating model is one developed by Professor Goro Uehara at the University of Hawaii. This model, called *Decision Support System for Agrotechnology Transfer (DSSAT)*, assesses crop planting alternatives and has garnered the support of more than a hundred research agencies throughout the world because it has been steadily expanded and enhanced to cover the twelve major crops that comprise the bulk of the world's staples.[6]

The second reason for this success was that DSSAT was modeled after known facts, not hypothesized notions. An example of the latter occurred when the Asian Development Bank sponsored creation of a model to improve water irrigation practices on the island of Bali. Scientists presumed that the local priests could not possibly have any sound idea of how to ration and allocate water. They were determined to show the uneducated locals how to do it better. As it turned out, this was one occasion when separation of church and state was a bad idea. The local priests proved to be among the world's best ecologists. Reluctantly, perhaps, the scientists modified their views.[7]

Whether these conventional models will eventually tame complex ecological issues is problematic and, if not, the holographic approach usable in physics and engineering could also be used for this class of research. However, unlike physics, this research can run headlong into economic and political problems. Many political leaders are concerned primarily with the exercise of personal power and will sometimes commit genocide to maintain it. Others may act more like statesmen, but they face the dilemma of short-term versus long-term survival of their countries. When rain forests are depleted, it is because citizens living off the land either need the wood as fuel and building material, or they need the cleared land in order to grow sufficient crops. Perhaps half the land mass on earth is inhabited by people living under such conditions.

In developed countries, the immediate needs may be less severe, but the various citizenries have grown so accustomed to higher standards of living that they are not always willing to make sacrifices on behalf of the environment. Short-term gains still govern. To restate the argument, then, if environmental problems are as potentially devastating as nuclear war, differing only in the speed by which they destroy their surroundings, it will take something more dramatic than position papers with multitudinous tables to convince decision makers otherwise.

Physiology and genetics. Research in physiology and genetics is immersed in empirical detail. Virtually every facet and dynamic of human anatomy above the molecular level has been mapped out in detail, although some of the underlying mechanics remain obscure. Furthermore, most serious viral diseases have been curtailed, at least in developed countries, and smallpox has been eradicated worldwide. Accordingly, the focus of research has shifted to those diseases and dysfunctions, which in part stem from the underlying mechanics of cells and organs. As far back as twenty years ago, deans of medical colleges joked that they spent the better part of their day resolving conflicts among eighteen departments of molecular biology.

These mechanics do not always yield to immunizations or conventional therapies. When they do yield, the side-effects may be more devastating than the prevention or cure. It's somewhat like trying to repair a fine watch with an ordinary screwdriver.

Perhaps the most well-known field of study within molecular mechanics is genetics. The chromosomes are being mapped out, which has led to an increasing number of links between specific gene segments and various disorders.[8] This biogenetic engineering has progressed so furiously that complex ethical issues have been raised earlier than in most sciences. Mankind, of necessity, is dabbling with the creative process and its natural automation, using man-made automation to probe even deeper. As in the inorganic sciences, three-dimensional holography combined with parallel processing of independent factors might improve this research.

The ultimate would be a model of the entire human organism. This would be the most intricate model every built, but it's do-able. The most complex organism operates by permutations and combinations of ordinary chemical reactions. In other words, the feasibility of the model is a function of the number of parallel processing chips that can be arrayed programmatically. Further, it would not be necessary to replicate every cell mathematically, only each type of cell. Actually, there would be a hierarchy of processors. The lowest level would mimic cells; the intermediate levels, subsections of organs; and the highest level, organs themselves. Each of the two lower levels would feed data into the next highest level. This is one situation in which the flat relational database design would be inappropriate.

This leaves the functioning of the organism as an entity. That would be achieved by three-dimensional holography driven by the processing chips representing organs, including the brain and its nervous system. The superintending logic, however, is not so much decision making by the brain (conscious or autonomous) but *homeostasis*, which means that every cell and organ strives to control its own forces analogous to a governor on an engine. As the engine accelerates, a centrifugal-force device swings wider and wider, eventually cutting off the fuel supply. Similarly, the tremendous forces operating in a cell—which dramatically display their clout in an embryo—are gradually brought under control by redirecting some of that force against itself. One example is called steric hindrance resistance, in which various molecules position themselves to act as a physical block to the action of others. Another is the immunological or anti-immune system, which dispatches antibodies to destroy or neutralize foreign objects (antigens) invading the host organism (although this system can sometimes turn against the host itself and destroy it).

In any event, once the model is working, the effect of various drugs and therapeutic regimens can be tested exhaustively in a matter of days, using millions of different parametric settings, if necessary, to cover the vast majority of the population. Furthermore, programmed calculations can be mathematically accelerated so that the long-term effects of a drug can be reduced to minutes.

This would not obviate the need for human testing, but it would save a great deal of time and suggest new avenues of approach that might not otherwise be discovered for generations.

At least one prototype model of this kind is already in operation: *BioCAD*. It was developed by Alejandro Zaffaroni at the Affymax Research Institute, Palo Alto, California, and is said to have cost only $50,000.[9] The algorithms are based on the fact that most drugs act on or otherwise influence various cells by so-called lock-and-key molecules and receptors—essentially a dynamic geometry problem. This is not the same thing as full-scale testing, but the technique eliminates a great deal of preliminary trial-and-error (heuristic) experimentation with potential compounds. The vast majority of these compounds eventually prove useless or at best replicative of what is already available. Worse, keep in mind that a typical drug takes twelve years and $230 million to develop by conventional methods.

Econometrics and geopolitical analysis. In 1849, Thomas Carlyle labeled economics the dismal science. Not much has changed since then, because getting any three economists to agree on the significance of data with respect to projections is difficult if not impossible. Yet this situation is changing. The field of econometrics attempts to lend scientific credibility to economic guesswork by methodical analysis and correlations of historical data with known events up to the present time. Although this technique has not yet arrived at the nirvana of programming, there is a logic to economic history and forecasting, and therefore it should eventually yield its secrets.[10]

Still, econometrics is plagued with the same chaos of all phenomena arising from the operation of independent elements or parameters, including in this case the psychological element. Moreover, economic history is filled with major swings within erratic cycles combined with numerous catastrophic events such as depressions and runaway inflation. Moreover, domestic and international economics are so interrelated that it is almost impossible to study either one in isolation. Finally, the problem of variable concentrations of wealth among nations, and within each nation among comparatively few individuals, can make a shambles of any set of equations.[11] When one considers that at least half of the world's wealth is expended on subsistence, the few nations that control the excess effectively control the world economy. In specific terms, the United States, western Europe, and Japan, with less than 10 percent of the world's population and roughly 12 percent of its land mass, control between 70 and 90 percent of the world's wealth above the subsistence level.[12]

On a more complex level, the matter of distributors versus parasites offers an interesting study. In an era of increasing specialization and widespread use of items produced in comparatively few locales, a complex pattern for the distribution of goods is unavoidable. Except for electronic transmission of information, this distribution requires middlemen. These middlemen always tack on expenses and take their cut, although given any serious competition, the goods are still much better and cheaper than in any regulated economy. Unfortunately, some of these distributors have become more like parasites over the past fifty years—for example, stockbrokers pushing clients to buy and sell more securities than prudent in order to swell their own commissions. This is a long list, albeit not all bad because taxes are paid on these profits. But what does it contribute to the wealth of a nation in terms of improving the means of production and formulating capital goods?

17. Breadlines in the Depression. Only a small fraction of the population remembers the breadlines and soup kitchens of the early 1930s, but no country has ever developed immunity from recurrences. More accurate econometric models could dramatize the consequences of bad economic policy and perhaps reduce the risk.

Then there is the variable role of government that tries by various measures to regulate the economy—to guide it directly or to influence it indirectly. These measures include tax and spending policy, interest rates and reserve requirements for financial institutions, the extent of welfare or mandating of benefits to be provided by employers, tariffs, deficit management, and a host of other levers. Some of these measures are invoked as a result of thoughtful decision making, and others by desperate manipulation in order to ameliorate the consequences of previous decisions.

Additionally, economic analysis sometimes flounders because it concentrates too much on money per se rather than on the forces behind it. Money is only a medium of exchange. In the larger sense of wealth, that which is exchanged, how much of value accrues and to whom, and how useful it becomes are more important issues than cash. This is Adam Smith's value theory pounding at the door again. In runaway inflation, currency may become worthless, yet the ability of the population to labor and produce goods continues. The question, then, is how something as abstract as economics can be demonstrated in a visual three-dimensional model. The answer is that it cannot, no more than one can draw a picture of energy except indirectly by showing the work it can do. What *can* be displayed are graphic representations of the various accumulations of capital, government programs, capital goods, investments, income, expenses to sustain life, distributions, and so forth, as the values representing various policies are entered in the model. This display can be made dynamic while symbolically depicting the flow of money (not entirely unlike the model of an organism).

Unfortunately, the problem doesn't end there. An accurate econometrics model is challenge enough, but because of human and international factors it is not the be-all and end-all of such analyses. Something called geopolitics demands a larger perspective. Geopolitics takes into account what might be called national power, of which economic strength is only one facet. National power also includes (a) population and other demographic characteristics, (b) geography to include natural resources and geographic position, (c) infrastructure of both transportation and political machinery, (d) technological prowess, (e) military power, and (f) the national ethos.[13] To be sure, some aspects of national power are a function of economic clout, but the total strength of a nation and its ability to exert influence in the world obviously goes beyond economics.

For example, all other things being equal, a country with three times the population of another will be much weaker because it must expend a greater share of its wealth to sustain itself. In another case—again other things being equal—a country with a favorable geographic disposition will exert its influence far more effectively than one that doesn't have such a disposition. Great Britain wielded enormous leverage until well into this century, even though its resources were small by world standards. Moreover, when nations band together under military or economic treaties, the world balance of power can unhinge in short order. That situation was especially true during the world wars of this century, at least until the much larger resources of the Allied

Forces were manifested in military terms. And it may happen again as major economic communities—some would say cartels—are developed in Europe, in North America, and possibly in Asia.

Restated, international behavior is not always compelled by economic interests. The lust for power was evident millenniums before Napoleon. The negative impact of armed conflict on economies has done little to abate war, with the obvious exception that the Armageddon consequences of thermonuclear weapons have so far deterred another global war. Thus analysis of national behavior and international relations would take a model considerably more comprehensive than econometrics can afford, and perhaps the latter will never be perfected until a geopolitical model is developed. As such, the model would be difficult to build, but there is ample historical data on which to base the computations until the model "predicts" what actually happened.

8

Health Care and Education

*Too often the new technologists are methodical and exact in
their specialized fields, but impressionable, naive, and opinion-
ated on broader issues of policy. Like the executives they ad-
vise, they lack a sense of relevance and analogy—the critical
common sense and trained judgment that mark the educated
man.*

—Harold L. Wilensky

Two of the things that America has most prided itself on have been the quality
of health care and the diversity of educational institutions. Without a doubt, no
other country spends more on health care and none have more schools. The
negative is that these resources are growing more expensive and hence con-
stricted, while what remains for distribution to inner-city clinics and public
school systems continues to decay at a deplorable rate. In some areas, teachers
and nurses take their lives into their own hands in these environments, especially if they are not of the same ethnic background as the neighboring community.

Accordingly, one hears endless political slogans about improving the
delivery of these essential services. That is a worthwhile idea, but neither
health care nor education can be delivered beyond the limited sense of prescriptions, inoculations, and correspondence courses. On the contrary, both are
lifetime propositions. The first stresses habits that can reduce but not eliminate
medical problems and at best can only slow the inexorable process of aging,
which takes its toll in the form of increasingly severe problems and disabilities
until death finally intervenes. The second runs the opposite course. Individuals
may be born with various instincts and the capacity to learn, but their knowledge and ability to control emotional reactions is close to zero at birth. Love

and nurture in the formative years are indispensable, but there comes a time when the mind must be educated. For most people, this takes long formal schooling in some form.

A different kind of generation gap. Given the declining availability if not the deteriorating quality of health care and public education, can automation make a difference? It could, if for no other reason than the long period of trial and error. Many, perhaps most, experiments floundered, but the few that succeeded have capitalized on proven commercial applications and seem capable of luring the necessary investment that will eventually place them in the mainstream. As such, these applications may follow the same path as image processing. That technology was ignored until it proved its investment potential, and a few major users pursued what became showcase examples of how to apply it well.

For noncommercial environments, the time span between idea and utility may be two, three, or four times longer. Accordingly, something needs to be said for this extended period of gestation. In the business world, a generation rarely runs longer than the human biological one. New technologies, once proven to have economic value, are readily embraced by at least a few business leaders, with all but the most recalcitrant minds falling in line within twenty years. Not so in academia or the medical profession. With a few exceptions, like vaccines, most new ideas take a minimum of ten to twenty years before anyone else takes serious note. The medical and academic communities, at least as entities, are not especially motivated by purely economic considerations. Keep in mind, for example, that the pioneering work in true computers and programming by Charles Babbage and Ada Lovelace remained a laboratory curiosity at best for a century.

The positive side to this is that proven methods are not readily discarded for potential fads, especially when the consequences may affect an individual's entire lifespan. The negative side is that effective remedies lie dormant for decades, thereby increasing costs or alternatively encouraging research that continues to bark up the wrong tree. As this situation is not apt to change much in the foreseeable future, the commentary in this chapter will likely remain dormant for many years.

Health care. The provision of health care on an equitable basis, whether or not it is considered a right, is plagued by a number of problems. Many of these problems can be traced to increasingly higher costs and the unwillingness or impracticality of placing sufficient resources in areas of poverty and rural regions. Additionally, physicians are somewhat maldistributed by medical specialty, although an increasing emphasis on family practice in medical schools is reversing this trend slightly. On the other hand, perhaps the majority of office visits have always been medically unnecessary, while malpractice litigation is motivating providers to perform more tests than appropriate.[1] For similar reasons, medical record documentation grows onerous. In turn, all of this adds to the increasing cost of health care. It will take drastic measures to curtail the price spiral, and even if that happens much still needs to be done to streamline the general process itself.

Medical records are an obvious first target. Imaging systems give providers instant access to records, worldwide if necessary. More advanced systems automate or semiautomate input during treatment. Thus when an order is placed for a service, that fact can be recorded in a database and later electronically transcribed to a "page" in the patient's imaged medical record. This also means that physician and hospital records can be linked no matter how far apart they are geographically. Ideally, then, an individual's medical history need be recorded only once. When a patient moves to a new location, copies of those records can be forwarded instantly. Alternatively, medical records could be maintained in centralized regional or area repositories to be accessed as needed. Granted, this type of system opens the door to abuse, a point covered at some length in Chapter 12.

Closely associated with medical records is prescription data. Most pharmaceuticals, when used for the problems intended and within prescribed dosages, are largely beneficial.[2] On the other hand, when several drugs are prescribed by different doctors, the results can be harmful. Or a patient may experience an anaphylactic reaction to a medication. Although these situations are not as common as the cold, they occur often enough and can be fatal; hence the need for a readily accessible prescription database. At least one retail pharmaceutical chain (Walgreens) uses this technique to prevent or at least warn against harmful combinations (and to permit customers to refill prescriptions regardless of where they may be in the United States). It wouldn't take much technology to extend this model into a general system.

The main benefit of automation support, however, is in diagnosis and prognosis. As mentioned in previous chapters, the prototypes have been successful, especially in the hands of doctors trained to use them. To review the bidding, a good program of this type accesses current and historical information so vast that only a few doctors, if any, could keep mental pace without automated resources. Far from usurping professional judgment, these programs demand the maximum exercise of it, but they do eliminate the need for a medical research librarian at one's beck and call. In time, therefore, many if not most doctors will latch onto them in order to provide more care for the same cost per patient, and possibly to have additional time to see more patients. They might also use them as a legal defense against malpractice because they would have an automated record that they queried the sum total of knowledge available to include the best sequence for ruling out alternative diagnoses.[3]

A good example of these programs is *DXplain*, developed by the American Medical Association. It has been available on the AMA computer network since June 1987. When a physician enters a set of symptoms, this system will generate a list of probable diseases within seconds, drawing on more than five thousand medical terms to interpret that input.[4] This is especially useful for rural doctors who do not have much contact with colleagues and quickly lose touch with advancing knowledge. Equally remarkable is a diagnostic system developed by Dr. Stephen Schueler, director of the emergency room at Holmes Regional Medical Center in Melbourne, Florida. This program, named *Home Medical Advisor*, is, as its name implies, intended primarily for home use, so that individuals can check with it before calling a doctor. It links information on 1,200 drugs and poisons, 450 diseases, 150 injuries, and 130 medical tests, and it retails for $70 (about the cost of a single office visit).[5]

Other programs include *Care* (Wishard Memorial Hospital in Indianapolis), which screens medical records and suggests treatments; *Attending*, which suggests optimal combinations of drugs for anesthesiology; *Oncocin* (Mount Sinai Medical Center in New York), ditto for cancer patients; and *PDQ* (maintained by the National Cancer Center), which provides current information on the latest cancer therapies. Another on-line database is *MedLine*, operated by the National Library of Medicine. It indexes 3,700 medical and related journals and includes more than one million articles and papers during the three-year period 1991–1993. That's a lot of reading to catch up on.

The next step would be house calls by electronic substitution. As described in Chapter 4 as part of the home workstation concept, a patient could telephone a group practice clearing house or triage center to describe symptoms, probably with a nurse practitioner who had access to both that patient's medical records and a general medical decision support program. This set-up would have special utility in rural areas, where it is impractical to place enough providers in reasonable proximity to all patients. It could also be extended to permit group consultation by specialists as appropriate without the need to route the patient through several offices. Interestingly, the Indonesian government has adopted this approach as a matter of economy, far ahead of developed nations.

This idea could then be extended to support patient care management for both inpatients and home-care patients. This is not a substitute for nursing care but rather a system to simplify note taking by automated recording as observations are made, possibly by voice recognition, and by generating patient care plans that are templated to specific requirements based on interactive input at the time of admission. For home-care applications, data could be entered from home workstations or by monitoring sensors linked (by transmitting capability) to ordinary telephone lines. This does not obviate the need for home-care nurses, but it would provide a continuous monitoring (if necessary) between visits. This practice might reduce the number of "emergency" calls for unscheduled visits.

As for the *practice* of medicine itself, without doubt the emphasis will continue on support of the physician rather than replacement in any sense of the word. In this regard, automation has already reached into the farthest corners of the profession—witness laser surgery, radiation therapy, automated laboratory tests, magnetic resonance imaging, and Robodoc (the hip replacement drilling machine).

Mental health, by contrast, presents a much different picture. Patients often need countless hours of therapy, but there isn't enough money in the national economy to pay for it. The alternative is to adopt experimental computer-based, multimedia programs for patients suffering from various neurotic disorders. This technique has some obvious and some not so obvious limitations, but when it does work it permits a psychiatrist or psychologist to see more patients in the same work hours, relying on these programs to fill in for the full amount of time the doctor might otherwise have to devote to each patient.

Ironically, it may be that more progress has been made in this aspect of health care than in so-called physical medicine, notwithstanding that psychiatry is anything but a rigorous science.[6] One of the more interesting programs is named *Plato*. It provides counseling in complex avoidance dilemmas and even teaches a method for problem solving.[7] However, the resistance to this technique is strong. The *Index Medicus* for 1991, a directory listing more than 300,000 articles and papers written that year, contained only ninety-one on the subject of decision support programs and expert systems, and most of those appeared in technical journals devoted to automation (although a far larger number of articles on conventional automation were indexed).

The last item is the one in which both physical and electronic-substitution automation play a major role—namely, prostheses and implants. This area encounters the least resistance to progress. The benefits are obvious, and with few exceptions each device is an improvement rather than a radical departure from earlier models. However, there are variations which do run into some resistance by those not familiar with the field. One example is the narcotic implant dispenser for terminally ill patients in constant pain. Some doctors are overly concerned that their patients will become addicted.

Education. President Garfield's preference for education was to put himself in a log cabin with a wooden bench, on one end of which sat Mark Hopkins and he at the other. In time, this ideal reduced to Hopkins at one end of a log and a student opposite him. With the steady decline in achievement scores, combined with increasing criminal behavior as low as the sixth and seventh grades (including conspiracy to murder a teacher in retaliation for being sent to the principal's office), the maxim has now evolved into sitting on the student and talking with the log.

If American colleges are still a bright spot, public education is not. Moreover, institutions of higher learning cannot compensate for inadequate preparation. For example, colleges that openly admit high school graduates standing in the upper half of their classes find that half of them require remedial education and that more than half drop out.[8] Thus if the high school dropout rate is 25 percent, and most college entrants come from the upper half of their high school classes, and half of them need remedial classes in the basic skills, then only the upper 25 percent of teenagers are sufficiently literate to navigate the watered-down courses offered during the freshman year of college.[9] All of this, mind you, after two decades of massive infusions of federal funds. This, of course, presumes that literacy goes beyond the ability to read a stop sign.

Furthermore, public secondary schools are plagued with deteriorating physical plants, drugs, increasing class sizes, and teachers burning out long before they reach retirement. How much of this is the fault of the schools, and how much is the fault of the individual student and his or her environment—and how much can be traced to lax social standards—is open to debate. What doesn't seem questionable is that the problems are likely to get worse, especially as funds get tighter. For example, a few years ago the Los Angeles Public Schools "asked" their teachers to accept a 12 percent pay cut—9 percent plus writing off the 3 percent pay raise from the previous year that wasn't funded. Because California has serious, long-term financial difficulties, the probability is that additional cuts will be demanded in subsequent years, eventually reaching the point at which most of the teachers could not afford to live on their salary.

Automation cannot resolve most of these problems, but it can make a dent in at least one area—reduction of class size. The critical ratio for students-to-teacher seems to be fifteen-to-one. Above that, the effectiveness of teaching deteriorates. Below that ratio, it improves exponentially.[10] The apparent reason is the time a teacher has to interact with individual students. Each student experiences his or her own learning difficulties, which are rarely addressed by a teacher lecturing to a class of thirty to forty students for fifty minutes a day per subject. With lower class ratios, not only is the time per student increased, but it's easier to keep mental track of how different students are progressing.

This only goes to show the importance of a good teacher. However, few school districts can afford to double or triple the size of their teaching staffs, and therefore the only feasible alternative is to harness computer-aided instruction to support many aspects of teaching and learning—ideally self-paced—and leave teachers free to spend at least a minute or two with each student each day. Fortunately, the prototypes are already in place and are improving each year. IBM and Apple Computers have together contributed more than $100 million (about one day's worth of fraud in health care billings) in funds and equipment to public schools. Moreover, the potential is so intriguing that Benno C. Schmidt, Jr. resigned his position as president of Yale University several years ago to head an institution dedicated to this work—the Edison project.[11]

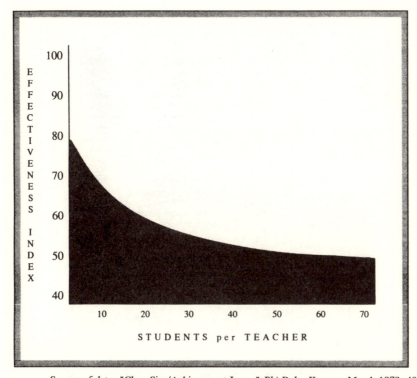

Source of data: "Class Size/Achievement Issue," *Phi Delta Kappan*, March 1979, 493

18. Teaching effectiveness as a function of class size. Student-teacher ratios above fifteen-to-one are ineffective. Below that ratio, they improve markedly, but anything less than thirty-to-one is unaffordable in public education. Computer-assisted learning at its best can increase the effective ratio to one-to-one.

Make no mistake, though. These systems are tremendously expensive to develop and take years to perfect, while many if not most subject areas require continual updating of material. However, once a system is operational, it can be replicated at a reasonable cost—certainly a lot less than doubling teaching faculties. And it is easy to extend the reach of these systems to rural areas, where educational resources tend to be lean.

To be sure, earlier attempts with technologically supported education were inadequate at best; hence critics are entitled to be skeptical. The efficacy of programmed texts and television in the classroom—learning by spoonfuls and even more boring lectures—was deplorable. On the other hand, newer systems employ extensive decision support programs. They operate by a large number of interactions with students, by access to vast amounts of information,

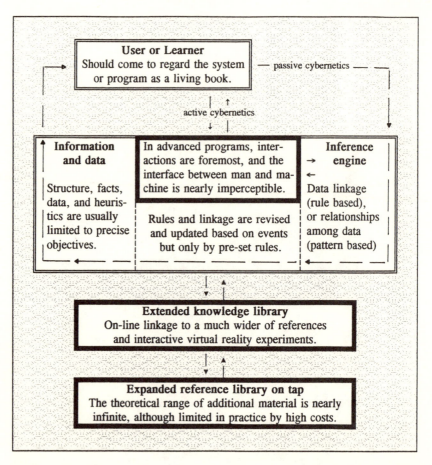

User or Learner
Should come to regard the system
or program as a living book.

— passive cybernetics — —

active cybernetics

Information and data	In advanced programs, inter-actions are foremost, and the interface between man and ma-chine is nearly imperceptible.	**Inference engine**
Structure, facts, data, and heuris-tics are usually limited to precise objectives.	Rules and linkage are revised and updated based on events but only by pre-set rules.	Data linkage (rule based), or relationships among data (pattern based)

Extended knowledge library
On-line linkage to a much wider of references
and interactive virtual reality experiments.

Expanded reference library on tap
The theoretical range of additional material is nearly
infinite, although limited in practice by high costs.

19. Educated computers. State-of-the-art decision support programs have become so sophisticated that it is not much of an exaggeration to think of them as being educated. It is not a machine you are dealing with, but the collective knowledge of mankind in an electronic library that can churn through millions of pages to find appropriate material faster than the eye can blink.

by being able to branch into related subjects, by responses that eerily replicate a human voice, and by assessing a weakness before a student is even aware of it and then directing that student to reinforcement practice as appropriate. Most of all, they provide each user with the opportunity to participate actively in his or her own education, regardless of how shy or reluctant that student might be in a traditional classroom setting.[12]

Furthermore, as these programs proliferate, school systems would be better able to relate, if not integrate, various subject fields; and hence continually build on and expand the knowledge base and reasoning powers demonstrated in earlier classes. The programs could emphasize different techniques or approaches for different subject matter. For example, mathematics, physics, and other hard sciences could be more fully integrated, and labs could be simulated by virtual reality. The aim is both to reduce costs and to provide far richer experiences. Regardless of the subject matter, however, the role of the teacher would still be paramount, but he or she would become much more of an active mentor than a passive lecturer.

All of this implies that student evaluation and records of progress would become far more substantial, based on the totality of learning experiences rather than just a few tests (although these programs need not dispense with the latter). This would be a fallout from the ability of these programs to detect weak areas and reinforce them. In turn, far more benefits would accrue. When students are ill at home for more than a few days, their education could continue almost as fully as if they were in the classroom, ideally supplemented by telephone links with the school but certainly infinitely better than what happens now.

When a student transferred to another district, he or she would have a record of achievement on tap and thus pick up where he or she left off. In addition, if these programs were started at an early enough age, there is some possibility of raising intelligence quotients.[13] At the least, they might restore what has been lost in a poor family environment or by watching too much television. The history of Head Start programs suggests that gains made in preschool years quickly wash out in inner city traditional schools. That would not be the case with computer-assisted instruction working at full tilt (more on this in Chapter 14).

University and professional libraries. Libraries are sometimes regarded as the centerpiece in any institution of higher learning, second only to the football stadium. The former are usually the only location that houses the collected knowledge of mankind, either directly or by some form of exchange or electronic interface with other repositories. Unfortunately, the proliferation of knowledge, combined with tightening budgets and increasing cost of books and materials, is placing these libraries in jeopardy.[14] It's not that they will close but that they will house fewer books and other materials, be open fewer hours, and offer less assistance. When that happens, a university must ask itself if it understands the implications of its priorities.[15]

However, priorities always come with price tags, which could be overcome by resorting to image processing (treading the same path as have insurance companies, banks, governments, and a host of other commercial users). The Library of Congress is already going this route, while the Navy has found this to be the only way it can cope with the mass of documentation (at times exceeding 20,000 pounds) it needs to operate the complex electronic gear on today's ships. Image processing has the capability to reduce the entire holdings of any university library to a large room, although that isn't necessary. The idea is to eliminate the need for any further expansion while increasing holdings at current budget levels. As a bonus, it makes material concurrently available to all scholars and students, regardless of their physical distance from the library or how many of them need to consult the same reference at the same time.

The issues are in the details. The two main options are whether to have optical disk copies in each library or access by network from central or at least regional repositories (not themselves libraries in the normal sense of the word). If materials are too centralized, the network traffic would be too heavy and too expensive, although this might be appropriate for seldom accessed material (especially older holdings and collections).

Regardless of the method chosen, the increase to efficiency results from improving the interior lines, which in turn can enhance automated indexing and searching. Present systems may not be bad, but there are too many of them operating from nonlinked terminals. No fundamental obstacle blocks the development of a master index for all reference material. A variation on decision support program logic could then be used to find, cross reference, compare, or otherwise compile all available reference material on any subject. Only one master copy of this index is necessary, updated weekly if not daily. In turn, library subscribers could obtain updates to their own database. Systems of this kind could also be linked with public schools, the anorexic libraries of which rarely have sufficient materials on hand to sate the needs of more serious students.

Many details still need to be resolved, but to date nothing has stymied commercial installations except for attempts to impose a decision support program over the images themselves rather than leave that task for human judgment. The U.S. Patent Office tried to add this feature while developing its current documentation search and retrieval system, but it gave up after spending an additional $100 million on this feature (and delaying implementation of the core project for a year). It made the mistake of attempting to supplant human judgment rather than support it.[16]

20. The stadium versus the library. The money poured into the least-utilized facility on many campuses—the football stadium—is in stark contrast to the severe budget limitations imposed on the most-utilized facility—the library. Automation may be the only way to compensate for this misplaced priority.

Another and perhaps more critical issue concerns copyright infringement. The problem is that current law does not fully take image processing and vast networks into account. For example, does *viewing* an electronic image on a screen constitute an illegal copy, presuming that no hard copies are made? The superficial answer would be no, but if such systems abruptly curtailed sales of copyright material, a different perspective emerges. One possible solution would be royalty fees included in subscription service payments, while single hard copies made for academic purposes (a legal exception to copyright protection) could be overprinted with copyright notices not to make further copies.

III. Problems and Their Ethical Perspective

In Woody Allen's film *Sleeper*, which was something of a comical variant on Aldous Huxley's *Brave New World*, the protagonist makes his confession before a decision support program embedded in a large machine. It whirls and spins for a few seconds and then displays the message "Absolved" and dispenses a kewpie doll to the penitent.

The setting of this comedy is two hundred years into the future, but today the profession of psychiatry offers a few programs that come tantalizingly close to the automated confessional, albeit not in religious terms. At least one of these programs—embedded in a palmtop machine—is popularly referred to as a computer teddy bear. In addition, Gary Garvey of Concordia University (Montreal) has developed interactive confessional software. As might be expected, the Roman Catholic Church did not express any interest, and Garvey admits that he wrote the program somewhat tongue-in-cheek. But perhaps it is only a matter of time before the number of priests shrinks to the point at which Catholicism will have to reconsider at least a variation on the idea.

It should be obvious, therefore, that automation will continue to raise and perhaps aggravate a substantial number of complex ethical issues, most of them with significant economic import and some that ask where mankind stands with respect to the ethos of his sociopolitical environment.

The common Uniform Product Code (UPC) scanner at a checkout counter exemplifies this problem today. Virtually every reader of this book has seen this technology in operation at least a hundred times, perhaps thousands. Without a doubt, use of UPC codes has doubled the productivity of checkout clerks and vastly improved inventory control for grocers and many other retailers. Yet that efficiency has eliminated tens of thousands of jobs and, in combination with credit and bank debit cards, has created vast databases of individual customer preferences—another major step toward an almost total invasion of privacy. Should we regress to earlier times or find some way to offset the insidious side-effects of automation?

21. Laser scanner at a checkout counter

The next four chapters examine some of these problems in detail. Chapter 9 looks at ethical factors in general as well as some aspects of human nature. Chapters 10 through 12 discuss three classes of problems associated with this technology: automation-related crime, socioeconomic issues, and psychological dilemmas.

9

Ethical Factors

Science, being pure thought, harms no one; therefore, it need not be humanistic. But technology is action and often potentially dangerous. Unless it is made to adapt itself to human interests, needs, values, and principles, more harm will be done than good.

—Hyman Rickover

An apocryphal story tells about the time the famed Notre Dame quarterback Johnny Lujack went to confession. He admitted to an especially foul deed on the field of play that the referees hadn't caught. His confessor was aghast, but before he could react, Johnny confessed to an even more serious offense. The priest started to lecture the gridiron penitent, only to discover that he had yet a third, unspeakable act on his conscience. At a loss for words, the priest stalled for time by asking who they were playing that day. Lujack answered "Southern Methodist, Father." There was a pause, followed by "Ah, well, boys will be boys." So it is with ethics. What constitutes a grievous wrong to some may not seem so bad to others.

There are many formal schools of ethics, and each must wrestle with dozens of factors in order to develop a consistent logical basis for its own perspective. Ethics without logic is mush. Furthermore, everything in ethics is said to be a matter of degree, and this is hard to refute. Almost everything is a matter of degree, starting with temperature. Seventy-five degrees is comfortable. One-hundred-fifteen degrees is miserable, even for desert dwellers. And one hundred-fifty-five degrees on a sustained basis is fatal. Will automation prove to be warm, hot, or scalding? That depends on how well the burners are brought under control, which requires knowing where they are and how they work. This chapter takes a stab at that prerequisite.

Keep in mind three points. First, automation is not the sole cause of the unfavorable side-effects associated with it. For example, while automation facilitates intrusion on privacy, this problem has been brewing for centuries. Second, some of the problems with automation are because there is not enough of it or because the components are not integrated more tightly than they are. This is most easily seen in the vast number of false arrests and credit denials arising from inaccurate and distended databases. Third, reaching a consensus on ethical issues, except for the most serious crimes, is all but impossible—and even that exception seems to be losing force.

By way of historical example, one need only consider the famed Pitcairn Island. This island was where the mutineers from the *Bounty* elected to go to escape prosecution and live out the rest of their days. Those days were not long. Within three years they slaughtered one another until only one survived. By contrast, their nemesis—Lieutenant (later Vice Admiral) William Bligh—had been set adrift in an open longboat with eighteen loyal crew members and compelled to sail more than four thousand miles to safety. It was the most harrowing voyage in the history of the seas, but under Bligh's able leadership and seamanship all but one of the men survived. This illustrates the difficulty of assessing the ethics of any event, even when murder intrudes.

That is as true today as it was circa 1800. On January 26, 1993, two seventh-grade girls in Lorain, Ohio, took umbrage at being yelled at and sent to the principal's office by their teacher. In retaliation, they *openly* conspired to murder her with a twelve-inch knife that they brought to school. Most of their classmates approved, because they agreed to pay a $200 reward if the two girls carried it out. The plot—a domestic *Lord of the Flies* situation—was revealed only when the teacher happened to ask one sobbing child what was bothering her.

Perhaps these things are bound to happen occasionally, but *The New York Times* allotted only four column-inches of space on page ten to reporting this item, while the front page bleated about the gays-in-the-military issue.[1] Obviously, the premeditated taking of human life has grown too commonplace to be of much interest. On the contrary, during that same week three mass murders took place, eliciting little more than a yawn.

The ethics buffet. Of the dozens of factors that impinge on ethics, at least seven are relevant to automation. All of them should be considered on their own merits, but a strong case can be made for regarding the consequences of acts as the primary factor when the perspective rises to the national level. If that is true, or at least if a strong argument can be made in its favor, then the other factors can be brought into some kind of focus. In this regard, consider the literary persona of Don Quixote. He was a fool of the first magnitude, yet in a strange sort of way his character can inspire an individual to seek a higher plateau of conduct. On the other hand, electing such a person as head of state of a nation would undoubtedly result in disaster. The seven factors are as follows:

• *Character of (or motive for) an act versus its consequences.* If an individual sets off a false alarm, and just as the firemen arrive a flash fire breaks out in a nearby building so fierce that only their immediate presence saves the occupants, the consequences of an inherently wrongful act are indeed favorable. Conversely, if an individual gives his life in attempt to save another but fails and leaves his family destitute, then the consequences of an inherently good act are mostly unfavorable. Supposedly, this is one of the great dilemmas in ethics and perhaps it is. On the other hand, the first instance is a rare occurrence. For every false alarm that has a happy ending, several hundred others put innocent people at risk and undoubtedly have led to unnecessary destruction and loss of life on a few occasions. So as the number of cases increases to which an ethical factor is applied, a kind of statistical averaging emerges which makes the consequences take on increasing importance. The proverbial road to perdition is still paved with good intentions.

• *Character of the individual.* Sometimes a very great person will do a little wrong. In extenuation of his or her reputation, that wrong is usually overlooked, downgraded to a mistake, or presumed to be an anomaly. Yet when those wrongs begin to accumulate or an especially bad judgment leads to ruination, the saving grace of character loses its effect. When the consequences linger on for generations after the idealism of the founder has long been forgotten, of what ethical value was the initial act?

• *Fixed standards versus situational interpretation.* The former posits a definite sense of right and wrong, the seriousness of which may vary with the circumstances. The latter argues that there are no standards, hence all ethical issues must be resolved pragmatically. This means that any act carried to an extreme, no matter how heinous, could still be justified simply by twisting the logic 180 degrees. Hitler was a master at this. Fortunately, this issue does not need to be resolved. In a nation of laws, the idea of fixed standards from which specific cases are adjudicated is assumed. This leaves only the possibility that where the law ends, ethics begin under a new paradigm of unbounded pragmatic quicksand. That, too, fails because as wrongdoing grows in intensity, it eventually comes under regulation.

• *State versus organizational versus professional versus personal ethics.* Some schools of thought hold that these various and sundry perspectives differ fundamentally (especially the Machiavellian school). Other schools see them only as variations. But all schools recognize that conflicts between perspectives will occur. Integrated databases serve the police function of the state while at the same time grow offensive to some professional groups and many individuals. Hence the conflict is not so much aligned with different ethical perspectives as it emphasizes different mixtures of the good and bad aspects of a common problem. That is, the interests of different levels of perspective will give different priorities to the various consequences. As such, this ethical factor cannot be resolved in isolation and therefore should be considered as part of the next one.

• *Greatest good for the greatest number.* Whenever this viewpoint is effected, it's a safe bet that the least number will lose out to some degree, no matter how well their rights are protected. Yet in a democratic nation, the whole concept of the franchise makes this inevitable. The ideal is to protect the rights of the minority, a point made crystal clear in the first ten amendments to the Constitution. Automation is not exempt. Individuals should be protected from excesses even when the overall consequences register for the good. Otherwise, the technology should be outlawed or at least curtailed. But don't expect perfection.

• *Means-to-an-end issues.* This age-old question asks if wrongful means can be justified if the outcome is favorable. This is not the same thing as motive versus consequences, and admittedly it is an especially difficult question to answer—perhaps the hardest in all of ethics. When the means are not especially wrongful and the benefits are significant and lasting, the issue is almost moot. (The so-called white lie common to social etiquette is the polemic here.) When the opposite is true, the conduct is subject to severe criticism. Between these polemics, most cases are a matter of degree and are often decided, if at all, on the value of the outcome—that is, consequences.

• *Dilemma or quandary ethics.* This occurs when all options to resolve a problem have serious side-effects and a choice must be made among them. This is especially relevant to automation because it cannot be easily disentangled from its excesses. But if there are standards and if one strives to generate the most favorable consequences for the majority while protecting the rights of those who are more subject to side-effects than benefits, the decision maker's reputation may survive history. Once again, he or she must consider the consequences.

In applying these factors to technology in general and to automation specifically, let us admit that *every* good has side-effects. Some side-effects are inherent; others result from the good being exploited by way of crime or abuse. Certainly, technology permitted the dictators of this century to expand war into global proportions with massive destruction of life and property, while in peacetime the automobile, especially in conjunction with alcohol, has become the deadliest single weapon in developed countries. As such, most of the resulting ethical issues are complex. On the other hand, that does not mean that they can be ignored, even if one holds to the situational ethics perspective. Will Durant once surmised that morals were relative and indispensable.[2]

Degrees of ethical complexity. If one accepts the argument that consequences are the dominant consideration for resolving a problem which increasingly occupies the attention of an entire nation, it is possible to develop what might be called a range of ethical complexity—that is, classification of the consequences in terms of the complexity of the remaining ethical issues. As such, each segment or degree in this range would be distinct in terms of the intent of the participants or perpetrators, and hence on whom to fix responsibility and therefore the appropriate countermeasures to curtail the excesses. As the responsibility defuses and good becomes intractably mixed with bad, the complexity of the ethical issues increases. In descending order of this complexity, these degrees are as follows:

• *Inevitable side-effects.* These effects do not stem from intent at all. They are primarily the result of trying to do what seems right or profitable in an honest way. The worst that can be said is that the participants are sometimes aware of these effects but do little about them, an imposed Faustian bargain of sorts. Hence it is virtually impossible to fix responsibility for them except on society as a whole, and that is a nebulous proposition at best. As to what can be done about it, the answer depends on the severity of the problem, the knowledge at hand, the ability to research for more, the willingness of the infrastructure to apply that knowledge, the resistance of the problem to the proposed remedy, and whether the remedy will introduce new problems.

• *Opportunistic misuse.* With the advent of color photocopiers, counterfeiting is said to have become a crime of opportunity. Individuals who never before gave a thought to personally decentralizing operations of the U.S. Mint may be tempted to do so on an ad hoc basis. Fortunately, that activity remains a felony and is rigorously prosecuted. Unfortunately, the same cannot be said for all of technology, especially when the opportunity has a legitimate purpose but is sometimes used under questionable circumstances. A common example occurs when an employer queries a credit bureau prior to hiring an applicant. The intent may be sound; the method in most cases is improper. In short, these side-effects are too homogenized in the context of their overarching use to be sorted out in anything less than a police state, and that would only usher in far worse abuses. On the other hand, partial remedies lie idle because of the difficulty and expense of proving anything except in a few cases. Last year, the Los Angeles Police Department disciplined a number of employees who used its database to obtain information improperly on individuals they wanted to date. But how many other police departments enforce this policy and how often?

• *Systematic exploitation.* This is opportunistic misuse grown to systemic proportions and can range from elevating the previous examples to standard practice, to political action groups exploiting databases in order to mail false or misleading material to voters. Regardless of any validity of the ultimate purpose, the intent to do wrong is clearly in evidence. However, the best that victims can do in most cases is file a civil suit, either as individuals or by class action. Only when abuses intensify to the point of rousing public sentiment can potential victims hope for the protection of criminal laws, and even that depends on how well those laws are enforced.

	Inevitable Side-Effects	Opportunistic Misuse	Systematic Exploitation	Criminal Conduct
Criminal			By definition, criminal acts are tantamount to malicious wrongdoing or exploitation. Automation does not significantly change this situation.	
Economic	Economic consequences of automation range from inevitable side-effects common to all technology, to the equivalent of systemic exploitation, for example, by reducing the size of the workforce, and by lowering the status of the balance to manual labor.			
Psychical	Psychical consequences of automation fill the entire range of ethical complexity because even the mere existence of massive databases can be unsettling at one polemic, while exploitation of this technology can easily cross the line into criminal behavior at the other. This unusual range underwrites the resurrection of the Frankenstein issue.			

22. Ethical complexity versus categories of side-effects. The scale from inevitable side-effect to malicious wrongdoing gauges the seriousness of problems stemming from the excesses of automation. As a problem gravitates to the left of this scale, ethical issues grow complex and remedies become tenuous.

• *Malicious wrongdoing.* At this point, the wrongdoing crosses over the line into conduct that is unmistakably criminal, more often than not for both the ultimate purpose and the method chosen to achieve it. Fraud is the most common example. Comparatively few individuals go this far, but they can be brought to trial in criminal court (and may also find themselves in civil court). The only snag is the lag time between new opportunities for wrongdoing and revision of the law to address advances in technology (e.g., existing copyright law versus image processing).

Another way of looking at these four degrees of complexity is by analogy to a marriage relationship. With exceedingly rare exception, couples are bound to have significant differences that they must accept in order to make the marriage work. That means a modest yielding of independence when it comes to personal choices and is thus analogous to inevitable side-effects. At the other extreme, a physical beating obviously constitutes malicious wrongdoing. If the victim has good judgment, she (seldom a he) would seek a divorce, if not prosecution. As for systematic exploitation, the analogy would be verbal abuse of an intentional and habitual nature, of which both sexes are guilty. This is not normally actionable in criminal court, but it is grounds for divorce and few healthy spouses would tolerate it for long.

This leaves the equivalent of opportunistic misuse, which includes arguments in which one or both partners say things in anger that they do not mean and later regret. This, too, is bound to occur in most marriages, and therefore it is an unforgiving spouse that would seek divorce on account of a few isolated incidents. Even when the incidents grow more frequent, the better solution would be to seek counseling first. Only when that fails or these incidents devolve into habitual conduct would divorce be appropriate.

The interesting point is the course of action that might be followed under any given set of circumstances. Some couples would forgive or make amends as the case may be; others would use the event as an excuse to feed an insatiable emotional discontent. In so many words, then, what should be done and what will be done may differ as a result of maturation or its lack among the principals. That is as true in marriages as in problems faced by a country, which suggests that some of these human factors be reviewed insofar as they are relevant to the excesses of automation.

Human factors. The most difficult question in the social sciences is: what is the fundamental nature of mankind beyond the physiological medium. Alexander Hamilton said that our greatest mistake was to suppose mankind more honest than they were. His colleague Thomas Jefferson had a much higher view of man, and single-handedly wrote the draft of arguably the most inspiring document in American history. Who, then, was closer to the truth?

Side-stepping that thorny issue, we still may be certain of one thing. The vast amount of fraud, embezzlement, and other crimes perpetrated today, combined with the unmistakable socioeconomic malaise prevalent in the national ethos, is far too extensive to attribute it to a few bad characters. Worse, the seeming public indifference and the unwillingness or inability of the political system to deal with crime clearly aggravates the situation. Thus even if only a small fraction of the population were intent on wrongdoing, the apathy and somnambulism of the balance has the effect of intensifying its toxicity.

Perhaps somebody will eventually compile a report on this general subject, which could prove to be one of the most pessimistic and depressing tomes ever written. It wouldn't solve anything either, but it might sober up the thinking of would-be social engineers who plan elaborate systems of government programs based on naive perceptions of the body politic. The prototype for such a study was completed in 1991. As cited in Chapter 4, the advertising agency J. Walter Thompson conducted a random survey of 2,000 people. Each person was interviewed and completed an 1,800-item questionnaire.[3] If the sample was accurate, 91 percent of the population regularly lies both at work and at home, and almost half admit to frequently calling in sick at work when they are not. This means between 50 and 90 percent of the population cannot be fully trusted.

A more depressing study was Stanley Milgram's experiments in obedience to authority conducted in 1961–1963.[4] In these experiments, persons from all walks of life were asked to administer increasingly higher voltage electric shocks to an individual who gave incorrect answers (or none at all) to simple questions. The voltage levels rose from 45 to 450 volts in 15-volt increments. The stated purpose of this "shock treatment" was to improve learning, and without exception every participant obeyed instructions at least until the "subject" (who was acting) indicated extreme pain. Most kept going to the limit.

To be sure, the conduct of these experiments met with intense criticism, notwithstanding that no actual physical harm was inflicted. Yet as Milgram argued in his book, the underlying reasons were that the results of the experiment contradicted optimistic perceptions of mankind. No technical aspects of the original experiment have been faulted by other scientists, and it has been replicated worldwide. However, one of those replications warranted criticism because it substituted live animals for humans and then used actual voltages (Milgram had nothing to do with it). Still, the fact remains that the vast majority of the participants executed those animals because of obedience to authority. Worse, when the intent and mechanics of the experiment were revealed, few participants had the slightest remorse over their behavior. To one extent or another, the vast majority believed that their behavior had been justified on the grounds of apparent authority. More than one participant was heard to say "I was just obeying orders."

The significance for the age of automation, of course, is that as decision support programs and their equivalents take on an ever-increasing aura of authority, the risk is that the vast majority of human beings will come to accept machine-generated decisions without question. That's food for thought.

The course of democratic resolution. Sir Winston Churchill was fond of saying that democracy was the worst form of government he had ever known except for all of the others. That was not an echo of Voltaire's Dr. Pangloss, who claimed this was the best of all possible worlds, but rather a realization that democracy was what the human race had to settle for if it wanted to survive with at least a semblance of self respect.

The reason for this situation is utterly simple. As Emerson put it, "Concentration is the secret of strength in politics, in war, in trade, in short in the management of all human affairs." Certainly, concentration is the basis for the age of automation, but politics has a difficult time following suit. Democratic institutions intentionally diffuse power in order to keep the excesses of corruption in check. The price of this, of course, is that concerted action against a danger is almost impossible until a substantial majority, for whatever reasons, perceive that danger as inimical to their own interests and then give high priority to resolving the matter. Thus the global aggrandizement spawned by the Axis powers in the middle of this century could not have realistically been opposed by the United States until the wolf was clearly at the door (i.e., Pearl Harbor).

On a more humdrum level, a good example of waiting for the crisis to develop is the growing concern over the invasion of privacy stemming from massive databases. As noted in Chapter 4, the *Marketplace: Households* database triggered a public reaction so negative that the product was withdrawn from general distribution almost immediately. Still, these and many other databases keep growing, many of them under the aegis of the federal government, in part to reduce injustices caused by inadequate coordination among separate systems.

In other words, not much will likely be done to curb the excesses of automation until those excesses are clearly recognized by the population at large as having reached an intolerable level. Even then, the polity will discover that it is almost impossible to separate the benefits from the likely abuses without instituting reforms so fundamental that it would take a more encompassing crisis to give reform a fighting chance.

The only alternative is the civil disobedience route. On rare occasions, this approach works with dramatic success—notably India's movement for independence in 1920–1947 and more recently in the civil rights movement within the United States. But how much effect would it have against automation? In 1700, loom operators rebelled against automation by destroying the machines. All well and good except for the fact that modern counterparts with incomparable sophistication abound in infinitely greater numbers.

More recently (1987), Katya Komisaruk—an M.B.A. graduate from the University of California, Berkeley—launched a one-woman attack on the NAVSTAR computer system at Vandenberg Air Force Base in southern California, believing (incorrectly) that it was programmed to launch a nonretaliatory nuclear strike against the Soviet Union. With crowbars and other tools, she methodically destroyed the central processing units of several mainframes and then readily admitted to her deed.[5] She pleaded not guilty in federal court, despite her voluntary confession, on the grounds that it was her ethical duty to destroy what she believed was an instrument of mass murder before it could be used. The judge was not especially impressed and sentenced her to five years in prison plus a $500,000 fine. She was paroled after serving three years and applied to a number of law schools without making any attempt to conceal her past. Three of them accepted her, including Harvard and Stanford. That's the hard way to get into one of those schools. The point, however, is that NAVSTAR is still there, and Katya will likely be paying for the repairs for many years.

Thus, civil disobedience succeeds only when it activates a latent but massive discontent. Unfortunately, and with the possible exception of the privacy issue, that discontent is too weak at the moment and at any rate is far more concerned with the economy. Fortunately—if that is the proper word—the eventual consequences of the metastasizing debt may serve to rouse discontent into action. This would be a painful experience at best, but in no other way will a democratic populace come to grips with the problems that contributed to it, automation among them. Napoleon at Austerlitz, when his staff advised him to seize an opportunity, is reputed to have said "Gentlemen, when the enemy is committed to a mistake, we must not interrupt him too soon."[6]

Granted, this perspective puts the horse before the cart. An economic meltdown would pose problems and dilemmas that reduce the excesses of automation to a playground squabble. On the other hand, a meltdown would be confronted head-on as a matter of dire necessity until it was reversed. Therefore, both problems might just as well be resolved as a package plan. On this point, there are three keys: (a) to expect no fundamental change in human nature, (b) to recognize that in the long run, the only permanent bulwark must emanate from the human mind, and (c) to identify the interior lines of specific problems and then address them at their key juncture points.

The reader may or may not agree with the first two assumptions, perhaps because they border on being contradictory, but at least they are self-explanatory. The third—harnessing juncture points in interior lines—is a technique derived from the essence of automation itself. In colloquial terms, this is a constructive variation of going for the jugular. Everything has a system. When it comes to human enterprises, those systems are more chaotic than orderly, but they are systems still. Successful reform in part entails finding the inherent center of gravity in a problem—its jugular—and applying pressure at that point. For example, some types of fraud can be identified by retracing the electronic transfer of funds with a decision support program that recognizes out-of-the-ordinary patterns among transactions. On a wider socioeconomic scale, automation can similarly be used to keep its own excesses in check so that priority can be given to the well-being of the individual without imposing on his or her right to seek fulfillment. In the final analysis, neither society nor a democracy exists apart from its constituents.

10

Automation-Related Crime

Money is a good servant but a bad master.
—H. G. Bohn

In an attempt to resolve the age-old question of which came first—the chicken or the egg—a student of evolution concluded that a chicken was the egg's way of replicating itself. That answer may not resolve the issue, but it does invoke a larger perspective. Similarly, the growing concern over automation-related crimes also needs a larger perspective. To date, the publicity has focused on computer viruses and hacking, with honorable mention to copyright violations and a handful of high-dollar fraud cases.[1] If a few enterprising felons were to build robots in order to reduce the risk of getting caught robbing banks at gunpoint, that technology would undoubtedly supplant viruses on the crime hit parade.

Yet automation-related crime is little more than a variation on what has transpired since the beginning of recorded history, and that history is to perpetrate wrongdoing. The new twist is the degree of stealth that technology offers and, with it, the ability to increase the magnitude of illegal gain. The reason is once again the interior lines afforded by various systems and the fact that funds and information (or programs) are represented by electronic symbols. Because those symbols move at nearly the speed of light, they can also be lifted or manipulated in a fraction of a second. The proof is that to date little crime has been associated with physical robotics, but hundreds of billions of dollars have been leeched out of computers.

These crimes are indeed a fascinating subject, but any detailed discussion of them runs headlong into three major obstacles. First, classifications of specific crimes are by no means standardized. Part of this stems from older laws that do not take the specifics of automation into account. This means that different jurisdictions rely on ad hoc interpretation of existing laws. Second, the data is in a state of flux, primarily because so much of the crime goes unreported or is lumped with other felonies not specifically linked to automation. Third, publicity has overemphasized the more technical and destructive aspects, notwithstanding that these headline hoggers account for only a part of the total losses.

Types of crime. Most crimes stem fundamentally from one of three roots: (a) *economic*, which is the desire to obtain something without earning or paying for it, (b) *psychical*, which occurs when some inner drive beyond greed propels an individual into wrongdoing in an attempt to sate that drive, or (c) *means to an end*, which entails an act of wrongdoing to achieve an ultimate goal that itself may range from noble to heinous. Economic crimes tend to be nonviolent, although the exceptions understandably garner more publicity (especially carjackings). By contrast, most psychical crimes typically involve violence or destruction. The motive is usually vengeance or comeuppance in some form or the need to exert power or exercise control over others. In this regard, the psyche seems to require concrete fulfillment of its abstract hunger, and violence is a handy way to do it. As for the third root—means to an end—the crime may be economic, or psychical, or merely a technical violation of an administrative law (e.g., improperly obtaining copies of information).

Economically motivated crime is the most common and includes many variations: larceny, fraud, embezzlement, burglary, hijacking, robbery, and others. By definition, some involve the *threat* of violence, but in most cases no harm comes to the victim if he or she complies with the perpetrator's orders. The motive is economic gain not destruction. Again, the exceptions command publicity and thus create a misconception. Not surprisingly, economically motivated crime also dominates the world of automation.

Crimes committed to sate psychical needs—lacking the singularity of economic gain—take one of three forms: (a) random violence and destruction, (b) targeted destruction, and (c) voyeurism. The first form is sometimes associated with madness and insanity as in pyromania, but more commonly it is a side-effect of wanton negligence, as when drunk driving results in injury or death.[2] The second may or may not involve madness, but the perpetrator always stalks his (or her) victim or target before acting. The third form—voyeurism—is commonly thought of in terms of peeping toms. The automation equivalent to voyeurism is breaking into a secured database just to prove it can be done.

As for means-to-an-end crime, something of an arbitrary dividing line is necessary. Stealing money in order to fund an even larger crime would qualify as a means-to-an-end type, but it is a distinct act and the rationale for it is not especially relevant in the prosecution, except perhaps to prove the intent of stealing. By contrast, the improper obtaining of information in order to sell it—illegal information brokering—is usually prosecuted as a package deal, despite any separate counts in the indictment. Another example is the freely admitted destruction of property in order to dramatize what is believed to be an unjust law or practice. Katya Komisaruk's single-handed assault on a NAVSTAR computer was cited briefly in Chapter 9.

In addition to these roots, organized crime sometimes uses automation to enhance its operations. This is no more illegal than bootleggers using trucks to deliver brew during the Prohibition era, but it poses problems for law enforcement. For example, with sufficient information recorded in an electronic database, a drug smuggler can optimize clandestine routes into a country.

As for the proportionality of computer-based crimes, one major study concluded that economic crimes consumed 74 percent of the pot; psychical-based crimes, 10 percent; and means-to-an-end crimes, 16 percent, assuming that alteration-of-data crimes are evenly divided between the last two categories.[3] Table 2 breaks this down in more detail. But even this data is misleading and doesn't include the massive fraud from claims that do not manipulate or damage to automated systems per se (more on this in the next section).

Table 2. Distribution of automation-based crime

Economic crimes

Theft of funds	36%
Theft of services	34%
Extortion	4%
Total economic	**74%**

Psychical crimes

Alteration of data (half)	4%
Damage to hardware	2%
Damage to software	2%
Harassment	2%
Total psychical	**10%**

Means-to-an-end crimes

Alteration of data (half)	4%
Theft of information	12%
Total means-to-an-end	**16%**

Source of data: Wood and Shriver, *Computer Crime: Techniques, Prevention*, (Bankers Publishing Company, 1989), 5.

Theft of funds. Bank robbery may have been a popular crime between the Civil War and the Great Depression, but it has since gone out of style except for drug addicts attempting to support their habits. As mentioned in Chapter 6, for every dollar taken at gunpoint, another fifty dollars of commercial funds are heisted by way of paperwork and computer systems.[4] This form of theft almost always comes under the heading of fraud or embezzlement, despite the many variations.[5] The common element is the practice of deception to extract money or its equivalent without having earned it or only part of it.

Although common perceptions of fraud are strikingly accurate, the term is difficult to define with precision because of the essentially infinite number of ways to practice deception. Yet from the perspective of automation-related crime, there are only two distinct types. One is *passive-automation* based and the other *active-automation* based. The difference is that in passive automation, the programs or databases themselves are not manipulated. Rather, the perpetrator relies on the sheer mass of transactions to slip in entries that are fraudulent. Common examples include padded insurance claims and intentionally incorrect income tax returns.

By contrast, active-automation crimes *do* manipulate software programs, databases, input instructions, electronic transmissions, or other aspects of a computer-based system in order to improperly or illegally extract or otherwise transfer funds or their equivalent to another account or receiver. That's a mouthful. Literally hundreds of different techniques have been used in this regard, and a few are so ingenious that they evoke the admiration if not the tolerance of law-enforcement personnel. The recent automatic teller machine (ATM) caper is a case in point (where two wanabe entrepreneurs installed a fake ATM in a shopping mall and collected all deposits made as personal profit).

But make no mistake in confusing this form of crime with data destruction. If anything, the idea of fraud is for the misdeed to remain undetected, and therefore the last thing the perpetrator wants to do is leave any more evidence as to source behind than unavoidable (and preferably no trace whatsoever). To achieve that, the perpetrator may use what is called "salami slicing," which means to shave off minuscule bits from various accounts and mass them in a new account.[6] Perhaps the most well-known variation on this entails rounding down account balances to the *lower* cent (rather than the *nearest* cent). Interestingly, a major case of international spying was throttled because of an unexplained discrepancy of seventy-five cents.[7] Another popular technique is charging a fictional service-processing fee.

Other perpetrators are more blatant about it. Some distributors occasionally bill credit card accounts of previous customers for comparatively small but fictitious orders, perhaps in the belief that many businessmen don't have the time to scrutinize every item on monthly billings. When a customer complains to the bank operating the card, that bank will file a letter of inquiry to the biller. If the latter backs off—inevitably on the grounds of a supposed computer error—that usually ends of the matter.[8] However, little attempt is made to prosecute, and hence this crime is seldom reported as such. Moreover, hospitals are notorious for rigging electronic bills with excessive charges, sometimes to compensate for inadequate Medicare and especially Medicaid reimbursements.

However, neither type of fraud is limited to surreptitious withdrawals. Some culprits use storefront businesses to sell goods and services with no intent to deliver or an intent to deliver less than agreed to. A variation on this is the use of credit cards numbers belonging to others to obtain goods and services without paying for them. In this case, success depends on getting victims to believe the operation is legitimate rather than depending on the sheer mass of transactions to mask the deception or using surreptitious manipulation of a program or data in a system. With nearly two hundred million credit cards in existence, the pickings are anything but slim. In addition, would-be counterfeiters are using desktop publishers to make illegal copies of negotiable instruments as a means of defrauding various accounts to the tune of at least a billion dollars a year.

Theft of services and programs. Theft of services and programs is more a variation on fraud than a different kind of crime; and, like fraud, its roots go back to ancient times. Most automation-related crimes here fall into categories: (a) copyright violations and infringements, (b) illegal or unauthorized use of systems and programs, (c) outright theft of hardware and programs (leaving no copies of the latter), and (d) failure of a vendor to deliver goods or services as agreed to in a contract. All involve economic gain, directly or indirectly; and, like funds-oriented theft, automation technology has opened new avenues of opportunity for wrongdoing.

However, of the four categories, two need not be discussed here. First, outright theft of physical goods differs little in the age of automation. Second, when a vendor fails to perform according to the conditions and specifications of a contract, that too is old hat, except for the occasional difficulty of distinguishing between a good and a service in automation (which is relevant to the remedies that can be sought). Moreover, with rare exception, lack-of-performance cases are tried only in civil court as either a breach of contract or a tort action and hence are not normally considered to be crimes.

Of the remaining two types, copyright infringement (sometimes called software piracy) is more widespread and incurs the larger dollar losses. By contrast, unauthorized use of systems, not amounting to copyright infringement, is less of a problem and in some cases is treated with benign neglect. For that matter, so are some copyright violations. To understand this situation, one should consider the difference between what might be called wholesale violations and those at the retail level.

A wholesale violation of copyright occurs when, for example, a vendor copies a program or part of a program intact and markets it under another name without paying a royalty or licensing fee. The intent to do wrong and thereby profit from it is almost always present. The only exception occurs when there is a bona fide doubt as to the extent of copyright protection. For example, while spreadsheet software published by Lotus Development Corporation is indeed covered by copyright, the concept of a spreadsheet per se is not. Thus there are many competing versions of spreadsheets on the market. But when Borland more or less copied the *Lotus 1-2-3* command menu into its *Quattro Pro* spreadsheet (de jure as an alternative to its own command menu and de facto as a means of attracting Lotus customers), Lotus successfully sued Borland to cease and desist and to pay damages for the copies already sold. On the other hand, not all infringement suits of this genre are successful.

A retail violation occurs when an individual makes a copy of copyrighted software for other than archival purposes without paying the appropriate fee (i.e., without buying it, or in the case of used software, without the former owner relinquishing all rights, copies, and documentation to the buyer). Collectively, this has become a serious problem, perhaps exceeding the cost of wholesale cases. One estimate puts the cost at $2 billion annually domestically, and another at $4 to $5 billion internationally.[9]

On the other hand, copyright law is anything but crystal clear and is deficient when it comes to electronic applications. To this must be added the tremendous variation in licensing agreements imposed by various vendors. This engenders confusion royal, especially when an individual uses several different software packages on a network and must transfer information among them. For example, one vendor may require a license for each computer in the network; another, only for each copy of the software in use at any given moment (called *booted*); a third, only for the number of computers that are in use at any given time regardless of what software is booted; and yet a fourth, to the number of registered users regardless of any other factor. Other vendors permit an individual to keep a second copy of software loaded on another computer (usually one at home or a travel laptop model) if the first copy is loaded but not booted at the time, perhaps making an exception for transferring data between the two electronically. You almost need a separate computer just to keep track of what is legal with the other computers.

The situation grows more complex when the material being copied is not software per se but merely information recorded in electronic form, sometimes as digital (character-by-character) data and sometimes as an image record. The difference can be significant. Text in the public domain cannot be copyrighted, but its arrangement on paper can be. Hence copying digitally recorded public domain text is perfectly legal, but to copy an entire book of public domain information, if it was electronically recorded in image format, may be a clear violation of copyright law.

Copyright violations, however, are not the only way to misuse software. Misuse also includes illegal or unauthorized use of *licensed* software. In most situations, it is perfectly legal for any number of different individuals to use a single copy of a software package, provided that: (a) they do so in succession, (b) the software is never loaded on more than one machine at a time (unless the license permits otherwise), and (c) each individual is authorized by the owner to do so. The misdemeanor in this situation arises when the last provision fails, although the loss, if any, is usually marginal. Software, per se, does not wear out.

Although the data on this practice is inconclusive, most offenses of this kind occur at the retail level. Parsing out illegally acquired blocks of time on systems is too risky, with the possible exception of repeated retail misuse of communications networks amounting to wholesale in sum. Finally, some employers regard minor misuse as a de facto employee benefit that might even increase their proficiency without training costs.[10]

Theft of information and espionage. The theft of information, regardless of the purpose to which that information is put, rarely results in damage to the original source. On the contrary, as in fraud cases, perpetrators go out of their way to leave no trace of their actions, at least none that can be traced to them. As such, this type of crime qualifies as a means-to-an-end type. The instances can be subdivided into two categories: (a) efficiency in the support of an external objective, which itself may or may not be illegal; and (b) espionage, which may be corporate or geopolitical. The former category—efficiency in support—has two variations: namely, where the perpetrator uses the information directly, and where he or she brokers it for a third party.

Illegal copying of information is not normally the same thing as massing of legitimate data. Once data is in the public domain or otherwise available upon inquiry to any citizen, the gathering and massing of that data can hardly be considered a crime. Indeed, a great deal of scholarly research, especially what are called meta-analyses, depend on this procedure.[11] This massing can and does lead to ethical issues, of course, but until widespread discontent results in new restrictions, it is legal. Illegal copying, by contrast, means that the individual or agency doing it does not have authorized access, and/or the act of copying it is illegal. Even when access is authorized, the use and copying are usually restricted to specific applications. For example, when a police officer checks a database to see if a traffic offender has any outstanding warrants, the application is not only legitimate but required. But if the officer does it to check on, or on behalf of, his or her personal friends, the access is illegal.

As for espionage, a case can be made that it is merely a variation on the more general crime of theft of information. That's a valid point, but the difference is the use to which the information is put—namely, to give the perpetrator an advantage at the expense of the possessor. In the corporate arena, this usually translates to gaining unfair competitive advantage by obtaining copies of proprietary data, information, or programs. A variation on this is insider trading. The extent of this kind of espionage is hard to estimate accurately because the amount of information lifted is difficult to ascertain. And gauging how useful it is (in order to assess damages) is even more difficult—somewhat like trying to evaluate objectively the marketing effect of a specific piece of advertising.

Finally, much proprietary information is gathered by the legal method of eavesdropping on conversations at conventions and parties, or by the even more honorable approach of carefully studying and analyzing published accounts. The defense intelligence community sometimes admits that roughly 80 percent of the raw information it gathers comes from open sources.

As for geopolitical espionage, the general albeit unofficial rule is that in the absence of an explicit statute to the contrary, there is nothing illegal or unethical about it regarding the perpetrator (although the methods may raise questions), whereas for the victim, espionage is wrong and possibly the source of grievous loss. Various codes of military justice throughout history have mandated capital punishment for espionage, even though the culprits are seldom regarded as criminals. In a few cases, the bravery may be so great that the prosecutor openly acknowledges it in court.[12]

The problem of reporting on this form of espionage is that many of the critical facts and techniques are themselves classified, and this applies even to some historical information. For example, the breaking of the German *enigma* code during World War II was not made public until the late 1970s, roughly twenty-five years after the end of hostilities. As a result, a great deal of history on that period had to be reassessed.

One last point—the Department of Defense often upgrades the security classification of lower level information once it is massed in a singular source. This may or may not provide legal precedence for regulating massed databases of information that is already in the public domain.

Malicious destruction and other forms of sabotage. Sabotage differs from espionage in that the intent is to inflict damage. However, there are times when the perpetrators don't want the victim to realize what has happened. In the case of automation, this means that the perpetrator intends for his or her victims to continue operations as if their programs and databases were intact and functioning correctly. The motive may be political dirty tricks, or economic gain, or just plain vengeance, but the motive is not especially relevant.

The act of destruction or wrongful manipulation is itself the crime. The motive and ultimate purpose can only serve to mitigate or increase the punishment meted out.

In the case of automation technology, this form of crime gained notoriety when Robert Morris unleashed a computer virus in the Internet system, disrupting its computing operations nationwide.[13] The virus did not destroy any programs or data (at least none that could not be readily restored), but it still came as a shock to professionals, who had hitherto regarded this danger as one step removed from fantasy. Since that time, thousands of these viruses and their kin (e.g., "worms" and "Trojan horses") have been unleashed worldwide.[14] As a result, virus-protection software has become big business. Unfortunately, the opportunities are immense, and new strains are developed each month.

Remedies. Because most automation-related crimes are variations of either theft or willful destruction of property, they pose few major ethical issues. In principle, the law stands firmly against them, and except for some necessary revisions to accommodate the technicalities of electronic data and images, there is little in the compendium of ethics that would stand in the way of prosecution. The exceptions, as noted, are a few incidents of civil disobedience and, more commonly, the subjective consequences of massed databases. The latter are covered in Chapters 12 and 14.

The civil disobedience exception is more easily dealt with; the perpetrator should willingly face the music for what he or she did in order to publicize what is believed to be a wrong. This type of heroism borders on martyrdom, and its practitioners should abide by the obligations of such conduct. In the final analysis, the act of civil disobedience does not excuse the crime but instead becomes a clarion call that may or may not be heard.

For the balance of automation-related crimes, the real ethical issue, if there is one, is the failure to prosecute these crimes sufficiently. As mentioned in Chapter 6, the Department of Justice declined to try 55 percent of the bank fraud cases investigated by the Federal Bureau of Investigation (85 percent in which the monetary loss was $100,000 or less). Clearly, that indifference demonstrates a lack of political will to do what is right, at least according to the laws that the department is obliged to enforce. Thus, until this situation changes radically, there isn't much that can be done. As numerous studies have concluded, the greatest deterrent to criminal behavior is assurance of punishment, preferably a prison sentence.[15]

On the other hand, if resources are limited, they should be invested where the concentration of crime is highest. Without a doubt, that concentration occurs in passive-automation fraud. Estimates of active-automation fraud, copyright infringement, and malicious destruction range from one to ten billion dollars, depending on the study one reads.[16] By contrast and as cited in Chapter 6, estimates of passive-automation crimes, such as fraudulent Medicare claims and income tax returns, start at a minimum of $200 billion. Every dollar that slips out of the federal budget in this way is added to the respective annual deficit and then to the cumulative debt. If borrowing is essential, it should at least go to worthy causes, not to swell the bank accounts of felons.

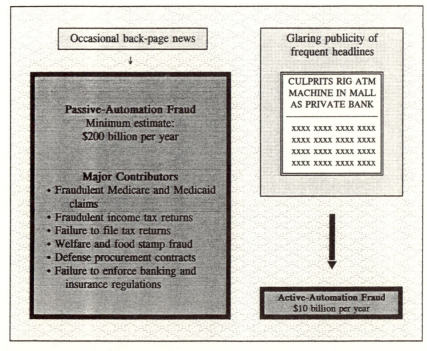

23. The deceptive appearance of automation-related crime. The popular conception of computer crime is that of manipulation or destruction of electronic data. This is a serious misperception. Most computer crime simply takes advantage of the impersonality of massive systems.

Socioeconomic Issues

All progress is based upon a universal innate desire
on the part of every organism to live beyond its means.
—Samuel Butler

Although automation-related crime generates the most severe economic losses at the moment, and perhaps the psychological issues will eventually dominate the age of automation, the socioeconomic issues have the strongest affinity to the malaise spawned by the federal debt. Furthermore, these issues work at cross purposes to any attempt to reduce that debt.

A reasonable amount of debt is tolerable *if* it serves as an investment to generate a return that is high enough to repay it. Unfortunately, this doesn't work, and indeed cannot work, for an entire country on a permanent basis. Few economies can sustain a rate of growth larger than 5 percent, at best. A nation cannot create wealth any faster than that. Beyond that modest growth, every gain made by one individual is another's loss or debt (or what is sometimes called a zero-sum game). The only exception occurs when a country has a surfeit of resources it can sell at high profits without risk or harm to itself (e.g., most of the oil-bearing nations in the Middle East). The United States is not among them, and automation is no substitute for oil. Oil creates jobs; automation—and technology in general—tends to eliminate them.

Job market outlook. Automation has reached a point of critical mass and now supplants human capability more than supports it. Various reports indicate that two-thousand jobs a day are replaced by technology, more often than not in the form of automation. This condition means that the number of jobs, proportional to the working population, will shrink and on balance the remainder will require less skill than at present, despite numerous prognostications to the contrary. In turn, the reduction will weaken the stabilizing influence of what is often called the middle class, so important to maintaining equilibrium in a democracy. As such, the consequence affects not only the economy but psychical and cultural attributes as well—the national ethos. Restated, automation is driving a wedge between the comparatively few who are capable of riding this wave of technology and the majority who, to one degree or another, are left in its wash.

Supposedly, this avalanche of technology should increase the demand for expertise. The landmark report *Workforce 2000*, published by the U.S. Department of Labor, paints that picture. But a more careful review of its data and projections reveals a different perspective. Although the fastest growing job categories are in the technical arena, that segment is only a small fraction of the entire workforce. The bulk of the new jobs are in more mundane areas. When combined with the larger replacement job market, the outlook is stagnant at best.[1] Furthermore, the report preceded the current and lingering recession and therefore could not deal with the widespread fear that many of the higher level jobs eliminated will not be restored if and when the economy recovers. A very good account of this situation appears in Barlett and Steele's *America: What Went Wrong?*[2] Another even more recent book on this subject is Wallace C. Peterson's *Silent Depression: The Fate of the American Dream.*[3]

In more specific terms, the Tables 3 and 4 depict the job market through the year 2005. Table 3 (page 142) is based on U.S. Department of Labor projections derived from 1990 data. The data has been annotated by the author to indicate the general relationship of occupations to automation, primarily in terms of use, that will likely occur by the year 2005:

A. *Imperative user.* Most people in these jobs need a commanding knowledge of automation in terms of applications, if not the technology.

B. *Journeyman user.* Most individuals require specific expertise in the use of computers or robotics (or both) but primarily in terms of immediate job requirements.

C. *End user (or not applicable).* No specific skills related to automation are required beyond some minor hands-on procedures, which are not much more difficult than using a typewriter or adding machine.

The imperative users probably constitute less than 9 percent of the workforce, a percentage that does not increase significantly in the interval between 1990 and 2005. At the other end of the range, nearly 70 percent of the workforce will continue as end users of automation at most.

Table 4 (page 144) takes the projected year 2005 job data from Table 3 and estimates the number of jobs in each occupation that could be eliminated by way of automation (beyond those considered in the original source) for any of various reasons, without any compensating jobs being created. At the extreme, this elimination could reach 11 percent, which, combined with the current jobless rate, would total at least approximately 18 percent—higher when the millions who have simply given up looking for work are counted. That percentage is close to depression-level unemployment, and arguably half of this loss would be middle class wage earners. They would be thrown into competition for lower class jobs with the seven-and-a-half-million lower-income workers who would have also lost their jobs.

Mechanics of job degradation. This net downsizing of job responsibility will be bad enough; but automation continues to exacerbate the situation with job degradation. To understand this phenomenon, consider how labor is employed in low-tech work, which was the mainstream of economic history as the Industrial Revolution took root. In most cases, the bulk of the population worked for a few overseers. Then came (a) quality control (which was initially created *to reduce* excessively skilled workmanship), (b) the assembly line, and (c) scientific management (e.g., minute control of employee work habits). As a result, high intelligence on the part of workers lost even more influence in the workplace. Automation restored some of this influence, but not always under favorable terms because it too can easily become another tool for overseers.

Now compare two groups of workers with different mental ability. Let us assume that one group has an average intelligence score of 80; the other group, 120. If the work consists of moving stones from point A to point B, both groups will finish in about the same time. If anything, the higher intelligence group might work slower. In high-tech jobs, by contrast, the high-enders (no relationship with the satire in Swift's *Gulliver's Travels*) will vastly outproduce the low-enders, simply because their intelligence becomes a major factor. Productivity often depends on stringing together different ideas or resolving conflicts among them.

Figure 24 (page 145) compares rock-movers with programmers. The average production rate of code for programmers is about ten lines of tested operational code per day per person. However, that figure is misleading. The most competent programmers can churn out fifty or more lines per day, whereas the output of the least competent is close to zero. Actually the situation is worse than that. The least able programmers seldom write any code that doesn't require major revision, and hence more proficient staffers must be pulled from their work to correct those deficiencies. In a very real sense, then, low-enders are counterproductive.

Table 3. Job outlook through 2005

Job categories	Year 1990	Year 2005	Relative index	ADP level
High-level management and professions				
General management	3,157,000	3,758,000	0.99	A
Science/engineer management	1,364,000	1,751,000	1.07	A
High-level corporate staff	1,509,000	1,989,000	1.10	A
Engineers/architects/scientists	2,816,000	3,875,000	1.15	A
Physicians, dentists, vets	855,000	1,101,000	1.07	B
Clergy	271,000	297,000	0.91	C
Attorneys and jurists	633,000	850,000	1.12	B
Subtotal	**10,605,000**	**13,603,000**	**1.07**	
	8.65%	9.24%		
Upper-level management and supporting professions				
Food service management	595,000	793,000	1.11	B
Construction management	183,000	243,000	1.11	B
Communications management	143,000	189,000	1.10	A
Other management	1,887,000	2,451,000	1.08	B
Teachers and librarians	5,687,000	7,280,000	1.07	B
Entertainers and writers	1,542,000	1,915,000	1.03	C
Social workers	778,000	1,079,000	1.15	C
Nurses and related fields	2,305,000	3,304,000	1.19	B
Other supporting fields	913,000	1,224,000	1.12	B
Subtotal	**4,033,000**	**18,478,000**	**1.10**	
	11.45%	12.55%		
Mid-level occupations				
Accountants and analysts	1,049,000	1,403,000	1.11	B
Adjusters and estimators	729,000	950,000	1.09	B
Inspectors	216,000	273,000	1.05	C
Personnel and labor relations	361,000	468,000	1.08	C
Purchasing and buyers	412,000	501,000	1.01	B
Other mid-level staff	846,000	1,097,000	1.08	B
Health technicians	1,833,000	2,595,000	1.18	B
Engr/science technicians	1,327,000	1,640,000	1.03	A
Other technicians	1,044,000	1,519,000	1.21	B
Sales	7,604,000	9,475,000	1.04	C
Records processing	3,809,000	3,795,000	0.83	B
Materials management	2,513,000	2,754,000	0.91	B
Technical operators	665,000	597,000	0.75	B
Adjusters and investigators	1,058,000	1,313,000	1.03	B
Secretaries/stenographers	4,680,000	5,110,000	0.91	C
Detectives and police	1,213,000	1,601,000	1.10	B

Table 3. (continued)

Job categories	Year 1990	Year 2005	Relative index	ADP level
Mid-level occupations (continued)				
Farming, forestry, fishing	1,314,000	1,152,000	0.72	C
Blue collar supervisors	1,792,000	1,912,000	0.89	C
Constructions trades	3,763,000	4,557,000	1.01	C
Extractive trades	237,000	247,000	0.87	C
Mechanics and installers	4,900,000	5,669,000	0.96	C
Precision workers	3,134,000	3,208,000	0.85	C
Other skilled trades	298,000	316,000	0.88	C
Subtotal	**44,824,000**	**52,152,000**	**0.97**	
	36.57%	35.43%		
Lower-level semiskilled and unskilled jobs				
Cashiers & retail clerks	2,848,000	3,607,000	1.05	C
Stock clerks	1,242,000	1,451,000	0.97	C
Other clerks	2,394,000	2,956,000	1.03	C
Information clerks	1,418,000	2,003,000	1.18	C
Mail and postal clerks	719,000	825,000	0.96	C
Other clerical	7,089,000	8,438,000	0.99	C
Building maintenance	3,435,000	4,068,000	0.99	C
Food preparation	7,705,000	10,031,000	1.08	C
Health service workers	1,972,000	2,832,000	1.20	C
Personal service jobs	2,192,000	3,164,000	1.20	C
Private household jobs	782,000	555,000	0.59	C
Guards	1,053,000	1,394,000	1.10	C
Gardeners	874,000	1,222,000	1.16	C
Machine setters	4,905,000	4,579,000	0.78	C
Assemblers	2,675,000	2,307,000	0.72	C
Transportation workers	4,730,000	5,743,000	1.01	C
Helpers and laborers	4,935,000	5,331,000	0.90	C
Other low-skilled jobs	2,143,000	2,452,000	0.95	C
Subtotal	**53,111,000**	**62,958,000**	**0.99**	
	43.33%	42.77%		
Totals	**122,537,000**	**147,191,000**	**1.00**	
	100.00%	100.00%		

Source (first 2 columns): U.S. Dept of Labor Bulletin 2401, *Occupational Projections and Training Data: 1992.*

ADP-skill requirements percentages	1990	2005	
A. Imperative users	8.42%	8.96%	
B. Journeyman users	23.03%	24.03%	
C. End users or none	68.55%	67.01%	

Table 4. Potential effects of automation on the job outlook

Job categories	Year 2005	Potential additional job loss		
		Percent	Number	Reason
High-level management and professions				
No significant reductions				
Job subtotal (from table 3)	*13,603,000*			
Upper-level management and supporting professions				
No significant reductions				
Job subtotal (from table 3)	*18,478,000*			
Mid-level occupations				
Accountants and analysts	1,403,000	40%	561,200	computers
Purchasing and buyers	501,000	30%	150,300	computers
Other mid-level staff	1,097,000	20%	219,400	computers
Engr/science technicians	1,640,000	10%	164,200	computers
Records processing	3,795,000	40%	1,518,200	image processing
Material management	2,754,000	30%	826,200	computers
Technical operators	597,000	10%	59,700	design efficiency
Secretaries/stenographers	5,110,000	30%	1,533,000	computers
Mechanics and installers	5,669,000	30%	1,700,000	robotics
Precision workers	3,208,000	30%	962,400	robotics
Other skilled trades	316,000	30%	94,800	robotics
Subtotal of above lines	26,090,000			
Job loss subtotal		**15%**	**7,790,000**	
Job subtotal (from table 3)	*52,152,000*	◄—┘		
Lower-level semi-skilled and unskilled jobs				
Cashiers & retail clerks	3,607,000	10%	360,700	robotics
Stock clerks	1,451,000	10%	145,100	robotics
Other clerks	2,956,000	10%	295,000	robotics
Information clerks	2,003,000	30%	600,900	computers
Mail and postal clerks	719,000	40%	330,000	electronic mail
Other clerical	8,438,000	30%	2,531,400	cmptrs & robotics
Guards	1,394,000	20%	278,800	cmptrs & robotics
Machine setters	4,579,000	20%	915,800	robotics
Assemblers	2,307,000	20%	461,400	robotics
Helpers and laborers	5,331,000	20%	1,066,200	robotics
Other low-skilled jobs	2,452,000	20%	490,200	robotics
Subtotal of above lines	35,237,000			
Job loss subtotal		**12%**	**7,476,300**	
Job subtotal (from table 3)	*62,938,000*	◄—┘		
Total potential job loss		**10%**	**15,266,000**	
Job total (from table 3)	*147,191,000*	◄—┘		

Source (1st column): U.S. Dept of Labor Bulletin 2401, *Occupational Projections and Training Data: 1992.*

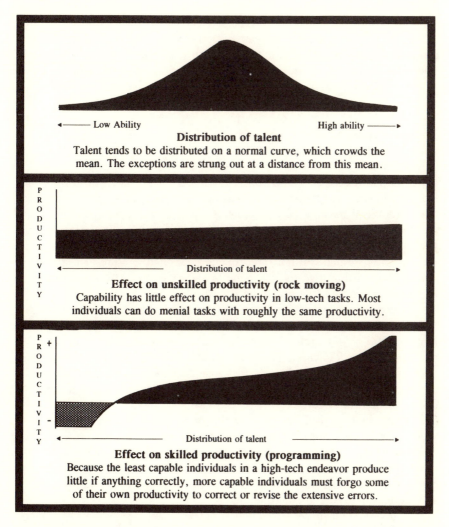

Distribution of talent
Talent tends to be distributed on a normal curve, which crowds the
mean. The exceptions are strung out at a distance from this mean.

Effect on unskilled productivity (rock moving)
Capability has little effect on productivity in low-tech tasks. Most
individuals can do menial tasks with roughly the same productivity.

Effect on skilled productivity (programming)
Because the least capable individuals in a high-tech endeavor produce
little if anything correctly, more capable individuals must forgo some
of their own productivity to correct or revise the extensive errors.

24. Low-tech versus high-tech productivity. Intelligence and related abilities are not
major factors in menial labor, but the opposite is true in high-tech work. As a result, technology—especially automation—can drive a divisive wedge among workers.

In other words, the productivity would increase if the least capable subgroup was transferred to menial jobs, and thus it is easy to see why management is restructuring the workforce. As such, the workforce will increasingly
be divided into low-enders assigned to structured, quasi-menial jobs with the
least requirement for judgment and exercise of initiative. Any failure to develop good workplace attributes will not affect productivity, as long as the

low-enders are supervised by a comparatively few more capable people that place maximum reliance on automation-supported management tools. This is a polemic, of course, and does not apply to all situations. However, the gap is bound to increase as the use of automation expands in the manufacturing plant, in the service industry, and in the marketplace, and especially while public schools continue to stress mediocrity.

Evolving class structure. According to many economists, a democracy requires a wealthy upper class; and large, profitable corporations to foot a good part of the bill for welfare, and a large middle class that can at least pay for the government services that affect its own well-being. It has also been said that this middle class is the primary stabilizing force within a diverse national ethos. Its members may be cognizant of the rich, perhaps begrudging their wealth at times, yet they do not lack for essentials and have at least a reasonable opportunity to obtain wealth on their own initiative. The middle class also sees the poor, is thankful not to be among them, and is more or less content that taxes are being used to ameliorate the worst poverty. This redistribution also limits revolution to a few isolated areas.

Unfortunately, technology in all its forms has wrought a major change. First, and by way of advances in medicine and health care, it has created a large and still growing retired class. Second, as discussed earlier, automation is driving a wedge into the middle class, pushing a comparatively few into an upper middle class status of professionals and technocrats, and the balance into a lower middle class status of workers. As such, the concept of the middle class may need to be replaced.

What has happened—as noted by Labor Secretary Robert Reich—is that society is now dividing into five groups: (a) the well-to-do; (b) professionals, executives, and technocrats; (c) workers; (d) retirees (except the wealthy and some poor); and (e) for lack of a better name, absorbers. This last group includes the traditional poor extended to include anyone who absorbs benefits and services in excess of contributions.[4]

A few individuals belong to two or more classes (e.g., a wealthy technocrat executive). The wealthiest person in the United States, Bill Gates, is the archetypical example. According to *Forbes* magazine, he owns more than nine billion dollars in assets, and there is no doubt about his role in technology as the founder and chairman of Microsoft Corporation.[5] For the most part, though, individuals belong to a single classification, and with two general exceptions they will tend to stay there. First, a significant but small number of workers and absorbers will by dint of effort or good fortune move up the economic ladder. Second, the vast majority of executives and workers will eventually gravitate to the retiree group, although the natural progression of birth and aging can leave proportional membership constant. The details are as follows:

• *The well-to-do.* Scripture advises that the poor will be with us always. It might as well have added the wealthy. Their numbers are comparatively small, yet on a per capita basis they provide the lion's share of investment, of taxes paid, and of charity. Whether this contribution amounts to the majority begs the issue. The question is at what point down the scale their cumulative contribution to the economic paradigm equals others. Depending on the set of data one reads and on how corporate taxes are factored in, that point occurs somewhere within the upper 10 to 20 percent of the population. As for exercise of financial clout, consider that if a billionaire lost 99 percent of his or her wealth, that person would still benefit from an annual gross income of nearly a million dollars from interest, dividends, and capital growth, without touching the principal of the "meager" remnant. That is equal to the total pay of more than a hundred workers earning the minimum wage.

As for influence, the well-to-do have always exerted more of it than other classes. Whether this is due to the money itself, or the aura that wealth projects, or the human attributes that led to that wealth is speculation, but there should be little doubt that it happens. Moreover, while the proportional size of this group may fluctuate slightly, that variation is much less a function of automation than it is of tax policy and other laws aimed at redistribution of excessive wealth.

• *Professionals, executives, and technocrats.* These make up the second group, in which income ranges from worker to well-to-do (although the majority are clearly distant from either polemic). These individuals collectively exert enormous influence by virtue of their jobs, or their ability to project their thoughts, or by their role in nurturing others. Of course, not all members depend on automation to make their living, but most of them use it, while the balance often find their native intelligence enhanced because of the advantages that this technology provides them indirectly.

• *Workers.* This third group includes both white collar and blue collar workforces in an economy that is increasingly service and information oriented. The general criterion for inclusion is that members exert little influence beyond their immediate work environment but they pay their own way, contributing roughly as much in taxes as they draw directly or indirectly in benefits. However, as their mere end use of automation and other technology sharpens in focus, their influence is bound to decline commensurate with a net drop in income. Despite this, the worker class is by far the largest of the five groups, and arguably workers are the backbone of any economy. The taxes they pay range between 40 and 50 percent of the total, depending on how the first two groups are defined. Still, their proportionality is shrinking due to the growing number of retirees.

• *Retirees.* Fifty years ago, the number of retirees was small and for the most part they had little money. Today, they exceed forty million, and most of them are drawing Social Security (or its equivalent). Many add pensions and interest from savings and investments to that income. They also have arguably the most influential lobby in the United States—the American Association of Retired Persons (AARP). What distinguishes this group is that its members contribute almost nothing to the *generation* of wealth directly while absorbing the bulk of entitlements. However, they sustain a great deal of the economy by way of expenditures and by paying taxes, albeit less per dollar than most workers.[6]

At this point, the critic will respond that retirees earned their Social Security benefits by way of contributions during their working years. Well, yes and no. The ratio of total benefits to total contributions for specific individuals can range from 50 to 1 to 1 to 50, and in a few cases from 1,000 to 1 (or to zero).[7] Moreover, the American economy works more like a sieve than a bank. The government is concerned with how much it takes in, and how much and to whom such funds must be redistributed. That is, the Social Security system is pay-as-you go, meaning that in reality it is part of a common income structure, from which all programs are funded.

Worse, the Social Security Trust Fund is a type of bank account, but its growing assets (currently adding about $53 billion per year) have all been lent to the Treasury to fund annual deficits in excess of the officially report deficit. Hence both the principal and interest have been reduced to IOUs. But because the debt continues to grow, the government has no way to repay these IOUs when eventually the swelling ranks of retirees come to depend on these reserves. Thus for all practical purposes the FICA tax is an adjunct income tax. This means that from the perspective of the Treasury, retirees constitute a large group that absorbs more benefits than they pay in.

• *Absorbers.* This final group contributes little if anything to the economy. Granted, many absorbers—perhaps most of them—find themselves members of this group through no fault of their own. They may have born retarded or with deformations or afflictions that require constant care. Others do not have the ability, character, or personality to hold down a steady job. Still other absorbers are hardened or habitual criminals. The list goes on and on, but whatever the cause they absorb wealth without contributing much in return. They are sustained by external funding. Even those who are supported entirely by their families are subsidized in part by tax breaks. In short, their existence is a reality that must be accommodated in economic terms. When the funds are less than the requirements, something has to give. Yet the current magnitude of benefits—direct and indirect—is enormous, and there is a great deal of pressure for more.

The capitalism versus socialism issue. The significance of these evolving socioeconomic classes is not so much their existence but their proportionality. To the extent that the retiree and absorber groups expand, the balance must be more heavily taxed to provide for them. Yet when taxes grow too high, productivity declines and hence the tax base shrinks even farther. This situation also means that the population will be increasingly bifurcated into payers and payees, making it almost impossible to obtain a political consensus except perhaps in times of great crises.

This section compresses a complex problem into a few admittedly oversimplified paragraphs. The intent is to make the fulcrum of these economic consequences clear. For in spite of the hordes of detail that affect it, this fulcrum seems intent on standing its ground. In plain terms, the bifurcation will eventually force the United States to decide between an infrastructure that is predominately càpitalistic or one that is predominantly socialistic. Although some analysts favor a mixture of the two, each model is based on its own fundamental premise. These premises do not mix well.

Capitalism is known best in the pejorative sense of its excesses, and these cannot be denied. Beneath those excesses, however, it is a system that considers the citizens and corporations of a nation as the source of wealth, impelled by the profit motive or at least the desire to advance one's standing. To keep capitalism functioning smoothly, a government regulates it to simultaneously improve those incentives and curtail the excesses (witness the antitrust legislation early in this century). Furthermore, the government can and does levy taxes to provide for those who, for whatever reasons, cannot cope with the system, but in no way does it attempt to provide economic equality. The reason is that unless a country has resources it can sell worldwide in almost any quantity at any price, there would never be enough capital to do it.

By contrast, socialism in its extreme form (which is theoretical communism) does not recognize the concept of wealth, at least not as a font. Money is regarded primarily as an accounting tool. The state controls the pot and doles it out in the form of allowances or paid services in equal measure to all citizens. Replacement is by way of confiscatory taxes on all profits and by the printing press. This system works in isolated circumstances—for example, monasteries that sustain themselves with little dependence on the outside world and a minuscule homogeneous population within. The system does not work on a larger scale, as demonstrated by the utter failure of communism in modern times and, for that matter, the Mayflower Compact within a few months of its creation.

So much for the polemics. The practical debate is between welfare capitalism, with an eye to more extensive redistribution of excess earnings, and so-called democratic socialism, which is communism modified to permit limited but heavily taxed corporate and individual earnings. At present, the United

States practices the former, while countries such as Sweden are essentially members of the latter. Sweden has a small, homogeneous population concentrated in a small area and maintains a favorable balance of trade. As such, it is closer to a monastery than a major player in a huge, free-wheeling marketplace. Moreover, a Swedish government commission recently proposed less welfare and more private enterprise.[8]

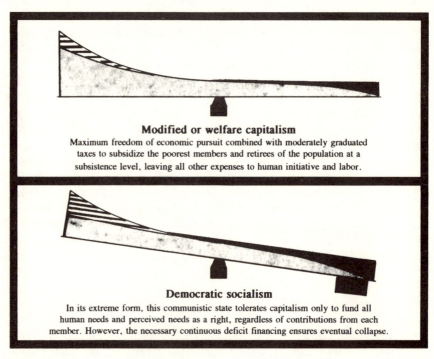

Modified or welfare capitalism
Maximum freedom of economic pursuit combined with moderately graduated taxes to subsidize the poorest members and retirees of the population at a subsistence level, leaving all other expenses to human initiative and labor.

Democratic socialism
In its extreme form, this communistic state tolerates capitalism only to fund all human needs and perceived needs as a right, regardless of contributions from each member. However, the necessary continuous deficit financing ensures eventual collapse.

25. Socialism's impossible balancing act. Excessive entitlements mandate higher taxes and, for the United States, massive deficit financing. It should be obvious, therefore, why socialism, by whatever name it may bear, must eventually overtax an economic system.

Unfortunately, in economic terms, the United States seems intent on following suit, and most of the reasons can be tied, directly or indirectly, to technology. The eventual consequence is that the generated wealth of this country will no longer be sufficient to pay the bills, while the capacity to borrow further will be strained at best. At that point—likely to be marked by an economic collapse in some form—the United States must choose between restoring capitalism with lowered expectations or going the socialistic route and micromanaging the money supply. The micromanagement alternative is feasible, given the advent of massive computer systems, but its operation would run headlong into a vast range of major problems, among them international trade deficits, foreign ownership and investment, and resistance of the population to such massive control, not to mention the abuses that would be inflicted by those in power.

The prospect of massive socialism is a sorry spectacle, but if it is to be headed off, the factors that propel the country in that direction must be understood. Unless dealt with, these factors will continue to fester and eventually immerse the United States in an undigestible mixture of capitalism and socialism that would please no one. A summary of the earlier-stated major contributing factors follows:

• *Redistribution among social groups.* Medical science has vastly increased the numbers and longevity of retirees. Furthermore, automation is reducing the number of jobs and net income of the balance, which throws more people into the absorbing group.

• *Personal economic needs perceived as rights.* The groundswell for national health insurance, the growing food stamp program, and continuation of a vast menu of other benefit programs attest to this. Once declared a right, the government must directly or indirectly ensure that the necessary funds are doled out. Technology is to blame only in part, primarily by its ability to process tens of millions of checks monthly and by intensifying public awareness of the dole by way of various public and private media.

• *Transformation to a service economy.* A service economy has less than an industrial economy to sell overseas. Moreover, the degree to which other countries have low wages or exercise unfair trade practices, is the extent to which domestic corporations farm work out across borders and individuals purchase more foreign goods. In turn, this imbalance leads to increased external investment and ownership of domestic corporations. The role of technology, of course, fosters service at the expense of manufacturing.

• *Fraud and waste.* Not all fraud and waste is attributable to technology, but vast programs managed by automation have so far led to even higher losses. In turn, this situation seems to encourage or at least tolerate waste. The annual total cost of fraud and waste may exceed the annual deficit.

• *Government share of gross domestic product (GDP) and the deficit.* It is a safe assumption that when the government share of the GDP passes a certain point, socialism will outgun capitalism as a matter of numbers. The turning point for a specific country depends on many factors, but if that share continues to increase, it is bound to reach the turning point sooner or later. Worse, if the initial funding of this socialism is by way of deficit financing, and the resulting debt eventually triggers an economic collapse, then the emergency measures invoked to control it could establish a massive precedence for micromanagement of the economy.

The last point deserves a closer look. Unfortunately, accurate data is difficult to find beyond the undisputable federal share of the GDP, which increased from about 6 percent in 1930 to more than 25 percent in 1992.[9] And when state and local taxes are factored in, the percentage exceeds 40 percent. Moreover, when—as inevitable—funding for the entire national health care bill is incorporated into the budget, it will add another 8 percent to the federal share of the GDP (i.e., the part of the existing 14 percent that is not already funded by the government). Hence Washington would directly control 33 percent of the GDP (and all governmental bodies combined about 50 percent).

Furthermore, a substantial slice of government funding is hidden. The best example is the earned income tax credit. Much of this credit does not show up as an expense because it is factored into net liability for individual income tax. Yet without question this credit is a formal income redistribution program. Moreover, the federal government requires that employers make certain investments for environmental protection and other programs. These programs may be essential, but that does not change the fact that the costs constitute a de facto federal expense. In addition, government policies greatly affect how other expenditures in the civil sector are made, while state spending—especially for welfare—probably consumes another 5 percent of the GDP. So the bottom line is that the American system of government either directly funds or effectively will eventually control perhaps two thirds of the gross domestic product.

12

Psychological Dilemmas

Disproportion is the root of all moral mistakes. . . . Within most virtues there lurks, waiting to slip its leash, a vice in the form of excess.

—George Will

The third class of ethical problems triggered by the excesses of automation are those that affect individuals psychically. As such, these problems come closest to the Frankenstein issue—namely that man *may* have created something that will do him in, despite any commendable motivations. This is not an easy matter to resolve because by the time sufficient objective evidence accrues it could be too late. Fortunately, the subjective perspective suffices.

The central theme running through many profound essays on this subject is that every individual needs a certain amount of space and time—privacy—in which to survive and grow. Erik Erikson and Eric Fromm both emphasized this point, but perhaps no one has put the case as succinctly as Cornelius Gallagher:

Every individual must have certain areas over which his sovereignty is absolute, as long as he is pursuing legitimate aims. Lower animals have a body buffer zone and, as Robert Ardrey has so compelling pointed out, a territorial imperative. Perhaps the need can best be represented by the bull ring where the bull himself outlines an area of his own called the *querencia*. This is a randomly chosen spot where the bull will always retreat when the pressure of his death struggle with the matador becomes too intense. But where can modern man go to gather his strength when his is gored by society? Techniques to assert the individual's right to a space of psychological control have simply not kept pace with technology's ability to disclose almost everything to almost everybody.[1]

Gallagher goes on to explain how he came to think of this need as "the intellectual imperative"—the need to discuss ideas and concepts freely with the assurance that it will remain private:

> Urban mass culture has destroyed for most of us the opportunity to exercise freely the Territorial Imperative; the advance of computer and other technologies threatens the Intellectual Imperative. Physically, we are constantly in a crowd; intellectually, technology has provided devices to make our forgotten actions and our unacknowledged thoughts known to the crowd. . . . It is extremely dangerous for a matador to violate the bull's querencia, and it may be equally fatal for society to presume that it can violate the space where the individual's basic nature resides.[2]

Actually, this intrusion can take one of two forms. The passive form arises from awareness of the mere existence of these automated databases. That situation alone, as a few writers suggest, may cause some people to attempt to modify their behavior under the pressure of assumed expectation—for example, to conform to various norms calculated from such data. The active form, of course, goes far beyond that and as a minimum constitutes abuse. This occurs when someone uses data to the detriment of an individual *without cause*. No one quarrels with police investigation of suspected felons, especially if the evidence is strong. By contrast, surveillance of innocent people in the name of national security are often met with outrage once discovered.

Both forms may frustrate the exercise of the intellectual imperative, leading to a certain amount of psychical disintegration. More common, however, is a reduction in the ability to exercise critical reason and judgment and to accept responsibility for one's decisions and actions. That is, the exercise of individual judgment seems to yield increasingly to machine logic. This may not be true for intelligent or creative individuals, but it does apply to million upon millions of others.

Note how many times people blame computers for their own mistakes or shortcomings, or demonstrate an unwillingness to rectify errors personally. Take into account the power of suggestion when a computer or automated system uses a voice supplement. If that isn't evidence enough, consider the numbing effect television has had on the American mind, or what's left of it.[3] Granted, television hardly constitutes automation, yet if a passive machine can capture the mind for seven hours a day on average—with material that oscillates largely between violence and swill—it would be surprising if "smart" machines fail to exert an even greater influence.

Passive invasion of privacy. Gallagher's observation was written twenty-four years ago. In the interim, the databases of which he spoke have increased somewhere between fifty- and a hundred-fold. Virtually everything one owns or does of significance today is recorded in an electronic database somewhere, and these databases are being increasingly linked. Additionally, data is being extracted and entered into ever more pervasive databases. However, because the intent is usually legitimate, containing this trend is difficult at best. This statement from a large insurance company soliciting new business tells the tale:

> As part of our routine procedure, we may request that an investigative consumer report be prepared. Such reports typically include information as to identity, general reputation, personal characteristic and mode of living. The information is usually obtained through confidential conversations with neighbors, friends and other acquaintances. . . . This is simply a standard precautionary measure to help assure fair and equitable treatment for everyone concerned. . . . In some situations, and in compliance with applicable laws, we may disclose items of information to third parties.[4]

The insurance is offered by Teachers Insurance and Annuity Association (TIAA), located in New York. Together with its sister company—the College Retirement Equities Fund (CREF)—it held $121 billion dollars (as of the end of 1993) in assets and other investments, primarily for individuals in the profession of teaching and education.[5] It is one of the most stable companies in the United States, consistently earning top ratings from A. M. Best Company, Standard & Poor's, and Moody's.

The prospective policyholder is invited to write for additional material on this subject. To those who so inquire, the company mails a flyer entitled *Description of Information Practices*. In part, it states the following:

> Information we collect about you will not generally be given to anyone without your written consent, except when the disclosure is necessary for us to conduct our business. In that case we will share information about you without your prior consent to the extent permitted by state privacy laws. Generally, information will be disclosed without your prior consent only to persons or organizations having a business interest in an insurance transaction involving you, having a contract with us to perform part of our insurance function, or having some other business relationship with us.

Because at least one member of each family in the majority of the population carries some form of life insurance (and almost all are eligible for it) and because there are hundreds of life insurance companies with thousands of contracts and other business relationships, it should be obvious that these consumer dossiers can be accessed by virtually any business in the United States, at least in the collective sense. The rationale appears sound and it is politely stated, but it doesn't take much imagination to recognize the potential for abuse. These consumer reporting agencies, combined with the expanding number of so-called information brokers, indicate that we are approaching the state of affairs portrayed in the novels *Brave New World* and *Nineteen Eighty-four*. For $24, one of these information brokers will supply the information recorded by all three major credit bureaus, which means it already has access to the whole nine yards.[6]

Another purpose for information gathering is to create a sense of equality among unequals. The government collects this data and statistically analyzes it to ensure proportional representation in activities directly or indirectly funded from tax revenues. Public schools, colleges, and universities follow suit with politically correct thinking, some of which has gone to such extremes that the courts have had to strike it down as a violation of the right to free speech. In theory, this equality is approachable in terms of justice, but it is obviously impossible in terms of talent, ability, character, and most other human attributes.

It would be remarkable if human nature and society could be otherwise, but no less a benefactor than Abraham Lincoln found it imperative to dwell on this difference at some length, especially during the exchange of views with Judge Stephen Douglas—a contest of wills that was initiated at least a year before the formal debates between these two men. In 1857, Lincoln said (referring to the *Declaration of Independence*):

> I think the authors of that notable instrument intended to include *all* men, but they did not intend to declare all men equal in *all respects*. They did not mean to say all were equal in size, intellect, moral developments, or social capacity. They defined with tolerable distinctness, in what respects they did consider all men created equal—equal in "certain inalienable rights, among which are life liberty and the pursuit of happiness." This they said, and this they meant. They did not mean to assert the obvious untruth, that all were then actually enjoying that equality, not yet, that they were about to confer it immediately upon [slaves]. In fact they had no power to confer such a boon. They meant simply to declare the right, so that the enforcement of it might follow as fast as circumstances should permit.[7]

In practice, of course, the ideal of equality before the law has never been fully attained. The wealthy have always been able to obtain better counsel than the poor, though as in the case of Clarence Gideon the courts will sometimes equalize the right, at least in theory.[8]

The point of all of this is that equality pushed too far leads to a homogenized society in which the individual loses his or her identity. It is not just an invasion of privacy but of the psyche itself. Figure 26 depicts the extent to which this invasion has reached. Some may say that is the price of democracy, but if so they have lost sight of a concept so fundamental that for them it may be beyond restoration.

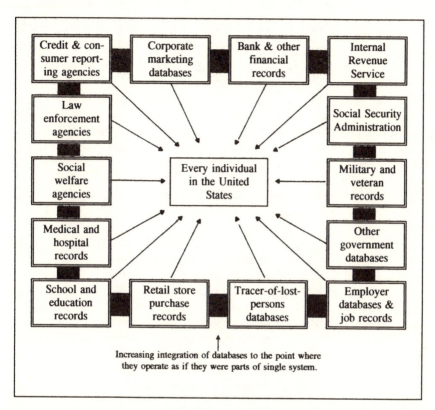

26. The imploding invasion of privacy. Until information is abused, the invasion of privacy operates almost by stealth, giving little evidence of its encompassing growth. But as these databases are expanded and linked, and as sophisticated statistical inference techniques are used to predict behavior, the environment described in the novel *Nineteen Eighty-four* will have been seeded.

Abusive invasion of privacy. The hopeful note on invasion of privacy is that the populace is becoming aware of it. A recent survey indicates that approximately 80 percent of the population is concerned about it, and that percentage is growing.[9] At least three books have been published recently on the subject:

- Dennis King, *Get the Facts on Anyone* (Prentice Hall, 1991),
- Edmund J. Pankaw, *Check It Out!* (Contemporary Books, 1993), and
- Jeffrey Rothfeder, *Privacy for Sale* (Simon & Schuster, 1992).

The first two books were not intended as commentary, but they serve that purpose. The third book was definitely a commentary. Unfortunately, little has been done so far. If anything, the pressure to create and integrate ever larger databases is irresistible. Moreover, it may be impossible to stop it legally, since the mere gathering of information would probably be protected by the First Amendment.

Abuses are another matter. Of the five categories briefly discussed in this section, the first is micromanagement. In this practice, employee performance is monitored in detail by a computer and evaluated by a statistical comparison of that data with locally disseminated criteria. This procedure may and usually is coupled with personal observation, but data is the primary tool, especially when it is a byproduct of the work itself. Thus telephone operators, reservations clerks, and anyone who operates primarily with computer workstations as end users can have all their work recorded. If (a) they agree to this surveillance as a condition of their employment, (b) it is applied equally and consistently to all similar job classifications, and (c) no one is singled out for disciplinary action, there is little recourse barring legislation that restricts such surveillance.[10]

The second category is improper obtaining of information, and this ranges from accidental to systematic exploitation. This abuse may be the most prevalent at this time though no comprehensive study has been made. On the other hand, few observers doubt its pervasiveness. Popular targets include Social Security records, credit bureau reports, medical records, and criminal or misdemeanor files.[11] In the case of credit reporting, all inquiries are supposed to be recorded on the credit report itself, and any individual is entitled to obtain a copy of his or her current report in return for an administrative processing fee.[12] A variation on this stems from the increasing reluctance of employers to write letters of reference on former employees for fear of litigation. As a result the gaining employers often resort to other sources of information to assess applicants, notwithstanding that the practice may be illegal.[13]

The third category of abuse involves marketing, and this ranges from perfectly legitimate techniques to unscrupulous exploitation. There is nothing wrong in principle with a vendor sending advertising material and brochures to individuals and families who are most likely to purchase its goods or services while avoiding those who are the least likely to buy them. Luxury car dealers do not advertise heavily among migrant farm workers, nor do insurance companies attempt to peddle sham burial policies in Grosse Pointe, Michigan. The abuse begins when these vendors tap into databases not intended for that purpose, and it culminates when that data is screened to exploit fear. Thus it is improper for a holding corporation that owns a credit bureau to use the bureau's database as a means of identifying the most likely buyers for the goods produced by other subsidiaries. And it is exploitative for insurance companies to peddle cancer policies by screening medical histories to determine which families have a history of this disease.

A variation on this is called porkware. In this situation, vendors exploit the ignorance of customers in order to sell them more technology than they need. In some cases, this could be considered good salesmanship, but if the sales pitch emphasizes false or misleading information beyond the level of mild puffery, the practice borders on fraud. Nevertheless, if the vendor delivers exactly what is agreed to and lives up to any warranty, it would be difficult to prosecute this kind of abuse in court. Actually, the whole computer industry would probably fall apart at the seams if it did not imply that updated products hopelessly outdated older versions.

The fourth category is a variation on marketing. This practice hawks a political bill of goods in lieu of more traditional wares. Again, the instances range from perfectly legitimate to exploitative. It is hardly a crime for the such-and-such party to send out material praising its candidates to voters who are registered with that party, or for ecology-minded representatives to seek support from members of the Sierra Club or the Nature Conservancy. But like some insurance companies that sell cancer policies, candidates and government operatives can exploit various databases to capitalize on voter fears by mailing out patently false or misleading information to garner support and votes.

Hitler parlayed the fears and prejudices of his country into the most virulent form of government ever witnessed by history. Because of this he is sometimes regarded as an evil genius, with the emphasis most assuredly on the adjective. Politicians in a democracy know that they cannot go this far, but with automated databases they can extend their influence in untoward ways much farther than in the past. A variation on this manipulates data from automated voting booths in order to change the outcome of an election.[14]

Fortunately, these four categories of abuse can be dealt with by legislation, at least in more severe cases, although that does not guarantee enforcement. Unfortunately, the fifth category presents a more difficult challenge. That category comprises the abuses which stem from inadequate or distended databases that nevertheless must be coordinated. For example, the Federal Bureau of Investigation depends on the cooperation of more than 60,000 criminal justice agencies nationwide to update their own databases.[15] As a result, researchers found that of 360,000 disseminations of information of this type (nationwide, not just to the FBI), approximately 165,000 were either incomplete or inaccurate. Among other things, this translates to more than 14,000 people at risk of being falsely detained every year.[16]

A similar situation occurs with the National Practitioner Data Bank. This database was mandated by Congress as a result of the Health Care Quality Improvement Act of 1986. It catalogs malpractice determinations, disciplinary actions, and similar derogatory information on physicians and other health care providers. One purpose is to make this information readily available to hospitals, which must check with it every time a doctor seeks admitting privileges. The idea is sound, yet apparently the process of collecting data from numerous sources is inadequate and the reputation of a number of doctors has been unfairly tarnished. That is bound to happen when nearly 900,000 inquires are made annually.[17] In other words, in order to reduce this unintentional category of abuse, existing databases must be further integrated, thus raising the ante on invasion of privacy.

Psychical disintegration. This brings the discussion to the ultimate risk of automation, and that is the potential disintegration of the human psyche in numbers too high and in degree too far for the psychical health of a nation. More than eighty years ago, Woodrow Wilson, then president of Princeton University, could see it coming:

> We have witnessed in modern business the submergence of the individual within the organization. . . . Most men are individuals no longer so far as their business, its activities or its moralities are concerned. They are not units but fractions. With their individuality and independence of choice in matters of business, they have also lost their individual choice with the field of morals.[18]

That observation is no longer limited to the workplace. It permeates life in general, and even if the source is a shortcoming in human nature itself, the decline is certainly accelerated by technology. As mentioned, television has lowered the average ability to concentrate and reason effectively and seems to have weakened the willingness of some Americans to pursue objectives beyond fetching another six-pack and a bowl of peanuts.

More symbolic of automation, however, is the debate of using calculators in school in lieu of learning mathematics more thoroughly. The analogy sometimes used is that one does not need to know how an engine works, much less how to repair one, in order to drive a car. On the other hand, the less one knows about automobiles, the more likely one is to be defrauded when a repair is necessary. By some estimates, 50 percent of all car repairs are unnecessary, and within that percentage the majority are fraudulent. In parallel, the argument in favor of the calculator is "that's the way it's done in the business world today." However, the old way is needed to learn the process, even if calculators are subsequently used to bypass repetition of a dull process. The rationale is that if the logic behind mathematics is not understood, an individual will often enter data incorrectly and then fail to recognize that the magnitude of the answer is out of whack.

It would be simple if the issue were limited to calculators. Unfortunately, automation has advanced far beyond number crunching, and thus reliance on it could atrophy the mind beyond the sclerosis of television. As automation gains sophistication—in logic, in content of information, and in mimicking human presence—increasing reliance will be placed on it if for no other reason than that the computer would often be more reliable than human estimates. This is Alan Turing's argument again; namely, that when an individual can no longer distinguish between a human and a machine response, the issue of whether a machine can replace human judgment is moot.

As emphasized in previous chapters, geniuses will not be affected by this. They are the ones who create, or at least can create, ever more sophisticated models. Occupants of the next rung down on the intelligence ladder will also escape the vacuum because they can make maximum use of the technology. All well and good, but what about the mass of the population that abides beneath those two levels? As automated systems gain de facto authority, combined with the force of peer pressure and the deplorable tendency of man to obey authority in questionable circumstances, where will he stand? Will he be regarded as the font of civilization or merely as a needy resource—itself an oxymoron—that society must continually feed?

One last point here concerns a decision support program named *Apache*. The name stands for Acute Physiology, Age, and Chronic Health Evaluation. In practice, *Apache* assesses the chance of survival for intensive-care-unit patients. As of the spring of 1992, fifteen hospitals worldwide purchased this program for $350,000 apiece.[19] The great benefit is that it can provide objective information to patients and their kin to support a decision on when and when not to terminate aggressive therapy. The obvious disadvantage is that insurance companies, and the federal Medicare program for that matter, might use it in order to cut off expensive benefits for patients with only a negligible chance of survival.

As funding for health care grows increasingly tenuous, this possibility should not be dismissed out of hand, grim as it may be. It would pit the individual against a machine that assumed a certain mantle of authority—in this case, the decision to live or die. Admittedly, the cases to which *Apache* apply involve individuals who are likely to die anyway in the near future, but it sets a precedent. If that kind of system arises from popular consensus, then democracy will only be doing what it was intended to do. But if such decisions osmose into the mainstream through electronic membranes, it would be the resurrection of Frankenstein enshrouded in a new edition of Stanley Milgram's experiments on obedience to authority.

The poet James Russell Lowell wrote, "Once to every man and nation comes the moment to decide." In perhaps not so strange a way, automation itself may confront mankind with the consequences of his creation before it becomes too late. Let us look, then, at possible ways to avoid that scenario.

IV. Amelioration

The making of the U.S. Constitution has been hailed as one of the most important events in political history, and well it deserves the accolade. On the other hand, it was written in a much simpler time. The population was only three million, and the vast majority lived and worked on farms. Thus for all but a small percentage of the citizens, economics had little meaning beyond real estate taxes and the local store. And most things that people had to learn were taught at home or in a few years in grammar school.

27. Constitutional Convention of 1787

Unfortunately, that situation no longer prevails. Only 3 percent of a population grown a hundred-fold remains to work on farms, and even they need a much more thorough grounding in practical economics. The problem for the vast balance of the American population is that functional illiteracy seems to be at an all-time high, while the federal government sinks ever more deeply into debt without making much of a dent in many, if not most, socioeconomic problems. Worse (and as stressed throughout this book) automation increasingly contributes to the economic and psychological degradation of all but the most talented individuals, by loss of jobs and demeaning many that remain, by invading privacy, by encouraging fraud measured in the hundreds of billions of dollars, and, more subjectively, by engendering an overreliance on computers at the price of personal judgment and a sense of responsibility.

This situation may not justify a new political constitution, but it does beg a socioeconomic one, though not in the sense of a formal singular charter. So in this final part of the book, we look for ways to reverse this trend, and, not surprisingly, the proposals seek to harness automation itself. For if that technology cannot be done away with, then it is up to man to put automation to work as his resource rather than watch himself degenerate into a faceless resource for an automated society.

13

Economic Countermeasures

Concern for man himself and his fate must always form the chief interest of all technical endeavors, concern for the great unsolved problems of organization of labor and distribution of goods—in order that the creations of our mind shall be a blessing and not a curse to mankind. Never forget this in the midst of your diagrams and equations.

—Albert Einstein

One of the reasons that nature is able to operate with high efficiency is that it eliminates the least fit and quickly kills off organisms that retire—that is, those that are no longer capable or willing to take care of their own needs. At one time, even a few Indian nations within this country practiced the latter with respect to older women who had lost their warrior. The tribe drove each widow into the wilderness without the wherewithal to survive.

By contrast, humanitarians want to provide for everyone, regardless of ability or condition. It is a noble goal, and people who champion otherwise, with the possible exception of declining to fund heart-lung transplants for patients with a terminal illness, face scathing criticism. The only problem is that somebody has to pay the bill for all this largesse. As the present annual deficit of $300 billion or so is not eliminating poverty, or expanding the availability of health care, or meeting a wide range of other social needs, it's a safe bet that under the present system of government financing, the humanitarian goal will fall farther behind realization. The polity could operate otherwise, and this chapter outlines four countermeasures that take aim at the roots of the current fiscal irresponsibility and, along with it, some of the excess of automation:

• *Ruthless prosecution of fraud.* Fraud and related crimes have become a luxury that the United States can no longer afford.

• *Semiprivatization of Social Security and welfare.* This would place these programs on an IRA-like basis, including antiabuse incentives.

• *Single-payer decentralized health care financing.* This is a variation on existing proposals, adding three measures to further drive down costs.

• *Increased employee ownership of corporations.* This may be the only way in which the conflict between man and machine in the workplace gets resolved.

Granted, these are big-ticket items, but at least each one attempts to resolve an undeniable problem while minimizing the role of the government *except at key juncture points*. In practical terms, when a redistribution of funds cannot be avoided and only the federal government is in a position to do so, it should go about it in the simplest, most direct manner with the minimum possible bureaucracy.

Unfortunately, the reader will find these countermeasures bereft of originality. Each measure has been proposed before, some numerous times with many variations. Even the superintending idea is old hat—to reconcile social requirements with capitalism without slighting the spirit and essence of the latter. Furthermore, three points need to be kept in mind:

• First, the looming economic meltdown and recovery will likely take at least ten years to run its course. In that period, the technology of automation will progress much further, and just about everything that is state of the art today will have become commercially viable, if not ho-hum.

• Second, some of the measures would require a transition period between ten to thirty years. That transition funding would be expensive, but it is perhaps the only way to effect fundamental changes rather than half-measures.

• Third, each measure requires a major application of automation. On the other hand, each measure also lends itself to detailed computer modeling so that the problems and inconsistences can be identified long before even pilot projects are implemented.

As to how these proposals would measure up on the bottom line, it's a safe bet that they would reduce federal expenditures and health care costs by an amount at least half a trillion dollars per year. That level of savings would more than cover the present annual deficit, but the excess must be used to retire the cumulative national debt and to pay for the transition costs. But could it be done? That's the wrong question. The better question asks how it might be done. The current way of doing business must eventually collapse—not falter, collapse.

Ruthless prosecution of fraud. The biggest waste in government are programs to eliminate waste. The roots of waste are too diffuse and seemingly too ingrained in human nature and organizations to do much about it. This perhaps explains why Friedreich von Schiller concluded that against stupidity the gods themselves rail in vain. For example, the Department of Defense (DoD) wastes $40 billion annually due to its lack of coordinated supply (i.e., it doesn't know what's on hand and what it really needs, and hence requisitions far more material than necessary). Furthermore, the General Accounting Office report citing this data noted that DoD already had major computer systems in place but they were not organized or programmed for the task.[1] However, there is no chance that anyone will go to jail as a result of such malfeasance.

Fraud is a different matter. It is committed with intent, for which individuals can be, and sometimes are, prosecuted. The problem is to gather sufficient evidence that will hold up in court, create the necessary infrastructure, provide adequate funding, and exercise the political willpower to see it through. Moreover, when it finally dawns on the country that deficit financing is a dead end and that there are limits to what can be provided, then ruthless prosecution of this type of crime will be one sure way to provide more service for the same dollar.

Fortunately—as discussed in Chapters 4 and 6—when information nets expand, they introduce interior lines among transactions, which enable decision support programs to track down the unusual patterns that are the signature of most fraudulent claims and operations. Furthermore, these databases provide a bonus because of their inherent capability to trap other crimes involving financial transactions, not just those directed at government funding programs. The best part is the payoff ratio. For every dollar invested in these types of programs, the return could be as much as a hundred dollars because once written the programs can be run indefinitely.

Semiprivatization of Social Security and welfare. This proposal would replace the current Social Security pay-as-you-go system with mandatory IRA-type accounts for every citizen yet retain the survivor and disability insurance functions. The concept would also supplant federal and most private pensions, unemployment compensation, and—in combination with a negative income tax—virtually all forms of fiduciary welfare. It would not prohibit additional pension supplements, but those supplements would have no tax advantages.

Every individual from the age of twenty would make mandatory contributions to a semiprivate IRA-type account, in proportion to earnings, within a minimum-maximum range pegged to the current cost of living and projections of national economic health and inflation. These accounts would be merged into a national pool, which in turn would be parsed out equally to ten or so regional investment trusts, but each account would remain fiduciarily inviolate. Distributions would then be processed in a manner similar to the existing Social Security administrative mechanics.

No withdrawals would be allowed before age sixty, except when income fell below certain levels. At that point, incremental periodic withdrawals could be made down to the point at which the balance would still provide the minimum mandatory benefits from age sixty to ninety. To the extent that an individual did not have insufficient income (that calculation would include the total income from married individuals and those cohabiting), the existing earned income tax credit could be expanded to fill the gap.[2] This plan would thus supplant the functions of survivor benefits, disability insurance, unemployment compensation, and welfare as well as payments for the small percentage of the population that lived past the age of ninety.

The key to funding this plan would be the compounding of interest as the accounts grew. This is in stark contrast to the present pay-as-you-go Social Security system. Moreover, when an individual died, that portion of his or her account that would pay the minimum retirement benefit would be transferred to a common pool, from which the negative income tax would be funded. Any balance above the minimum could be willed to the accounts of whomever the individual or next of kin designated (up to the maximum limits for each account). Another key is the simple fact that this set-up would reduce the tendency to seek welfare and unemployment benefits. Until the individual's account above minimum levels (proportional to age) was exhausted, there would be no supplementary benefit. That is, individuals who chose to drift through life would have to do so at a subsistence level, leaving comfortable lifestyles to those who were willing to work for it. The socialistic alternative is a nation of economic zombies.

The main advantages of this proposal are that (a) each individual would have his or her own portable pension and insurance package that provided higher benefits for lower contributions, (b) an enormous pool of investment money would be generated, (c) the government's role would be limited to enforcing the necessary provisions, and (d) the inevitable financial collapse of the present Social Security system in the next century would be avoided.

The first two advantages are self-evident, except for the low cost/higher benefits aspect. The present contribution for a person making $25,000 per year is $3,100 (including the employer's share but excluding the Medicare portion). The benefit (in today's dollars) would be about $9,100 per year (less for individuals under age fifty).[3] In the proposed plan, a deposit of $1,000 per year—one third the FICA tax—invested at a mere 6 percent for forty years would accumulate a nest egg of $180,000. This balance would provide an *annual* payment of $12,960, starting five years earlier and extending to age ninety. If the individual were married, both would have paid into the system and in return would have an annual benefit of nearly $26,000. Moreover, as every individual would have a minimum-balance account, there would be no need for a negative income tax for those between the ages of sixty and ninety.

As for the collapse of the existing system, that will likely occur when the ratio of workers to beneficiaries reaches three to one sometime between the years 2010 and 2035 although, as discussed in Chapters 4 and 11, the break-down may easily occur earlier because of the government's future obligation to raise taxes to pay back its massive borrowing from the Social Security Trust

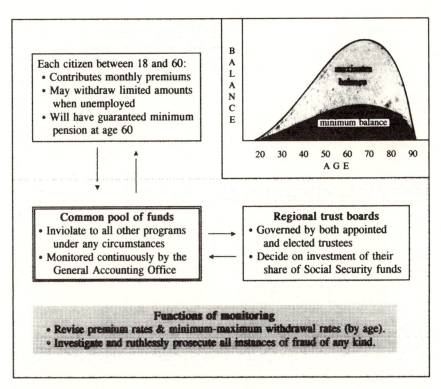

28. Semiprivatization of Social Security. The current Social Security system could be integrated with basic pension plans, welfare, and a negative income tax, provided that the model is based on annuity investments rather than pay-as-you-go and that seed funding is obtained indirectly by a ruthless prosecution of fraud.

Fund. The only other solution would be to reduce benefits severely (or to tax them heavily) for all but the indigent, a movement which is already underway. At first, Social Security benefits were untaxed, but between the ages of sixty-two and seventy, benefits were reduced in proportion to income earned above certain very modest levels. Then 50 percent of the benefits were taxed for persons who had incomes above specified middle-income levels. Now 85 percent of the benefits are taxed for upper-middle-class income levels. So it is just a matter of time before all income at all ages is used to reduce benefits for all but the indigent.

The disadvantages are (a) very high transition costs to fund the existing Social Security benefits for retirees as younger wage earners began to contribute to their own plans, (b) funding to offset the effects of inflation, (c) ensuring that funds are invested in accounts that met stringent safety requirements, (d) ensuring that no account is depleted below certain levels, (e) privacy issues, and (f) fraud.

Transition costs would be funded by the enormous surplus that would be generated if all four proposals were invoked as a package. Moreover, the initial contributions could be set equal to the present FICA tax tables and then be decreased over a period of ten to fifteen years. Inflation would be covered by (a) an increase in quarterly premiums pegged to the cost of living, (b) the compounding of interest on the account, and (c) revision of minimum account balances periodically. Note also that upon death, the minimum required balance in each account would revert to a common fund that would in turn fund the negative income tax. Finally, to control losses on regular accounts, the regional investment trust boards would be limited to investing funds half of the funds in FDIC-insured accounts and all but a small fraction of the other half with those companies that had received the highest possible ratings by Standard & Poor's, Moody's, and A. M. Best Company. A small fraction—say less than 5 percent—could be reserved for venture capital investment.

It is true that until recent times, this approach would have been all but impossible to oversee. However, today's computer technology can track hundreds of millions of accounts with ease, reviewing all accounts in detail every five minutes, if necessary, to ensure that they are being maintained according to Hoyle. The same is true of the health care funding system described in the next section.

Privacy issues are a harder nut to crack. This massing of financial information would be accessible to a large number of people. On the other hand, the plan would be fairly standardized. Furthermore, no individual would be required to reveal his or her entire financial history to a welfare agency factotum—there is perhaps no more degrading experience visited upon citizens in this country.

As for fraud, it must be admitted that a program of this kind would be a vast target for it. On the other hand, intolerance of fraud in all its forms was put at the head of the list of problems earlier. Given a comprehensive financial safety net, all possible justification for any kind of fraud would evaporate. Therefore, any attempt to *fraudulently* understate or hide actual income on one's annual return in any amount above $1,000 could be greeted with a strictly enforced, mandatory, no-parole, no-probation minimum prison sentence of two years, plus one month for every $1,000 over that amount, up to a maximum of five years. Double that for second and subsequent offenses.

Single-payer decentralized health care funding. Health care is already the single largest expense in the United States, consuming 14 percent of the gross domestic product and projected to reach two trillion dollars by the year 2000, especially if the government subsidizes the forty million uninsured Americans. Moreover, as cited in Chapter 6, the government already pays 42 percent of this bill directly and indirectly subsidizes much of the balance in one form or another, especially by income tax deductions for excess medical expenses.[4] Given the pathetic record of the government at controlling these costs, any general program to provide coverage for the uninsured (or underinsured) will only worsen this picture.

Thus the task becomes one of providing more services at a lower total cost. The only way to do this is to eliminate the four aspects of health care that add hundreds of billions of dollars to the annual tab without providing a whit of health care. The first is the profit and administrative overhead of health insurance companies and the attendant accounting systems required by providers. That surcharge ranges between $100 and $200 billion annually. Second, while Medicare is largely exempt from the first problem, it has become the target of enormous fraud and is perhaps the second largest single category of fraud in the nation (after income tax fraud and nonpayment). Third, excess hospital capacity encourages administrators to pressure doctors for more admissions and to buy duplicate expensive equipment as an incentive. Fourth, many physicians and other fee-for-service providers have been charging far above the reasonable rates set by most insurers.

All four sink-holes could be eliminated with a single-payer insurance system coupled with mandated closure of all hospital excess capacity (with some left in a ready capacity for disasters and the like), a cap on all reimbursed fees, a ruthless prosecution of fraudulent claims, and a per-diem rather than a per-patient reimbursement to the hospitals that remain, adjusted for the severity of average patient load. In addition, aggressive therapy for the terminally ill with a life expectancy of a year or less could be deleted from coverage. (The author developed this concept in *The Ethics and Economics of Health Care*, St. Louis: Warren H. Green, Inc., 1992.)

The elimination of most insurance and accounting overhead, as well as excess hospital capacity, would reduce the total bill on a one-time basis, thus freeing more than enough funds to subsidize the indigent. The cap on fees and the intense prosecution of fraud would further reduce the cost, in this case on a continuing basis. This leaves the question of who would pay the bill, even if it were less. The answer, more or less, is the same parties that are paying it now. These include the Medicare tax, the funding of Medicaid and Veterans Administration hospitals, employer-paid health care insurance, individually paid policies, and copayments.

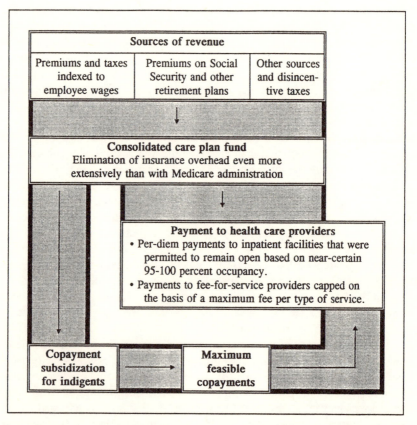

29. A single-payer decentralized health care system. Health care already claims 14 percent of the gross domestic product. If services are to be expanded *and* costs cut, then anything that does not contribute to health care must be eliminated. In practice, that means excess hospital capacity and the bulk of insurance overhead.

To be sure, the idea sounds too simple, but once again automation makes it possible. Moreover, automation would accelerate payment to providers, probably by preset periodic payments adjusted for actual billings in the previous period. Another feature is that the government would get out of the health care profession except in those areas in which it had a business to be—for example, military field hospitals, the National Center for Disease Control, and other programs that are beyond the capacity of a private agency to provide.

Increased employee ownership of corporations. The story is told about the factory worker recently laid off and desperate for work. He responded to an ad from the local zoo, where the zookeeper explained that the zoo's gorilla had just died, and someone was needed to wear a costume and play the role until a new one could be obtained. The animal was the most popular attraction, and without him revenues would likely decrease. The applicant accepted the job reluctantly and spent the first day moping around in his cage feeling sorry for himself. That evening the zookeeper counseled him that he must become much more active, or else another applicant would be given the job. He complied, whereupon the crowds encouraged him to do more. Taking the bait, he swung furiously until he went too high and landed in the adjacent lion's den. After one quick look at its denizen, he immediately yelled to the crowd for help. The lion looked at him and said "Be quiet, you fool; don't you know a displaced executive when you see one?"

Automation may not have been the main cause of corporate integrations, but many (if not most) of them would have been impossible without computers to manage the diverse financing. Moreover, as middle management positions are eliminated, senior managers have come more and more to look upon the workforce as resources to be managed, controlled, and perhaps eliminated. The three methods for reversing this trend are (a) legislation that directly or indirectly restricts corporations from excessive employee layoffs, (b) a pervasive resurgence of unions, and (c) increased employee ownership.

The first is so impractical that it doesn't warrant further discussion. The second is likely to occur in the absence of a more constructive solution, motivated by the need to survive. The third is almost too ideal, but at least it places the people most directly affected in a position to decide their own fate. Going about it is another matter. Vaguely reminiscent of antitrust legislation, the government could develop policies and incentives that would eventually lead to the break-up of large corporations and the offering of stock to employees until they gained control of the companies they worked for. The advantage is that these companies would be less inclined to replace workers with automation. On the other hand, in order to remain competitive—hence profitable and a continuing source of wages—the new owners would realize that there are limits to feather-bedding.

To date, the evidence on the effectiveness of employee ownership through stock purchase is insufficient to make any firm projections; too few companies are involved and, except for the 1994 employee buyout of United Airlines, they do not include any of the largest corporations. On the other hand, the supposed business acumen of seasoned executives hasn't been all that good either. After losing money in 1991—which should have been a warning—IBM continued policies that led to a record-setting loss of $5 billion in 1992, which is roughly $16,000 per employee. The solution, of course, was to invoke massive early retirements and forced layoffs of more than 150,000 employees, many of whom will never be able to find comparable jobs.

In summary, this would be the most difficult of the four proposals to implement. Yet if preservation of free enterprise and capitalism are long-term objectives and arguably the only means by which a country can continue to fund its insatiable appetite for welfare, then its methods should follow suit. As mentioned, the motivation would be reversal of deterioration in the job market. As jobs are lost to automation, the tax base shrinks and therefore the wage-earner tax base atrophies, which reduces purchases, which reduces profitability, and so forth in a vicious cycle.

On the other hand, even if all of these proposals were put into effect, there is no guarantee that they would achieve the intended goal. Perhaps every major nation is destined to have its time in the sun and then fade in comparative importance in the global scheme of things. If so, it would be because it no longer had the right mix of resources and attributes to compete. That is a grim thought, but not one to accept without a concerted effort to reverse the trend.

14

Reversal of Psychological Degradation

Resistance to the organized mass can be effected only by the man
who is as well organized in his individuality as the mass itself.
—Carl Jung

The economic countermeasures proposed in the previous chapter aim as much at reversing economic pitfalls as at curbing the excesses of automation. Unfortunately, those measures depend on an expanded use of this technology, which would only aggravate the psychological side-effects. Because the mix of good and bad is so entangled, the task of amelioration would become all the more difficult.

Napoleon had an interesting way of dealing with such problems. He placed all related correspondence in a desk drawer without comment. In time, 90 percent of the problems took care of themselves. The other 10 percent did not, but he could easily identify the holdouts by the repeated entreaties on the part of their originators. This approach would not curtail invasion of privacy, but a twofold variation on it might. First, given the fact that there is no stopping automation, it is essential to draw a line between what can be tolerated and what cannot be, and then live with the former while prosecuting the latter. Second, the process of education (a phrase borrowed from Jerome Bruner) could itself become a means of comeuppance against this new adversary.[1] The young can be educated to outsmart the insidiousness of automation by harnessing its own ground rules.

This does not mean mechanical learning. Far from it. It would entail a sophisticated learning environment, bearing in mind that the most effective education is one that continually builds a reservoir of knowledge and skills in a methodical fashion.[2] The dividing line between this approach and mechanical learning may appear fuzzy on the surface, but once students are in an environment that emphasizes the enlightened approach, there is no comparison. Furthermore, students who came to appreciate its value would not likely tolerate a relapse into the mechanical counterpart. This is a critical point, and we will return to it after looking at the privacy issue.

Reconciliation of privacy versus automation issues. Although the systems necessary to manage the proposed economic measures would be complex and extensive, they succumb to straightforward logic and algorithms. The same is not true of the conflict between massed automated information and the right to privacy. On one side, the need for ever more massive databases is evident. On the other, these databases will almost certainly engender even more severe abuses, while their mere existence poses a subtle threat to psychical integrity for weaker minds.

The sticking point, as mentioned, is that much of the information on each individual is public knowledge and is available to anyone willing to make the effort to search for and compile it. Therefore, automating and integrating that information into electronic databases by itself is not an invasion of privacy. Abusing that information is another matter, but that would be true with or without automation. Automation only facilitates the process. As for private information, mere possession of it by an individual or agency that is not so entitled *is* wrong even if the information is not abused. However, a number of practical problems arise when attempting to separate these two types of data:

• First, the two types are typically commingled in most databases.

• Second, there are many classes or degrees of private information (e.g., business versus personal correspondence).

• Third, some types of private information are legally accessible to thousands of individuals and many different agencies, at least under specified criteria.

• Fourth, with the advent of image processing and optical disk storage, the tendency is to keep obsolete data on file permanently.

• Fifth, private information for some individuals may be public for others (e.g., juvenile versus adult criminal records). Or one jurisdiction may declare an item private that another specifies as public.

• Sixth, a great deal of private information can be inferred statistically with a high degree of accuracy from public data. It may not always be on the mark in a specific case, but corporations are more interested in playing the odds. The insurance industry is based on actuarial calculations, while banking practices, especially the criteria for making loans, are based on probabilities of not defaulting.

• Seventh, it is exceptionally difficult to establish damage or harm in a court of law from the mere existence of databases that contain private information, especially if the agencies maintaining them have the full weight of the law supporting the practice.

In short, the potential solution of labeling data as public or private is impractical. Attempting to enforce the law would itself widen access to private information, and in the event no law is worth much unless it can be enforced. One need only consider the endless conflicts between the Freedom of Information Act and the Privacy Act when it comes to specific requests for information from government agencies. It is all but impossible to get any two of these agencies to agree on the dividing line. The only practical approach, therefore, is to concentrate on abuses rather than the potential for abuse. Otherwise by analogy, the state could incarcerate individuals whose psychological profile indicated a high propensity toward violent crime.

Even this limited approach encounters many obstacles, among them (a) the definition of abuse itself, (b) the extent to which individuals consented to the information being collected and used, (c) defining at what point wrongdoing became a criminal and not just a civil offense, and (d) paying the tab for enforcing what is agreed upon. For example, the use of computers to micromanage employee performance is thought by many to be abusive. Yet, as mentioned in previous chapters, there is no wrongdoing if (a) all the data collected in fact pertains to the work, (b) the evaluative procedures are applied without bias or prejudice, and (c) the criteria for promotion, retention, and firing are delineated in objective, quantitative terms as free of subjective judgment as humanly possible.[3]

Moreover, the amount of fraud arising from the opportunities afforded by automation—not to mention the pervasiveness of violent crime—is so massive that priority should be given to reducing such opportunities. The right to privacy, worthy as it may be, would not be worth much if you have to expend all your energy just eking out a living for a decade in a collapsed economy or defending yourself against fraudulent operators. Even if that environment can be avoided, how many more cases can the judicial system tolerate? According to some surveys, the year 1992 witnessed approximately 20,000,000 civil suits or their equivalent filed or pending.

Restated, while the laws against abuse should be brought up to date in line with technology, and while these laws certainly need to be enforced more rigorously, the excesses of automation will continue to mount and thus exacerbate the problem. The psyche needs to be strengthened against this onslaught or, as the homily written into the play *Inherit the Wind* has it,

> Progress has never been a bargain. You've got to pay for it. Sometimes I think there's a man behind a counter who says "all right, you can have a telephone, but you'll have to give up privacy, the charm of distance. . . . You may conquer the air; but the birds will lose their wonder, and the clouds will smell of gasoline."[4]

In other words, the world is not especially user friendly, and automation is making it less so. The ultimate appeal, therefore, is to oneself and whatever beliefs, tenets, philosophy, and character one may possess to draw on as resources. That can only come about from lifelong education.

Automation as a model of learning. As mentioned in Chapter 3, the prolific author Isaac Asimov wrote a science fiction tale entitled *I, Robot.*[5] In it, he presumed that technology would eventually lead to androids that possessed most, if not all, human attributes and characteristics. To counteract the risk of another Frankenstein, he programmed his literary robot with moral standards. It was taught not to injure a human being or through inaction to allow a human being to come to harm. So much for independence. It was then programmed to obey all human orders unless they came in conflict with the first rule. Finally, it was also programmed to protect its own existence unless that forced it into a conflict with either of the first two rules. Those aren't bad rules, and if they had been in effect in Vietnam, there would have been no My Lai.

But that is not the point. Rather, the pure mental processes of the individual are essentially equivalent to a computer (or vice versa). Accordingly, they can be programmed, in a manner of speaking, *provided that it is recognized that the human computer is embedded in an overpowering psychical reality that, once educated, doesn't give a damn about automation unless it supports what is held to be in its own interests.*

More to the point, the ultimate value of decision support programs at their best depends on how well they support human decisions. While they take over the chores of research, they can also compel the user to consider a much wider range of options and factors. And barring the equivalent of negligence or fraud, neither these programs nor their programmers can or should take responsibility for user decisions. As such, the ultimate in education may be to develop the sound methods of decision support programs within each individual, so that the mental processes are sharply honed, while at the same time recognizing the psychical, often subjective component and its crucial role in making learning effective or ineffective. Figure 30 depicts this relationship.

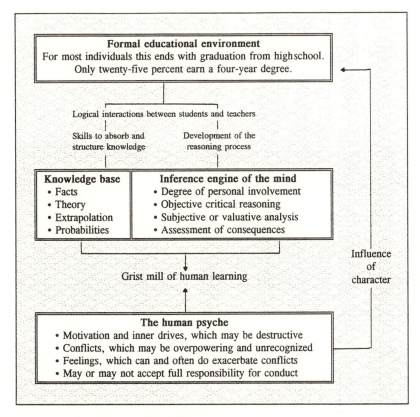

Formal educational environment
For most individuals this ends with graduation from high school.
Only twenty-five percent earn a four-year degree.

Logical interactions between students and teachers

Skills to absorb and
structure knowledge

Development of the
reasoning process

Knowledge base
• Facts
• Theory
• Extrapolation
• Probabilities

Inference engine of the mind
• Degree of personal involvement
• Objective critical reasoning
• Subjective or valuative analysis
• Assessment of consequences

Grist mill of human learning

Influence
of
character

The human psyche
• Motivation and inner drives, which may be destructive
• Conflicts, which may be overpowering and unrecognized
• Feelings, which can and often do exacerbate conflicts
• May or may not accept full responsibility for conduct

30. The human decision support program. Decision support programs replicate human thought processes with increasing efficiency, often outdoing the latter in terms of spade work. Perhaps it is time to reverse this process with one critical addition—to recognize the overpowering reality of the spiritual or psychical aspect of an individual.

The relationship between the psyche and the mental processes is a profound inquiry and probably constitutes the Rosetta Stone, if not the godhead of all philosophy, psychology, and ethics. Spinoza attempted the issue in his immortal *Ethics*, and perhaps Kant did the same in his battery of treatises. Whatever the answer may be, the two fonts obviously affect one another. For example, the psychoanalytic process is based on a conscious review of one's history and recognition of associations that preside over the pieces. The effect of transference provides the human succor, but the analysand must come to grips with his or her own life.[6]

Public education is not psychoanalysis, notwithstanding psychiatrist Karen Horney's oft quoted remark that "fortunately, analysis is not the only way to resolve inner conflicts. Life itself remains a very effective therapist."[7] On the other hand, a formal education should prepare an individual to continue learning on his or her own. Thus while it may be unnecessary and perhaps even dangerous for schools to integrate personal in-depth analysis into the curriculum, they can hardly be faulted for teaching students to think through the potential consequences of a decision, be it historical, current, or personal. That is where automation can play a critical role because it can be programmed to demand this kind of applied reasoning from every student.

However, one caveat begs recognition. While a structured learning environment works best, that approach doesn't always mean learning by discrete increments. Some concepts take years to gel in the mind, and sometimes this occurs by way of an unpredictable, eureka-type experience or insight. Therefore, to the extent that automation is adapted as a model of learning it should emphasize the trial-and-error heuristics of pattern-based analysis, not the stimulus-response drills associated with mechanical cybernetics and old-style programmed-learning texts. This is not so much an attempt to evoke a ghost in the machine as it is to build patience into its programming.

A superintending criterion for education. The aims of education have been debated for millenniums without much consensus, perhaps because the needs of individual students are often unique and because of uncertainty regarding what is ethical. It is true that ethics have little bearing on mathematics, or on the hard sciences per se, or on the mechanics of language, but they permeate the literature, history, civics, current affairs, psychology, law, and the extent to which experimentation in the sciences should proceed, especially with the advent of biogenetic engineering.

To bring this subjectivity into focus sufficiently to be supported by automation, the author posits a superintending criterion for education: *Every graduate of every public high school should be able to recognize the consequences or at least the likely consequences of decisions made—their own and those of others, historical or current—when it is their obligation or in their interest to consider them.* This presumes that when the decision is personal and made with any degree of bona fide choice, one must accept responsibility for that decision and the consequences that follow.[8] It is not enough to cram knowledge into a student's head, and even the development of critical reasoning is almost irrelevant unless it can be put into practice in ways that have meaning and value to an individual.

Time and time again, a few educators have pleaded for a more vocational oriented curriculum. Unfortunately, because that idea is so often equated with shop courses, the idea dies a thousand deaths. However, there is something to be said for the vocation of life and the choices one must make in it and for understanding why the unfolding of history leaves much to be desired and why most plans to improve society fail miserably. The reason is that each decision has its consequences, and those consequences are largely a product of the environment in which they are made, certainly more so than the hopes and aspirations of decision makers.

Assessing the consequences of a decision, then, bridges the gap between knowledge and reasoning ability on the one hand, and morality or ethics on the other. Granted, as discussed in Chapter 9, a consensus on ethics is impossible. Some hold to fixed standards of behavior, others see almost everything as situational, still others consider primarily the consequences, while a fourth group concentrates on the character of each act. Furthermore, there is something to be said for partially situational ethics. Murder is wrong; killing in self-defense when there is no other recourse is justifiable. So when a terribly abused wife kills her husband under extreme duress but without *immediate* danger to her own life, is she guilty of murder or was her conduct a matter of self-defense?

To answer that kind of question requires some mental bearings from which the logic of jurisprudence can be applied. But who is to define those standards in any situation beyond that framework in which most laws are historically in agreement? If there are such standards, there must be reasons for them. Arguably those reasons are primarily a function of the consequences or likely consequences as attenuated by (a) the character of the individual or nation making the decisions in order to assess motive, and (b) situational factors in order to assess an appropriate criminal or civil penalty when the consequences prove harmful. When you think through consequences, therefore, you develop a strong sense of morality and character or are at least forced to admit—if only privately—the inadequacies of your make-up. Even Napoleon, eking out his last years on the forlorn island of St. Helena, came to that painful realization.

At present, this approach is seldom seen below the graduate level. The photograph of a senior defending his thesis at St. John's College in Annapolis, Maryland (Figure 31) is an exception, and it also bespeaks a larger message. The older professor is perhaps testing the wisdom of a lifetime against that of youth, while the younger one depicts the rise of women into this arena. Their expressions suggest both firmness and forebearing, demanding that the student confront facts and adhere to the parameters of logic. At the same time, both are obviously intent on preparing students to stand on their own feet.

In the film *Animal House*, which few would consider as a paragon of education, the character of Dean Wormer does make one statement of import. In expelling the denizens of Delta house from the college, he turns to freshman Kent Dorfmann and advises him that being drunk and stupid is no way to go through life. Unfortunately, public education in the United States, irrespective of where the blame may lie and regardless of substantial dedication and unselfishness on the part of most teachers, seems more inclined to produce hordes of Kent Dorfmanns. Dorfmann was a likeable if nerdy character and, as portrayed, had the capacity to learn. Yet Wormer's assessment of his conduct was essentially correct.

Courtesy of Kevin Fleming, Annapolis, Maryland

31. Defending one's thesis. Of what value is an education other than to apply it to problems and to continue personal development and maturation? This means being able to defend one's decisions in terms of the likely consequences.

A real college may operate with more positive refrain, but it is not the place to remedy this situation. First, only about 25 percent of the population earns a baccalaureate degree. Second, undergraduate courses are increasingly taught by graduate assistants who neither know the subject well enough to present it effectively nor have the experience to integrate it into other learning experiences. Third, a college education is increasingly expensive, and hence the college population is likely to shrink. But could a vastly improved public school education reverse this pathetic situation? The mass of facts say no; the exceptions plead otherwise.[9]

The great problem is extending the exceptions to the point at which they become the rule. Automation, in the form of computer-assisted learning, offers this potential, provided that it remains subordinate to the exercise of human judgment and ethics. Unfortunately, precision has a tendency to displace subjectivity. For the latter to prevail, it must have a consistent access and a theme that at least has a chance of attaining a consensus. Furthermore, that theme must coincide with democratic ideals.

In a democracy you can do whatever you want to do, but you must be prepared to accept the consequences of those decisions—be they favorable or unfavorable, constructive or destructive, enlightening or degrading. An individual is free to commit any crime he or she wants, but that crime will be subject to prosecution, and that could result in the death penalty. Thus to elevate assessment of consequences to a superintending criterion links the freedom of democracy with the discipline of learning, reasoning, and the acquisition of knowledge. In short, schools are better used to overcome ignorance than to provide a stage for displaying it.

With that thought in mind, the process of education could be more thoroughly integrated. In turn, this integrated approach could hone mental ability and fill one's reservoir of knowledge more deeply than is common today. It could also enhance the willingness to listen and the perseverance to be heard and, perhaps strengthen character insofar as schools can imbue it indirectly. Furthermore, it would serve to prepare the citizenry to react more forthrightly to the excesses of automation on two levels.

First, education would focus on consequences, which could lead to a stronger ground swell of political action to throttle those excesses. Second, it would make clear the inevitability of technological progress. This means accepting *some* of the unfavorable consequences as inevitable and then recognizing that only a certain inner strength of mind and character can offset the angst. The remainder of this chapter attempts to outline an approach to reach this goal.

Thematic public school curriculum. The ancient adage of "the three R's" (reading, 'riting, and 'rithmetic) could not have survived as long as it has unless there was some truth to it. On the other hand, reading and writing must be useful for something beyond arithmetic or solely as a linguistic skill to play solitaire with one's mental deck of cards. Assuming that the first two—reading and writing—can be lumped together under the heading of *linguistic expression and ability* and that arithmetic is a harbinger of *critical reasoning and the sciences*, this leaves two other themes to consider. The first has always been taught in public schools, albeit in many different forms, and that is history in the broadest sense of the word—*ethos and valuative reasoning*. In addition to history, this theme includes law and, in part, literature. The second—*psychology, ethics, and subjective reasoning*—is also covered, but only in uncoordinated, piecemeal fashion with introductory courses in psychology, literature, and, in a few cases, philosophy.

Yet with the exception of the fine arts, these four themes corral just about every academic subject in secondary school, and undergraduate college for that matter. An entire twelve-year public school curriculum can be derived from them that would be both richer in content and more versatile in terms of the different needs of different students. To this end, consider how each fits under assessment of consequences.

• *Linguistic expression and ability.* This means the ability to express oneself, both orally and in writing, in terms that are clear and understandable by those with whom one works or attempts to influence. It is a skill that can be mastered by the time of graduation from high school, not in terms of authorship but more than adequate to work and conduct most business. Hence there should be no need to continue this educational area afterward. In specific terms, every student should be able to write a clear sentence by the time he or she completes middle school and a cohesive and equally clear paragraph by graduation from high school. These may sound like watered-down goals, but they are not. Even Sir Winston Churchill, a bona fide genius when it came to expression, admitted that he struggled for years to master these skills.

• *Critical reasoning and the sciences.* There is much that is unknown in science, but what *is* known, or at least what is commonly accepted, is either subject to replicable experimentation or is a theoretical explanation that adheres to the rigors of mathematical logic. This kind of knowledge is largely external to the individual, and a student must learn to subordinate himself or herself to facts and rigor. The exception occurs when a current theory or explanation is challenged, but that is rarely applicable at the public school level (excepting the ludicrous attempts to put creationism side by side with evolution in the science classroom). Even if it were, it would require an even greater self-discipline with respect to facts. Revolutions in science aim at strengthening order, not expounding personal philosophy.

• *Ethos and valuative reasoning.* Unlike the hard sciences, the fields of history, law, and literature have always been subject to interpretation, but they are more interrelated than commonly presumed. As such, they fill the void between the objective world of mathematics and science—and the subjective world of the self. Granted, few students will write significant works, much less masterpieces, in literature or legal commentary. Certainly, very few will singularly change the course of history, but all are and will continue to be affected by those who do, and virtually all will become eligible to vote. Thus it is critical to assess the consequences of historical decisions and to understand the role of law and literature in order to make reasoned decisions for whatever influence may be exercised, even if it is limited to exercising the franchise.

• *Psychology, ethics, and subjective reasoning.* This is where individuals come into their own. In understanding themselves, they either develop a philosophy of life and accept the consequences of decisions, or the combination of the environment and their inner drives will do it for them, usually to their detriment. Never underestimate the ability of students, even in elementary grades, to grasp some fairly significant philosophical concepts.

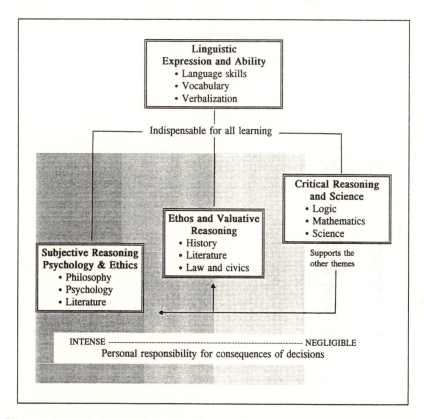

32. Four themes in formal education. Most academic subjects adhere to one of four themes. The relationships among them are based on the degree to which the individual is involved and therefore the extent to which the consequences of his or her decisions in later life should be considered.

Adapting automation. Computer-assisted learning would not supplant how an exceptional public school system and its faculty might carry these themes into practice but rather (a) extend it to all schools, (b) place much greater emphasis on the continuity of learning over a twelve-year period, (c) reduce the discontinuities upon transfer, and (d) above all, involve each student so deeply in his or her own education that the severe drop-out rate would abate significantly. Much progress has been made with this technology, but few advocates make it the centerpiece of education. That would mandate resolving any issues. Seven of the more pressing are summarized here.

• *How can machines replace teachers?* They would not, yet because good decision support programs are the equivalent of dynamic books, they extend the influence of a good teacher from one student at a time to thirty concurrently, and that process can be replicated in thousands of classrooms. Restated, a machine is only a medium, and its intelligent programming only mimics what good teachers would do in trying to bridge the gap between ignorance or indolence on the one hand and accumulated learning on the other. Moreover, teachers would always be present in the classroom.[10]

In this regard, give some thought to the effects of a good book on an avid reader. Ideally, that reader will enter into an imagined conversation with its author, not in the psychiatrically dysfunctional sense but in an attempt to deduce how the author—and others who have written on the subject at issue—might have addressed a related problem, especially those that have done so since the book was written. Computer-assisted learning at its best tries to enhance that potential, primarily by linking the subject matter with related material. That is no small matter when the technology can extend this reach to potentially millions of references.

• *How can machines manage the hundreds of thousands of elements that a formal education should draw on?* In the twinkling of an eye—the fraction of a second it takes to scan indexes of material related to the issue. These indexes work by logically relating the necessary files in any and all paths that are reasonable. Granted, this capability operates only in the laboratory and it is still too expensive for widespread use, at least with the necessary operating speed for learning. But like all technology, the capabilities will improve and the cost will drop. Today, one can buy a palmtop computer for a few hundred dollars that is a thousand times more capable than prototype mainframes in the 1940s, which in today's dollars cost $20,000,000 or more.

• *How can automation be used to teach consequences, not to mention ethics and valuative reasoning?* That is the wrong question. The better question is, "How can computers encourage students to think about consequences and ethics, and thus hone their reasoning thereon?" At least two methods are available. The first is to counter responses to ethical or subjective questions with a slate of background material—pro and con—from a library of files and then prompt for reconsideration. If the response is different, additional references can be fetched and displayed. The second method would have students respond in writing anonymously to a situation and then have those responses displayed as a set to the entire class (or subgroup if too large). Here the computer is just being used as a message center; the judgment remains entirely with the students. On the other hand, this would be all but impossible without automation.

• *How can machines sense where a student is weak or evaluate his or her progress?* Pattern recognition. When the weakness goes beyond a mere lack of knowledge on a fact or point (which is corrected immediately), the responses create logical patterns or, more accurately, flawed patterns. Recognition of these patterns may not be absolutely on the mark, but they come close. Furthermore, the programs operate interactively. If the weakness continues, the learning program would try other combinations.

To be sure, learning of concepts is anything but a smooth process; understanding them often comes by quantums, sometimes rather suddenly. Yet those moments do not occur until a sufficient set of facts and their relationships accumulate—critical mass, so to speak. And the reason why some students grasp concepts faster than others, presuming that they can absorb facts to the same degree, is the ability to draw the associations faster—interior lines, as it were. So the advantage is that automated programs can reinforce the same concept for each student at his or her own speed of comprehension, for years if necessary, until it does gel.

• *How can machines that rely on logical programming accommodate cultural diversity and the subjectivity of the human mind?* First, logic, mathematics, and virtually all of the so-called hard sciences are not culturally based, nor are the facts of history, nor the existence of laws, nor what exists per se in the annals of literature, ethics, and psychology. Second, while education aims at developing individuality, it does not or at least should not advocate doing so at the expense of ignoring masses of facts or the logical sinews of critical reasoning. Third, information concerning hundreds of different cultures can be included in the resources accessible to the programs, thus vastly widening a student's perspective early in life. Fourth, teachers must continue to interact with students on these important matters. Fifth, the mere existence of different ways of thinking and acting does not necessarily justify their continuance unabated. If that were true, murder would be an acceptable alternative lifestyle.

• *How can machines accommodate the fact that some learning is a process that consumes years?* Where appropriate, they can be programmed to track progress along various lines rather than in sequences of discrete units, and do a far better job of it than could four or more teachers, often in different districts that the student may move among.

• *How could anything this sophisticated be implemented on any widespread basis in less than thirty years, perhaps forty?* It probably can't, except
in prototype form, and even that can take ten to fifteen years. It took nearly
forty years before electronic computers made it from the laboratory to the
home desktop. In more philosophical terms, educators accept the fact that what
they impart or inculcate may not come to fruition for decades. Similarly, educational planners should keep the longer view in mind.

• *If machines can live up to this billing, would they not overwhelm individual teachers and turn students against them?* That's an interesting point—
another instance of a potential electronic Frankenstein. The only way out of
this problem is to make the profession of teaching so enticing that it would
attract only the best minds who also have the patience to work with younger
ones, many of whom are not able to follow suit. Moreover, it is possible that
teaching will slowly transform into a second profession. That is, people would
enter the profession after they reached the age of forty and had accumulated
significant experience and knowledge. At that point, their preparation would
focus on expanding their own education. This would also do away with the
pathology of current schools of education.

In sum, then, automation can be used to restore and enhance that which
its own technology has weakened. There is, however, one major caveat: No
system of learning, no matter how comprehensive, can ever fully live up to its
expectations; nor would that be necessary. If the widespread adoption of computer-assisted learning resulted in only 1 percent of the population being willing to think through the consequences of decisions, that alone might evoke a
major change in the national ethos. When candidates for public office have to
answer to searching questions from 2,630,000 people who refuse to equate the
usual palaver with anything of substance, the chances are that government will
improve. If 10 percent of the population reaches that level of ability, the improvement would be guaranteed.

Furthermore, the process is all so simple. You stop emphasizing automation as a substitute for human endeavor and instead use it as a means to entice
that endeavor, harnessing its capabilities in order to train the mind to concentrate on the resolution of relevant issues. Computer-assisted learning can bring
about that concentration, for that is the hallmark of interior lines, and interior
lines are what automation offers without limit. As Sir William Osler said,

> Concentration, by which is grown gradually the power to wrestle success-
> fully with any subject, is the secret of successful study. No mind however
> dull can escape the brightness that comes from steady application . . .
> the failure to cultivate the power of peaceful concentration is the great-
> est single cause of mental breakdown.[11]

Glossary

A complete glossary of automation would have more than five thousand terms. However, a mere hundred or so are adequate to develop an informed perspective of the field. Further, most of those terms fall into related groups or concepts, which themselves have a distinct structure. This brief glossary takes advantage of that situation, primarily by grouping related terms. Finally, it emphasizes terms related to computers more so than robotics because a robot is essentially a computer program that performs physical work rather than symbolic work representative of information and its processing.

GENERAL TERMS

Abstractions. *Energy* is the capacity to do work. When it is doing work, it is *kinetic energy*. All other energy is *potential*, but in any situation whether that potential is available (and in what amounts) is another matter. The measure of this unavailability is called *entropy*. *Chaos* is the science of phenomena attributable to nonlinear (independent) factors, wherein the resulting behavior does not adhere to a set of conventional equations. *Catastrophe* is when a system, chaotic or nonchaotic, undergoes a sudden change, beneficial or destructive. *Critical mass* is a specific instance of catastrophe, and strictly speaking it describes nuclear fission. However, the term is now used in the more generalized sense of any impending catastrophe (again, beneficial or destructive). *Interior lines* describes the physical or logical distances among objects in a system, and the degree of interference or its absence along those paths. This is the basis for critical mass within a configuration or system because it permits a single reaction to cause more than one new reaction.

Automation. *Automation* is a generic term applied to making any system or process operate without external influence except as a source of energy. *Robotics* is automation applied to the replication of human physical activity, while *computer science* is concerned with replicating mental activity. A *system* is any organized set of objects or items designed to work together to produce some result or achieve some objective, with or without automation. *Systems analysis* is used at the front end of a project to discern the system that either underwrites the objective or would be necessary to effect it. *Systems design* translates this analysis into a robotic or computer-based system, analogous to architecture. *Systems engineering* refers to procedures, techniques, and similar aspects to implement a design, analogous to construction. *Artificial intelligence* refers to any attempt to mimic human intelligence with machine logic. *Cybernetics* means the process by which a machine or organism "learns" by analyzing the feedback it receives as it performs its functions, with the implied assumption that it is programmed to do so. *Heuristics* describes trial-and-error learning. An *algorithm* is a segment of logic that will generate one or more answers based on input and rules for processing that input.

Forms of automation. These terms have been defined arbitrarily for use in this book. A *physical system* is synonymous with robotics. An *electronic substitution system* includes computers but also extends to combining computers with additional electronics so that the result can substitute for more traditional robotics (of which UPC code scanning systems are the best- known example). A *psychical system* is one whereby its mere existence and mode of operation suggests the presence of human intelligence and judgment, even when limited to a recorded or programmed voice. This form is usually a facet of one of the other two forms, but it can be created on a stand-alone basis (a recording) and is especially strong when virtual reality is used to project images in space.

COMPUTER SCIENCE

Types of systems. These are common types of systems. A *transaction system* processes specific transactions (e.g., accounting and inventory control). A *management information system (MIS)* is used for the orderly presentation of data in a readable format and is often satellited on a transaction system. A *decision support program*, often called a decision support system or an expert system, goes far beyond MIS by using data to gauge trends, make predictions, evaluate the quantitative advantages and disadvantages of various courses of action, or almost any other structured mental activity. An *executive information system* is something between an MIS and a decision support program and typically consists of on-line management information and a slate of analytical tools (or tool generators) that users can apply to the data as appropriate. *Rule-based* and *pattern-based* models are types of decision support programs. The former relies on a set of rules and direct logical relationships (sometimes called "cookbook" decision making). The latter formerly stressed image patterns but is now evolving into imprecise patterns of logical relationships among facts that can be compared for similarity. *Scientific modeling* employs mathematics or imagery to simulate actual or hypothesized conditions in order to discover causes and relationships, or to make predictions, or to otherwise experiment with options when the use of real elements or actual times is impractical.

Types of processing. *Batch processing* is periodic processing of a number of records or programs without user intervention once activated, whereas *interactive processing* means that the user participates in the processing interactively, typically by entering additional data and/or commands based on intermediate output, or at least having the opportunity to enter additional inquiries. *Realtime* is the measure of how long a user intervention takes to execute.

Robotics. Many physical robots mimic a human arm and hand, in which case the *manipulator* is the arm and the *effector* is the hand. The *control device* is its mechanical "brain," and *articulation* refers to the versatility or flexibility of the robot. A *nonservo* robot means that it can only do what it is programmed to do without respect to subsequent effects. By contrast, *servo-programmable* means that stimuli or reactions will cause the robot to change its response cybernetically, either on a one-time basis or by modifying its programming.

Integrations. These terms describe various methods of getting two or more independent systems to work together. The definitions used in this book are arbitrary, but they adhere to a scale ranging from a lesser to greater degree of relationship. *Linkage* means that two or more systems remain essentially independent while sending and receiving information between or among themselves. An *interface* links existing systems to exchange data and perhaps software to the point that the separate systems become interdependent although they still retain their identities. An *integration* is an interface carried to the point of an alloy or merger wherein the components no longer have any independent standing except for physical separation of any terminals or nodes. A *database integration* is a logical if not a physical merger (or consolidated library) of the databases from separate systems, leaving the programmed applications somewhat more independent. *Standardization* means limiting the type of hardware, operating systems, languages, etc., that can be used within a organization. It is a not an integration per se, but it often facilitates the other forms. *Emulation* is hardware (typically a circuit board added to a computer) or software that effects translation of data and programming from one system to another in order to achieve linkage.

HARDWARE

Types of computers. For the most part, these terms describe different "sizes" of computers. A *supercomputer* has the greatest capability and costs upward of ten million dollars, sometimes more. Less than 400 of them exist. *Mainframes* are the mainstay of commercial systems and cost $500,000 to several million dollars. A *minicomputer* (frequently called a "mini") is a miniature mainframe (more so than a "super" desktop) that costs in the range of $25,000 to $300,000 and does not normally require the operating staff that mainframes need. A *microcomputer* or *PC* is either a *desktop* or *portable computer* priced in the $1,000 to $10,000 range. When networked to access common data or software, it is often called a *workstation*. The computer to which workstations are linked is often called a *server*. *Laptops* and *notebooks* are portable computers (the former term having fallen into disuse as they grow smaller and lighter). *Palmtops* are even smaller portables, typically weighing between one and two pounds, which can be held in one's hand while being operated, though the emphasis is on maximum portability rather than how they are held.

Computer innards. The *central processing unit* is the heart of any computer. It accepts input (from many sources), carries out programmed instructions, and directs output (to many destinations). *Registers* are small memory segments that are incorporated into the CPU to hold, for example, the next instruction to be executed. *Random access memory (RAM)*, also called *operating memory*, temporarily holds software and active files, from which instructions and data are copied into the registers for execution or for the temporary recording of interim results within a sequence of calculations. *Read only memory (ROM)* means instructions that are permanently recorded and hence can be read only. However, some versions of ROM can be reprogrammed (called EPROM, for Erasable Programmable ROM).

Storage media. All these terms refer to "permanent" storage of software, files, and data. *Storage memory* (or *secondary memory*) is the generic term. *Disk* is the generic term for *hard disk*, which is built into a computer, and *floppy disk*, which is removable (although some hard disks are also removable). An *optical disk* substitutes optical technology for magnetism and occupies much less space per bit of information stored. *Tape* is used for sequential file storage (rarely with PCs), and a *tape cartridge* is a fast tape device used for back-up copies of software and files. A *punchcard* (or *punchtape*) substitutes paper, cardboard, plastic, or other visibly written material (in the form of visible holes or slits) for magnetic or other media. However, these punch-type media are seldom used beyond a few residual robotic applications. *On-line memory* means that the storage device is immediately available to the computer. *Off-line memory* means that a system or operator must first link the device to the computer in some way before it can be accessed.

COMMUNICATIONS and NETWORKS

General communications terms. *Communications* is a generic term that refers to the method used for exchange of information among elements in a system. *Network* is an electrical or electronic form of communications that links multiple computers and terminals (or telephones) together. *Transmission density* is the measure of how many bits per second (*baud* or *baud rate*) can be transmitted over a line. *Distributive processing* describes how processing and data storage are subdivided among units in a network. *Modems* convert digital data to and from modulated data for transmission over ordinary telephone lines. A *digital network* eliminates the need for modulation and typically offers much higher transmission density. A *protocol* is software that controls traffic in a network, and *packets* are segments of messages subdivided for transmission.

Types of networks. A *wide-area network* serves a geographical region or larger and may be owned and used by a single organization, but more commonly by a service company leasing lines or charging for time to various users. A *local-area network* is usually one installed to effect communications among specified computer terminals at one location. The configurations of networks vary. The *star network* has a central or main computer through which all traffic is routed. A *bus network* routes traffic typically, but not always, in a circuit through many terminals. A *token-ring network* is similar to a bus network except that the circuit passes just outside of each terminal, with a path from the circuit to each terminal. Each messages is given special headers (the token), which is then checked by each terminal as it passes by. Note, however, that wide-area networks almost always have compound configurations.

INPUT and OUTPUT

Nonautomated input. *Manual input* is a generic term meaning emphasis on the user typing data in order to enter it into a computer or program. *Keyboard* input means direct key-press-to-computer input. Early computers required that the keyboard input first be transcribed to a punchcard, which was then fed into a computer. A *mouse* is a small external device that substitutes for the cursor and arrow keys on the keyboard.

Automated input. These are methods of bypassing or reducing the role of a human in entering data into a computer. *Optical character recognition (OCR)* translates printed characters by way of pattern recognition into digital data, while *Neural OCR (NOCR)* uses both pattern recognition and code-breaking logic to do the same with handwriting. A *scanner* translates a document into a raster image. The *Uniform Product Code* is a system of vertical lines of specified thickness representing digits that can be read by a laser scanner and converted to digital data. A *magnetic character reader* is the equivalent of OCR for characters recorded in magnetic ink. It reads the magnetic rather than the visual pattern. *Voice recognition* translates patterns of sound waves into digital data. *Pen computing* combines NOCR with scribing on an electronic tablet to convert handwriting to digital data. This technique can substitute for a mouse. Virtually all forms of storage media can be used as input (and output).

Output. *Output* is the result of processing. Typically, output is directed to a television-like *monitor,* or to a *printer,* both of which can take many forms. Output is also frequently directed to a database. *Multimedia* means that the output affects at least two senses, commonly sight and sound.

Types of printers. A *font printer* is essentially a typewriter controlled by a computer and uses a daisy wheel or other hard font to press preformed characters on paper through a ribbon. A *dot-matrix printer* forms characters by controlling a vertical column of pins that strikes the paper through a ribbon while the head moves horizontally. An *ink-jet printer* substitutes jets of ink for the pins and eliminates the ribbon. A *laser printer* operates like a photocopier, except that the input is an electronic bitstream rather than a physical document. An *array printer* is any printer that prints more than one character at a time, usually an entire line or an entire page. In effect, it is a set of printer heads arrayed in parallel.

DATA and DATABASES

Types of databases by access. A *direct* or *random-access file* lets a user access any record in the file without accessing any other record, whereas a *sequential file* can only be accessed in sequence from the first record until the record sought is found (although new records can be appended to the end). A *view* is an access to selected fields from records in a file and may include new fields of data generated from existing data in the file.

Types of databases by structure. These terms describe three common formats for databases. A *hierarchical database* has a main file, with all subordinate files accessed by linking data in that file to other files tiered below it. A *network database* is a variation on the hierarchical model. The user can enter it at different points and proceed up or down along several paths. A *relational* *database* places all of its files on the same level under tight logical criteria but with minimum formal linkage. The linking (relating) is done by applications programming.

File structure. These terms describe the logical hierarchy of record files. A *character* is a byte of data, one or more of which comprise a *field*, such as "Social Security number." A *record* is a set of fields of information pertaining to one individual or unit. One or more records comprise a *file*. One or more files, normally related in a logical sense, comprise a *database*.

Data structure. A *bit* is the smallest unit of information and can have only two values: 0 or 1. A *byte* is a set of bits (commonly 8). A *word* is a set of bytes (commonly 4). *Binary data* is a way of storing numbers to facilitate making calculations (usually in a half-word, word, or dual-word), whereas *character data* is the subdivision of data into its constituent symbols, letters, or digits, each of which is stored in one byte. *Text data* is a string of character data, usually without any prescribed length.

Data correctness. These terms are not standardized, but they run parallel with common definitions in test and measurement science. *Validity* means that the data on file represents what it purports to represent. *Reliability* means that the data recorded is the same as the data that was entered (a problem in some networks). *Accuracy* refers to the precision of the data (e.g., so-and-so many decimal places of accuracy). *Legal range of values* means the range of values that may be recorded in a specific field. Any value outside this range is inherently invalid. A *compatibility check* compares data entered with data already on file when there is a logical relationship between them.

SOFTWARE and PROGRAMMING

General software terms. *Software* is a generic term used for all instructions written to control or make use of a computer or robot. *Programming* is the act of writing software, and *programming languages* are the means of writing it. *Procedural language* refers to language that is closer in form to the way a computer operates. *Object-oriented language*, by contrast, can be written with the objective of the program foremost in view. *Higher level languages* edge toward the object-oriented form. However, some professionals restrict the meaning of *object oriented* to a specific programming technique that more closely links instructions and databases. See also *programming levels*.

Types of software. *Systems software* refers to programs that control the computer, including operation of various input and output devices. By contrast, *applications software* is software written to make use of the computer to meet user requirements. An *operating system* is a specific form of systems software that is central to the operation of a computer, whereas *utilities* can vary from specialized software to simplify the use of operating software, to application-level routines that are used by different applications programs, to emulations for linkage among separate systems.

Programming levels. *Machine language* is the language that computers use directly. It consists solely of strings of zeros and ones, or their equivalent. *Assembler* is a barely readable version of machine language. A *third-generation language* employs cryptic but understandable commands that a *compiler* later converts (as a set) to assembler (which then converts it to machine language). An *interpreter* works like a compiler except that it converts and executes one line of code or instruction at a time. *Natural language* is a variation on third-generation languages that more closely approaches conversational English (and is sometimes called a *fourth-generation language*), while so-called *fifth-generation software* uses automation to facilitate the development of other software, often in the form of an interactive decision support program that prompts the user for specifications rather than detailed logic. *Code* is a generic term that refers to any program in any language. This term was indeed an accurate description of machine language programming when that was the only way to control a computer. *Pseudo code* (occasionally one word) is a structured way of drafting lines of programming in the vernacular before translating them into actual code.

Fifth-generation software. *Productivity software* is software (e.g., word processors and spreadsheets) that has a menu-driven or a key-driven (or both) array of practical utilities. This lets the user concentrate on applications. However, many professionals are reluctant to categorize productivity software as fifth generation. *Proprietary software* is highly specialized productivity software designed for explicit purposes and is usually ready-to-run. *Program generators* are, in effect, decision support programs that build programs based on interaction with the user. *Computer assisted software engineering (CASE)* uses programs, such as schedulers and partially automated testers, to support the development of (usually) large systems. However, the dividing line between program generators and computer assisted software engineering is growing thin.

Subprograms. *Subprogram* is a generic term for *subroutine* and *function*. A subroutine is a segment of code called by a higher (hierarchically) segment. It accepts data, processes it, and returns answers (or writes them to a file). By contrast, a *function* returns only one answer and can be used like a command in a higher segment of the program rather than being formally called like a subroutine. A *module* is typically a subprogram or set of subprograms stored in a separate file (and which requires additional programming steps to activate).

IMAGE PROCESSING

General image processing terms. *Image processing* is the storage of documents as images rather than as text. A *folder* is the electronic equivalent of a paper folder of documents. A *pixel* (or *pel*) is an abbreviation for "picture element" and is the display unit of an image, analogous to a dot on a dot-matrix printer. *Resolution* refers to the number of pixels per unit of length (and lines per unit of height) that a scanner reads or an output device displays. A *raster image* is captured as an image, whereas a *vector image* is one that is generated by software (e.g., a graph in a spreadsheet). A *compression/decompression algorithm* is a logical technique for reducing the amount of data it takes to store or retrieve an image record, usually by recording any changes to succeeding lines of pixels rather than every pixel on every line. *Fax*, which stands for facsimile, means the transmission of an image record over a network rather than to a storage medium, though both can occur in sequence. *Virtual reality* is a vector image, usually a dynamic one, that mimics phenomena or a person to the point at which the artificiality is immaterial for the purpose intended. A *hologram* (or *holograph*) is an image that gives the appearance of three dimensions. It may be printed on a physically flat medium or projected into space.

Types of image records. These terms refer to raster images. *Bi-level* (occasionally one word) reduces a document to a series of so many dots per line and then records each one as either on or off (i.e., light or dark). The color used is immaterial. *Graytone* (or *greytone*), by contrast, registers each pixel as a shade of one color, not necessarily gray. A *color image* is in effect an overlaid three-part graytone image, with each part representing one of the three primary colors. A *bitstream* describes the raster image when it is being transmitted, vaguely analogous to a text file.

Software

Each of the four programs described in this section illustrates a major theme in this book. All four are available through Internet as a single package with a shell menu. The programs were written in *Microsoft Professional Basic 7.0* but will run in *QuickBasic*. The package includes both compiled programs and ASCII source listings for experimentation. The source listings, of course, can be read directly into any version of *Professional Basic* or *QuickBasic*, noting that the abbreviated version of *QuickBasic* that comes with DOS 5.0 and later cannot compile programs. It can run them only on a slower, interpreted basis. Note also that these programs are samplers intended to illustrate a point or principle, not to provide comprehensive, all-inclusive models.*

Invasion of privacy (*Huxley*). This program—named after Aldous Huxley—will likely raise a few eyebrows, as it will demonstrate just how easy it is to amass—and abuse—information on anyone, simply by drawing on linked databases and statistical inference techniques. This is especially troublesome as DNA digital "fingerprints" begin to work themselves into various databases, not to mention responses to ethical questions that some doctors now ask their patients.

The national budget (*Collapse*). This program depicts the national budget, especially the metastasizing national debt and why essentially very little can or

---

* To obtain a copy of these programs (in compiled, ready-to-run form), send an IBM-formatted 3.5-inch disk and self-addressed, stamped mailer to the author at Pima Community College, Department of Computer Science, 2202 W. Anklam Road, Tucson, AZ 85709. The files are *not* available via Internet at this time.

will be done about it before it eventually causes the economy to collapse. *Collapse* draws on some concepts in econometrics but relies more intensely on the empirical budgetary data of the last twelve years. The model does not predict when the collapse will occur, only that the debt has passed its point of critical mass and can no longer be controlled, at least not given the way a democracy operates. A nation cannot borrow to infinity. The program also depicts the per capita share of the debt in terms of the fraction of the population that has any significant disposable income.

Computer-assisted learning program for ethics (*Ethics*). This program presents the user with three options on what should be done about the growing problems with automation. From a larger perspective, this program suggests that if computer-assisted learning can be utilized for ethics, it can be adapted to any subject. However, while this program is about as objective as possible, the user is warned that it could be reprogrammed with a bias.

Automation in genetics (*Oparin*). This program was named for the Russian biologist A. I. Oparin and, as mentioned in note 14, Chapter 1, the genetics and evolution program written by Dr. Thomas S. Ray (a plant biologist at the University of Delaware) was based on algebraic algorithms. *Oparin* demonstrates that physical arrangement is the only factor necessary to effect the evolutionary process. That is to say, arrangement *is* the basis of genetic programming, not just a mathematical model.

Suggested Reading

In excess of a million books and articles have been written on automation and computer science. If 99 percent of them are considered too technical for this book, that still leaves ten thousand worth reading. Hence the short list here cannot do justice to that library; it can only emphasize a few key points, namely (a) advanced applications of automation, especially in so-called artificial intelligence, (b) the fact that the use of automation is expanding exponentially (and the reasons why), (c) educational applications, and (d) ethical issues related to man versus machine.

* * *

Andriole, Stephen J., and Gerald W. Hopple, editors. *Defense Applications of Artificial Intelligence: Progress and Prospects*. Lexington, Massachusetts: Lexington Books, 1988. No single use of automation has more diverse requirements and opportunities. Thus, notwithstanding its focus, this book provides as good an overview of decision support programs and systems.

Barlett, Donald L., and James B. Steele. *America: What Went Wrong?* Kansas City, Missouri: Andrews and McMeel, 1992. This thoroughly researched book demonstrates clearly why the middle class in America is shrinking, the principal reasons being the substitution of service jobs for manufacturing and the vast manipulations of company stock and ownership common to Wall Street, both of which depend heavily on automation.

Berry, Dianne, and Anna Hart, editors. *Expert Systems: Human Issues*. Cambridge, Massachusetts: MIT Press, 1990. This book probes the line that should exist between decision support programs and human responsibility.

BloomBecker, Buck. *Spectacular Computer Crimes*. Homewood, Illinois: Dow-Jones-Irwin, 1990. BloomBecker directs the National Center for Computer Crime Data. His book offers case studies and psychological profiles of perpetrators.

Burke, James. *Connections*. Boston: Little, Brown and Company, 1978. This book, which was made into a Public Broadcasting System television series, amply illustrates the relationships among most aspects of science and technology, and therefore how automation was a natural outcome of general progress.

Burnham, David. *The Rise of the Computer State*. New York: Random House, 1983 [with a foreword by Walter Cronkite]. As the title implies, this analysis narrates how state and federal agencies have steadily developed a mantle of authority to amass and use automated information on citizens and organizations, and how this trend has been consistently upheld by the courts, especially the U.S. Supreme Court. Attempts by the legislatures to reverse it have seldom amounted to more than a delay. The book also explains why this has occurred.

Business Week: The Information Revolution. May 18, 1994. The underlying theme of this special issue is that automation has more or less integrated itself into society, and especially business, at large.

Business Week: The Quality Imperative. October 25, 1991, especially Evan I. Schwartz, "Turning Software from a Black Art into a Science," 80–81. This special issue explains why programming has come of age in the business world.

Cherbuck, David. "Computers' New Frontier," *Forbes*, November 26, 1990, 257–264. The *cover* for this cover story stated "Don't Dump Your Computer Stocks: Image Processing Will Expand the Market Explosively in the Nineties."

Dejoie, Roy, George Fowler, and David Paradice, editors. *Ethical Issues in Information Systems*. Boston: Boyd & Fraser Publishing Company, 1991. This is one of the best collection of articles and essays on this subject. Of special importance are James Rachels, "Why Privacy is Important," 110–117 and Arthur Miller, "Computers and Privacy," 118–133.

Ferris, Timothy, editor. *The World Treasury of Physics, Astronomy, and Mathematics*. Boston: Little, Brown and Company, 1991, especially the following three articles: (a) Lewis Thomas, "Computers," 475–477, (b) John von Neumann, "The Computer and the Brain," 478–491, and (c) Alan Turing, "Can a Machine Think?," 492–519.

Freedman, Warren. *The Right to Privacy in the Computer Age*. New York: Quorum Books, 1987. This book is an extensive review of the legal right to privacy in light of intrusions arising from computerized databases and electronic surveillance. It is based almost entirely on case law.

Girifalco, Louis A. "The Dynamics of Technological Change," *The Wharton Magazine*, Fall 1982. Girifalco demonstrates the discontinuities, cycles, and other nonlinear aspects of technological development. His thesis is that technology sputters along until it reaches a kind of critical mass, when it mushrooms.

Jaki, Stanley L. *Brain, Mind and Computers*. South Bend, Indiana: Gateway Editions, 1969. Jaki was one of the few writers that traced artificial intelligence to its roots in Ramon Lull's *Ars Magna* (1303).

Johnson, Deborah G. *Computer Ethics*. Englewood Cliffs, New Jersey: Prentice Hall, 1985. Written by an ethicist rather than a computer professional, and somewhat academic in scope, this is still one of the most comprehensive books on the subject of ethics related to automation.

Koestler, Arthur. *The Ghost in the Machine*. New York: The Macmillan Company, 1967. Koestler posited that man was a fluke in the evolutionary process and that science should find some sort of pill to bring him in line with other animals. This was a seminal work and perhaps contributed to the emphasis in psychiatry on psychoactive drugs. (The book is included in this list only to illustrate the extent to which some analysts want to reduce mankind to some sort of controlled benign robots.)

Lasch, Christopher. *The True and Only Heaven. Progress and Its Critics*. New York: W. W. Norton, 1990. The author argued that the most important values worth tending are exemplified by a working class whose influence is being gradually eroded by large corporations and automation.

Levitan, Karen B., editor. *Government Infostructures: A Guide to the Networks of Information Resources and Technologies at Federal, State, and Local Levels*. Westport, CT: Greenwood Press, 1990. If the reader has any doubts as to the massive extent of government information networks and their expanding reach, this book will eliminate them.

Liebowitz, Jay, editor. *Expert Systems for Business and Management*. Englewood Cliffs, New Jersey: Yourdon Press, 1990. This is a good representative sample of operational decision support programs.

Marshall, Ray, and Marc Tucker. *Thinking for a Living*. New York: Basic Books, 1992. The authors point out that the educational environment in the United States aims at rote and is inadequate for dealing with the ramifications of technology, especially automation.

Milgram, Stanley. *Obedience to Authority: An Experimental View*. New York: Harper Colophon Books, 1974. This well-known research established that most people are prone to carry out orders, no matter how despicable, if they are issued by those perceived as having authority. The application to automation is obvious.

Moravec, Hans. *Mind Children: The Future of Robot and Human Intelligence*. Cambridge, Massachusetts: Harvard University Press, 1988. This is another thoughtful book on the problems that are likely to arise as programming grows more sophisticated.

Morris, Anne, editor. *Application of Expert Systems in Libraries and Information Centers*. London: Bowler Scur, 1992. The applications in this field have progressed extensively, at least among a few leaders.

Oz, Effy. *Ethics for the Information Age*. Dubuque, Iowa: Wm. C. Brown, 1993. This case-study textbook is one of the first books to examine all of the ethical issues associated with automation, though it does not quite come to grips with the exponentially increasing magnitude of them.

Penrose, Roger. *The Emperor's New Mind: Concerning Computers, Minds, and the Laws of Physics*. Oxford: Oxford University Press, 1989. Taking the scenic route through virtually the whole of physics, Penrose argues that no machine can ever fully replicate a human being, although that safeguard has little to do with the excesses of automation. Much of the text is overly technical, but readers can skip over these sections without losing sight of the main theme.

Perry, Nancy J. "Computers Come of Age in Class," *Fortune Special Issue*, 1990, 72–78. See also Rogers, Michael, "MTV, IBM, Tennyson and You," *Newsweek Special Issue*, Fall/Winter 1990, 50–52; and Toch, Timothy, "Wired for Learning," *U.S. News & World Report*, October 28, 1991, 76–79. These articles depict the potential for computer-assisted instruction in public schools.

Plant, Richard E. *Knowledge-Based Systems in Agriculture*. New York: Mc-Graw-Hill, 1991. This good account of agricultural-based systems also explains how decision support systems are developed in general.

Postman, Neil. *Technopoly: The Surrender of Culture to Technology*. New York, Alfred E. Knopf, 1992. Postman argued that culture is shaped by technology more than it relies on it. As such, this supports the argument that automation, as perhaps the ultimate technology, will have an overbearing affect on society.

Sieber, Ulrich. *The International Handbook on Computer Crime: Computer-Related Economic Crime and the Infringements of Privacy*. New York: John Wiley & Sons, 1988. The long title is self-explanatory, and in general this book includes more than enough hard evidence and data on these crimes and abuses.

Sochurek, Howard. "Medicine's New Vision," *National Geographic*, January 1987, 2–41. See also Ward, Fred, "Images for the Computer Age," *National Geographic*, June 1989, 719–751. These two articles graphically illustrate the power of automation applied to constructive objectives.

Time Special Issue: Beyond the Year 2000, Fall 1992, especially the article by Michael D. Lemonick, "Tomorrow's Lesson: Learn or Perish." This issue also goes a long way to illustrating the extent to which automation permeates almost all aspects of business and life in general.

Toffler, Alvin. *PowerShift*. New York: Bantam Books, 1990. This is the third volume in Toffler's trilogy (the other two were *Future Shock* and *Third Wave*). He posits that success in the future depends on instant communications and dissemination of data, but he recognizes the need for free expression and personal growth in this otherwise stifling situation.

von Neumann, John. *The Computer and the Brain*. New Haven, Connecticut: Yale University Press, 1958. Although this book was compiled thirty-five years ago as von Neumann was dying from cancer, it remains a valid treatise on the relationship of automation and cerebral physiology.

Wagman, Morton. *Computer Psychotherapy Systems. Theory and Research Foundations*. New York: Gordon and Breach Science Publishers, 1988. This book is an eye opener on how far automated systems have evolved in the subjective fields of psychiatry, psychology, and personality assessment. It is also a good general description of decision support programs.

Weston, Alan F., editor. *Information Technology in a Democracy*. Cambridge, Massachusetts: Harvard University Press, 1971. Although compiled more than twenty years ago, this remains one of the best anthologies on computer ethics available, especially the essays by Cornelius E. Gallagher ("Computing Power in Real Time," 214–221) and Harold L. Wilensky ("The Road from Information to Knowledge," 277–286).

Wiener, Norbert. *Cybernetic or Control and Communications in the Animal and the Machine*, 2nd edition. New York: John Wiley & Sons, 1961. [The original 1948 edition was published by MIT press.] This seminal work described, among other things, how machine logic learns and reprograms itself based on the parallel process used by organisms. However, the sweep of the book also pokes into most of the nooks and crannies of information theory in general. Wiener is generally credited with creating the term *cybernetics*.

_____. *God and Golem, Inc.* Cambridge, Massachusetts: MIT Press, 1964. Wiener died just as this short book was published. Its profundity touches upon many of the issues central to ethical problems in automation and exemplifies the idea that when a true scholar writes his spiritual last will and testament, he brightens the insight of others without diminishing the reputation of his own.

Notes

CHAPTER 1

1. The Castilian spelling of his name is Raimundo Lulio, and later authors used the same title for different purposes. Frances Bacon came to despise the *Ars Magna*, but Liebnitz praised it as the harbinger of a "universal algebra" (i.e., a unified theory of all science and knowledge).

2. John of Calabria is credited with developing the first programmed loom. His designs were improved upon by Bouchon, Falcon, and Jacques de Vaucanson. Jacquard's later improvement was not all that profound, but it was critical. Earlier models used scrolls or a fixed number of cards on a belt to activate the pins on a drum over which the belt or scroll passed (like a piano roll player). Jacquard's modification—making the number and type of cards variable—was analogous to the difference between printing by etched blocks, which goes back millenniums, to printing by movable type. Thus for similar reasons Johannes Gutenberg is generally credited with inventing the printing press, whereas in reality, he developed movable—programmable—type. James Burke's *Connections* (Chapter 4 in that book) provides a good account of this aspect in the history of technology.

3. Her feat was even more remarkable than it appears, because (a) the machine was never built, (b) she was only twenty-seven at the time and beset by personal problems (among them adultery and losing a small fortune betting on horse races), and (c) the opportunities for women of the day to write for scientific journals were rare. The photograph of Babbage's apparatus (actually a reproduction) frequently seen in textbooks is his earlier "differential machine" and was the forerunner of geared machines that could multiply, divide, and even find square roots. He never built his "analytical machine" because he always started on the design of an improved model before the current one was completed.

During that period of development, Babbage traveled to Italy, where he lectured on his machine at a number of universities. At one of them, Dr. Luigi Frederico Menabrea took extensive notes and made drawings, which he then published in a French journal. Menabrea's paper was republished in Richard Taylor's journal *Scientific Memoirs* (1843), translated by Ada Lovelace. She added a series of seven extensive notes (labeled A through G), which collectively comprise the first treatise on programming. These notes (which were reviewed in some detail in Joan Baum, *The Calculating Passion of Ada Bryon*, Archon Books, 1986, 1, 67–83) were so prescient that a century later, Alan Turing, working at Bletchley Park on the Colossus computer, found them to be the best reference on the subject available. Mrs. Lovelace has been duly honored for this by having the programming language Ada (a registered trademark of the Department of Defense) named after her.

4. See the previous note. The quotation is from Ada Lovelace's note A. It is also quoted in David Burnham, *The Rise of the Computer State* (New York: Random House, 1983), 5.

5. Peter Rentzepis, a chemistry professor at the University of California, Irvine, developed an optical storage device the size of a sugar cube that holds 6.5 trillion bits of information, which equates to approximately 800 billion characters (*The New York Times*, September 1, 1991, I43). Processing trillions of instructions per second is easily done by mounting a thousand or so miniature central processing chips in parallel.

6. Taking advantage of terrain to enhance defensive positions also contributes to this favorable (from the defender's perspective) ratio. Hence there is some justification for the remark of a battalion commander overheard in World War II: "They've got me surrounded again, those poor bastards!"

7. An even more dramatic incident occurred at Rorke's Drift (a river ford) in South Africa in 1879. Eighty English soldiers, half of them recovering from wounds and sickness, held out against numerous murderous charges by four thousand Zulu warriors. This battle was portrayed in the popular film *Zulu* (1964). The heroic defense resulted in the award of eleven Victoria Crosses (the equivalent of the Medal of Honor), but no amount of heroism by itself can account for that victory against all odds. The defenders had to rely on the advantages of interior lines, though they were probably not aware of it at the time.

8. It is true that virtually all of the charges were subsequently dropped, but this was not due to any lack of thorough investigation.

9. The inventors, Jack S. Kilby and Robert N. Noyce, received the first annual Draper award by the National Academy of Engineering for their achievement. Noyce died shortly after the award.

10. In nuclear power reactors, the idea is to produce an arrangement that fissions exactly on a one-for-one basis. To achieve this, early models used graphite control rods to absorb excess neutrons before they triggered a chain reaction. As the control rods were slowly pulled out, the rate of fission picked up until it reached one-for-one. Had the rods been pulled out further, a violent nuclear reaction would have occurred. Today more sophisticated mechanisms are used, but the principle is the same. Furthermore, critical mass also depends on the specific type of material. The more radioactive the element or isotope, the less mass that is required. But the rate of fission in some isotopes is so low that it is impossible to sustain a chain reaction no matter how many tons of it are amassed.

11. Catastrophe theory, which is more science than theory, studies the phenomenon of sudden or radical change and uses topology (what is sometimes called "rubber-sheet" geometry) to plot the effects. It is not quite the same thing as the science of chaos. Chaos studies the behavior of independent or nonlinear elements

when that behavior does not fall into neat patterns predictable by equations, though one may argue that catastrophe is a special case of chaos theory.

12. The basic mechanics and process were deduced by the Russian biologist A. I. Oparin in *The Origin of Life on Earth* (1928). This book was largely ignored until the 1960s.

13. This idea is not original. It is known as the *anthropic principle* and was formalized by the British physicist Brandon Carter. He posited that the universe must have been designed with certain properties in mind that enabled life to develop amid the chaos.

14. The program was written by Dr. Thomas S. Ray, a plant biologist at the University of Delaware, and won a $15,000 prize from IBM (*The New York Times*, August 27, 1991, C1). On page C8 of the same issue, the *Times* also mentioned that John von Neumann had conceived of a similar if more abstract model in the early 1940s.

15. Jonathan Miller, *The Body in Question* (New York: Random House, 1978), 203–212. There is no way to prove Miller's conjecture, but he pointed out that many other scientific discoveries also coincided with development of engineering applications. Incidentally, Harvey published his thesis *De Motu Cordis* in 1628. It gained academic respectability after a mere twenty-five years, lightning speed by most standards of scientific discovery (although he was soundly condemned by his colleagues in the interim).

16. A recent introductory textbook written by Professor Alan Lightman at the Massachusetts Institute of Technology stresses just four principles. Two of them are the first and second laws of thermodynamics. Lightman points out the influence of these principles on such diverse nonphysicists as Immanuel Kant, Edgar Allan Poe, Vladimir Nabokov, and Henry Adams (Connie Leslie, "From the Lab to the Library," *Newsweek*, December 7, 1992, 58). The other two principles covered are relativity and the dual wave-particle nature of subatomic particles, neither of which has much practical bearing on other sciences. For example, a spacecraft would have to attain a speed of approximately 93,744,000 miles per hour before the passage of time (its internal molecular beat) slowed by 1 percent.

17. This modification is the theoretical significance of relativity. Relativity means that the mass of an object is relative to its velocity (while its width decreases and the passage of time slows). However, any increase in mass would violate the principle of conservation of mass. The only way to preclude this is to assume that some of the energy expended to accelerate the object is converted to mass and added to it, like a tax.

The relativistic equations were first posited by Hendrik Antoon Lorentz in 1895 in his book *Versuch einer Theorie der elektrischen und optischen Erscheinungen in bewegren Körpern* [*Theory of Electrical and Optical Phenomena in Moving Bodies*], Leiden, sections 89–92. He later derived them more formally in a 1904 paper "Electromagnetic Phenomena in a System Moving with any Velocity less than that of Light" (*Proceedings of the Academy of Amsterdam*, 6, 1904). Einstein then derived the same equations a year later, albeit using a different set of assumptions ("On the Electrodynamics of Moving Bodies," *Annalen der Physik*, 17, 1905). A few months later, he recognized the mass problem and wrote a brief supplement (two pages) published in the same journal ("Does the Inertia of a Body Depend upon its

Energy-Content?"). It was from an equation in this paper that the famed $e = mc^2$ was later derived. Interestingly and according to one of his biographers (Ronald Clark), Einstein regarded Lorentz as the greatest physicist in this century.

18. The third law of thermodynamics is greatly misunderstood principles. The original law concerned only substances at near absolute zero in temperature, positing that some reactions at those temperatures were fully reversible, and hence the second law of increasing disorder did not apply. In time, this law evolved by intellectual osmosis into the general concept that nature could reverse the process of entropy. No formal proof for this exists, but even a cursory review of evolution and genetics demonstrates that it must be true. For while every organism must eventually die, it reproduce itself beforehand and usually in ever increasing numbers.

19. Paul Saffo, "The Trend Toward Connectivity Brings the PC Revolution Full Circle," *PC Computing*, November 1992, 92.

20. *The Washington Post*, May 17, 1993, business section, 5.

21. At times, even this safety net seems weak. The *GenBank* database at the National Center for Biotechnology Information (National Institutes of Health) has been used many times to solve major problems that were seemingly beyond man's ability to solve (Newsweek, September 5, 1994, 64), while Todd Wipke's *Invention* software (University of California) is quite capable of inventing new molecules that no human ever thought of.

22. Daniel Boorstin, *The Discovers* (New York, Random House, 1983), 408–412.

23. James R. Newman, editor, *The World of Mathematics*, volume 1 (New York: Simon & Schuster, 1956), 277.

24. *The New York Times*, September 7, 1994, D1.

25. *The New York Times*, August 27, 1993, B9.

26. "What Price Privacy," *Consumer Reports*, May 1991, 356–360.

CHAPTER 2

1. Alan M. Turing, "On Computable Numbers, with an Application to the *Entscheidungs* Problem," *Proceedings: London Mathematical Society*, vol. 42, 1937, 230–265. A correction was printed in vol 43, 544–546.

2. In practice, numbers intended for mathematical computation are usually stored in a variation of the one-byte-per-digit format. Typically, four or eight bytes are joined in what is sometimes called a word. In a thirty-two bit word, numbers up to 2,147,483,647 can be stored (i.e., all possible combinations of thirty-one bits), leaving the thirty-second bit to indicate whether the number is positive or negative. However, that is not exactly how negative numbers are represented. Instead, the bits are reversed, but the effect is the same in the sense that the last bit is always turned off for positive numbers and on for negative numbers. For larger numbers, the choice is between longer words or approximation. In the latter, only the first so-and-so many digits of a number are recorded and then multiplied by some power of ten (positive or negative) to put the decimal point in the right place. The word is then divided and used to store both the significant digits (called the *base* or *mantissa*) and the power (usually called the *exponent*). Normally, program instructions

must be written so that the computer is told which form is being used, or else erroneous answers will be generated.

3. In the base-2 system that computers use, it is also necessary to add the quantity 1 to the result before the correct answer is obtained.

4. Most chips have circuits that perform multiplication and division directly.

5. Military applications provided an impetus for this, not because of cost savings but because the problem of repair under battlefield conditions by personnel with less than adequate electronic skill can be bypassed. The cost is higher, but it is a choice between maintaining critical equipment or having none at all for unacceptable periods of time.

6. The machine, known as Technasonic Weight-Talker III, is made by the Technasonic Corporation and retails for $119 as of this writing.

7. Paulette Selmi et al., "Computer-Administered Cognitive-Behavioral Therapy for Depression," *American Journal of Psychiatry*, January 1990, 51–56. The study was part of Selmi's doctoral dissertation, which relied on thirty-six patients, twelve per group. One group received traditional therapy, a second the computer-based version, and the third none at all. The first two groups progressed equally well; the third, poorly.

8. This categorization is not standard in any sense of the word. The author developed it in *Strategy, Systems, and Integrations* (Tab Books, 1990) as an analytical tool to evaluate the problems of linking existing systems.

9. Ross Perot was the chairman of EDS, but apparently he and General Motors did not get along well. GM bought his interest for $700 million.

10. The Open Standards Interface Architecture agreement categorizes the seven levels as (1) physical compatibility, (2) reliability, (3) packet length, (4) pacing, (5) synchronization, (6) formatting, and (7) accessibility. Thirteen parties signed the agreement, including virtually all of the major computer and software vendors.

11. For obvious reasons, the Social Security Administration keeps track of numbers that have been used more than once. The Internal Revenue Service and the recordskeeping functions for military personnel and veterans are also mindful of this situation, but few other organizations are concerned.

12. Number of dependents refers to the number of individuals dependent on a another individual for their sustenance. But whether those dependents can be claimed as exemptions on income tax returns depends on many factors. For example, grown children living at their parents' home cannot as a rule (there are exceptions) be claimed as exemptions on income tax.

13. John Schwartz, "The Highway to the Future," *Newsweek*, January 13, 1992, 56–57. See also "Eyes of the Future," *Newsweek*, May 31, 1993, which highlighted interactive automation with massive databases.

14. There is a third way, usually called a network configuration. The idea is to arrange the data in several different intersecting hierarchies so that it is convenient for more than one user. This is done by linking data fields that logically radiate in several directions, somewhat like a house with three main doors and therefore several different traffic patterns. But because major changes are extremely difficult to make, this design has fallen into disuse.

15. The concept of relational databases has grown into a subfield within computer science. There are five degrees of adherence to strict formatting rules, called

degrees of normalization (although the first two are inadequate to achieve the intent). Some practitioners admit that on occasion the two highest levels can prove too exquisite for the circumstances.

16. In a compression algorithm, the first line of dots is recorded dot for dot. After that, each succeeding line records only the changes to the previous line. In many documents, there is very little change between most pairs of lines. However, for pictures and photographs, this algorithm often increases the storage required. Other algorithms are available to compress these kind of images, but there is usually some loss of definition.

17. Using algorithms analogous to code-breaking programs, a technique known as neural optical character recognition (NOCR) can translate handwriting into digital text. However, the accuracy varies and is poor with small samples. To be sure, NOCR technology is improving, but when high accuracy is needed it would still require time-consuming and expensive human comparison of the handwriting with the text output.

18. This technology was envisioned more than thirty years ago. The problem was both bulk and cost. The only readily available medium to record image data was the magnetic disk, and workstation terminals cost hundreds of thousands of dollars. In the intervening three decades, optical disk technology reduced the bulkiness to negligible dimensions, while hardware technology drove the cost of the workstation down to $10,000, often less.

19. The experiment was conducted in Ohio during 1992 (for the 1991 tax year), and in practice the technique is not that much different from systems that allow users to query the status of their checking accounts or any specific check by telephone. Interactive recorded instruction directs the account holder to enter the necessary information via buttons on a touch-tone phone.

20. When business documents are used in court, the two general criteria are that (a) they are the best evidence available, and (b) the documents submitted are typical of the normal course of business. In most instances of commercial image processing, both conditions are automatically met. Furthermore, the use of so-called WORM (Write Once Read Many) optical disks, combined with some intricate control algorithms, makes it almost impossible to modify an image document without leaving a tell-tale signature.

21. The key is the existence of registers in a central processing unit. These operate at extremely high speeds. Assembler programming lets the programmer make maximum use of these registers, whereas most higher level languages swap data in and out of registers more than necessary. However, the popular programming language known as C lets the programmer control the registers directly.

22. Originally, almost all programming languages were written in English. This has changed, and they now exist in more than thirty languages.

23. More commonly, these programs are called decision support *systems*. This book substitutes the word *program* for *system*, because they do not or should not be considered a system until the user and the exercise of human judgment is included.

24. The name *Pluto* was chosen in honor of Percival Lowell, the first two letters being the same as his initials, though Lowell had predicted that the "missing" planet would be heavier by at least two orders of magnitude compared to Pluto's actual weight.

CHAPTER 3

1. Alan Turing, "Can a Machine Think?" in Timothy Ferris, *The World Treasury of Physics, Astronomy, and Mathematics* (Boston: Little, Brown and Company, 1991), 492–519. The original article appeared in *Mind*, published in 1950 by Oxford University Press.

2. The case originated in Mount Rainier, Maryland, just outside the city limits of Washington, D.C. The boy (it was not a girl as in the novel, but a similar case in Earling, Iowa, in 1927, did involve a girl) lived at the corner of 33rd Street and Bunker Hill Road. (Later the house burned down and was never replaced, so it is now the only vacant lot in the general area.) In late 1948, he was brought to Saint Louis to be with relatives. When his condition worsened, he was taken to the Alexian Brothers Hospital at 3933 South Broadway. At the time, it was a male-only hospital with a large staff of Brothers who were also registered nurses. The exorcism was performed in the rectory immediately around the corner from one of the two psychiatric floors. It took approximately seven weeks, presided over by Father William S. Bowdern, S.J., St. Louis University. No one was killed, but a few arms and noses were broken, and Father Bowdern lost between forty and fifty pounds during the ordeal. Furthermore, there was nothing in the boy's medical records that remotely presaged this condition. To this day he has not the slightest recollection of what occurred, and there have been no relapses.

3. "Golem," *Encyclopaedia Britannica*, vol. 5, 1992, 348. In ancient Israel, it was (and still is) considered an offense against God to utter His name, and hence only a sort of acronym was used. However, the name could be spelled out by separate characters if they were not physically joined.

4. They were *Haunted Summer, Gothic,* and *Frankenstein: The True Story*.

5. The woman's name was Trisha Marshall. The baby, named David Marshall, will be a ward of California's Child Protective Services, as are his three brothers and sisters. The cost of bringing the embryo to term under these conditions has been estimated at between $250,000 and $500,000. A similar case occurred in 1982, when a pregnant woman who died from a brain hemorrhage was kept "alive" for fifty-three days until the fetus reached viability. A third case happened in Germany in 1992, involving a pregnant woman (Marion Ploch) who was killed in an automobile accident. Although the doctors were unable to stabilize the cadaver, the case attracted far more media attention than did Marshall.

6. Norbert Wiener, *Cybernetics or Control and Communications in the Animal and the Machine,* (Cambridge: MIT Press, 1948), 37.

7. For example, see Roy Dejoie, George Fowler, and David Paradice, editors, *Ethical Issues in Information Systems* (Boston: Boyd & Fraser Publishing Company, 1991), especially Chapter 5, "Ethical Issues in Artificial Intelligence."

8. Mary W. Shelley, *Frankenstein, or the Modern Prometheus* (Philadelphia: Courage Books, 1987), 9. Incidentally, the creature becomes the most erudite and eloquent of the characters in the story. He is a truly sensitive individual who initially desires nothing more than to do good and be loved (his one request of his creator is to make him a mate). However, when his horrible deformities repel all those with whom he comes in contact, his dominant feelings turn to rage and vengeance, and he kills his maker's younger brother, next his best friend, and then on

their wedding night his bride. He also provokes his maker into pursuing him to the point of death. Throughout the tale, many of the powerful themes exemplified in the *Great Books of the Western World* are brought to fore, incorporating a number of them by name in the dialogue.

9. See note 3 in chapter 1. She made this point in note G.

10. Franz G. Alexander and Sheldon T. Selesnick, *The History of Psychiatry* (New York: Harper & Row, Publishers, 1966), 14.

11. These ideas are brought out in his essay *What is Life?*, which is combined with another essay *Mind and Matter*, republished by Cambridge University Press in 1967. Schrödinger makes allowances for the incredible complexity of the human organism, but in no case does he acknowledge spiritual attributes that can redirect the course of events.

12. As early as 1960, researchers realized this. Confronted with inadequate commercial hardware and software, they created what was known as LISP (for LISt Processing) machines. Some of these machines are still in use to today, but modern hardware and languages can do the job more efficiently.

CHAPTER 4

1. See "The Premier 100: The Most Effective Users of Information Systems," second section of *ComputerWorld*, October 8, 1990. The AMR corporation spent $1,244 million on automation in the preceding year (11.46 percent of gross revenues), while Boeing spent $1,164 million (5.74 percent of gross revenues). The average was $274 million (median = $158 million), which means that these one hundred companies spent in excess of $27 billion dollars on automation.

2. In practice, open architecture does not always live up to its billing, despite the intent. The technical details of any image system can be rather aggravating even when a customer continues with the same vendor. By analogy, there is a kind of open architecture among various General Motors products. Some parts are interchangeable but there is a limit, and each division publishes its own shop manuals.

3. This division of American Express is located in Arizona. The story was reported by Bob Christman, "American Express Improves Its Aim," in the *Arizona Daily Star*, March 15, 1989. A variation on this occurs frequently by advertisers who place ads in newsmagazines only in issues mailed to certain sectors of the country, or alternatively to ZIP codes in which the residents have certain income ranges.

4. James I. Cash et al., *Corporate Information Systems Management*, 2nd edition, 146–162.

5. For example, Philip Elmer-Dewitt, "Dream Machines," *Time Special Issue*, Fall 1992, 39–41. Also see Loraine O'Connell, "Computerized Sex is no Longer Just Science Fiction," *Orlando Sentinel*, April 3, 1991.

6. "The Quality Imperative," *Business Week*, the special issue of October 25, 1991.

7. For example, see Jay Mathews, "The Cost of Quality," *Newsweek*, September 7, 1992, 48–49.

8. "Introducing 'Robodoc,'" *Newsweek*, November 23, 1992, 86. As of this writing, Robodoc, developed under the aegis of surgeons, has been approved by the Federal Drug Administration only for experimental use.

9. Much debate surrounds this point. Perhaps the strongest indicator is the number of office visits per year, which has reached approximately 700 million. This means that the average family of four made twelve visits to doctors (in 1993). If every one of those visits was medically necessary, the United States would be a very sick country in ways more than economic. Even the most conservative providers readily admit that between 25 and 33 percent of all procedures are unnecessary (at a cost approaching $150 billion per year).

10. Reinhold Messner, "At My Limit—I Climb Everest Alone," *National Geographic*, October 1981, 552–566. Messner was the first of two individuals (the second was Jerry Kukuczka) to climb all fourteen peaks over 8,000 meters (roughly 26,000 feet), always without supplementary oxygen.

11. Norman Boucher, *PC Computing*, October 1988, 42.

12. Passive sonar only "listens" and therefore does not give away the position of the tracker to a submarine. By contrast, active sonar emits waves that can reveal the source location and permit the submarine to fire antiship missiles (from underwater) before it becomes the target. Many other factors play into these decisions, far too many for most humans to cope with using paper and pencil or rules of thumb. Hence the utility of decision support programs.

13. For example, see Leo S. Mackay, Jr., "Naval Aviation, Information, and the Future," lead article in *Naval War College Review*, Spring 1992, 7–19.

14. The two most prevalent DoD systems here are the Computer-Aided Acquisition and Logistics Support Program (CALS) and the Engineering Data Management Information and Control System (EDMICS). See William G. Beagley, "CALS and Its Impact," *Inform*, October 1990, 12–14, and Gregory E. Kaebnick, "EDMICS Goes to Work," in the same issue, 15–18.

15. *The New York Times*, September 23, 1992. The Birth Defects Prevention Act was introduced in Congress in July of 1992, but it did not include provision for a national registry. The need stems from the fact that between 10 and 64 percent of different kinds of birth defects go unrecorded on birth certificates.

16. *The Washington Post*, September 6, 1992, A19.

17. "Computerized Billing Planned for Medicare," *The New York Times*, October 20, 1992, A8, A16.

18. The Brady Bill was subsequently enacted in 1993, but not the child-abuse database.

19. The program was aired on CBS, NBC, and PBS, on September 4, 1992, at 10 P.M. EDT. ABC aired it two nights later at the same hour. According to *People* magazine ("Not Scared, Not Silent," September 7, 1992, 48–49), the insurance and financial services company USAA funded the program.

20. Many commentaries have been written on this. For example, see John R. Wilke, "Lotus Product Spurs Fears About Privacy," *The Wall Street Journal*, November 13, 1990, B1, B9. Also see "LOTUS Cancels *Marketplace*," *Lotus*, March 1991, 20. One of the main figures behind these national marketing and other databases is Mitch Kapor, who founded Lotus Development Corporation and has been active with the Electronic Frontier Foundation.

21. *The Washington Post*, January 2, 1993, E1.

22. M. Scott Peck, *People of the Lie* (New York: Simon & Schuster, 1983), 255–273. Interestingly, the first line of this book advises that it is a dangerous one.

23. Another point to note is that at least 7 percent (and likely higher) of male psychiatrists have sexually abused one or more patients, as reported in Nanette Gantrell et al., "Psychiatrist-Patient Sexual Contact: Results of a National Survey, I: Prevalence," *American Journal of Psychiatry*, 1986, 143:1126-1131. At the time there were 27,875 psychiatrists in practice, the vast majority male. Every fifth one was sent a questionnaire. A total of 1,314 were returned. Of the 1,057 returns from males, 7.1 percent admitted to having sexual relationships with patients, notwithstanding that the profession universally regards such conduct as unethical. Of the female psychiatrists, 3.1 percent made the same admission but in almost every case it was as a patient with her own therapist. For a more comprehensive look at this problem, see Glen O. Gabbard, editor, *Sexual Exploitation in Professional Relationships* (Washington, D.C.: American Psychiatric Press, 1989).

24. *Newsweek*, November 16, 1992, 63. The company, located in Kansas City (Kansas), was Kansas City PM, a Jiffy Lube franchise. The incentives included both cash and tuition assistance at college.

25. For an insightful commentary on this situation, see Gary S. Becker, "How the Disabilities Act Will Cripple Business," *Business Week*, September 14, 1992.

26. Paul Taylor, "'Dow Jones of the National Soul' Sours," *The Washington Post*, January 16, 1992, A25.

27. *Newsweek*, July 30, 1990, 64.

28. The most widely read are Revi Batra, *Surviving the Great Depression of 1990* (New York: Dell, 1987), and Harry Figgie, Jr. & Gerald Swanson, *Bankruptcy 1995: The Coming Collapse of America and How to Stop It*, revised edition (Boston: Little, Brown and Company, 1993). Batra predicted a recession by 1990 that would persist and eventually lead into a deep depression. As of this writing, the first part of his prediction proved correct, while the current minor economic improvement doesn't seem to have had much effect on the core problems. Batra also correctly predicted the demise of communism about two years before it happened. These, of course, are the two books that have been on *The New York Times* best seller list.

29. According to *Statistical Abstract of the United States: 1992* (U.S. Bureau of the Census), 326 (table 509), 112,136,000 personal income tax returns were filed in 1989. Assuming that 10 percent of the population did not file a return that year (mostly retired persons living on small incomes and/or Social Security who may not need to file), the adjusted gross income at the sixtieth percentile was approximately $22,000. After taxes, that would net between $16,500 and $20,500. That isn't very far above the official poverty level, and furthermore only about a fourth of this large group had a net income exceeding that level.

30. Draft Commission Findings, Bipartisan Committee on Entitlement and Tax Reform (Senator J. Robert Kerrey [D-Nebraska] chairman), July 12, 1994, 1. The entire federal budget will be required to fund entitlements and debt service by 2012, and hence taxes must be increased at least by 85 percent to cover other existing federal spending, or even further if the deficit financing is to be reduced.

31. National Research Council Committee on Law and Justice, *Understanding and Preventing Violence* (Washington, D.C.: National Academy Press, 1992), which indicated a figure of six million. A subsequent survey by the Department of Justice increased that figure to 10,900,000. The discrepancy was attributed to *unreported* violent crimes.

32. James Patterson and Peter Kim, *The Day America Told the Truth* (New York: Plume/Truman Talley Books, 1992). The authors are respectively the chairman and the director of research for the J. Walter Thompson advertising agency. The survey was based on interviews and on-site questionnaires of two thousand individuals chosen at random. The questionnaire contained 1,800 questions.

33. For example, see Ray Marshall and Marc Tucker, *Thinking for a Living* (New York, Basic Books, 1992). The authors argue that corporate America still relies on the outdated scientific management theories of F. W. Taylor, circa 1910, who developed the well-known time-motion studies technique. As such, he regarded employees as little more than robots.

34. "Your Hamburger: 41,000 Regulations," *U.S. News & World Report*, February 1980, 64. As of 1980, there were also 111,000 relevant precedent-setting court cases.

35. Cornelius E. Gallagher, "Computing Power in Real Time," in Alan F. Westin, editor, *Information Technology in a Democracy* (Cambridge: Harvard University Press, 1971), 214.

36. Abba Eban, "Camp David—The Unfinished Business," *Foreign Affairs*, Winter 1978.

CHAPTER 5

1. One of the best references on this is Jay Liebowitz, editor, *Expert Systems for Business and Management* (Englewood Cliffs, New Jersey: Yourdon Press, 1990).

2. G. Vedder, "Expert Systems for Crisis Management: The HIT Project," in ibid., 235–244.

3. The current product is called GroupSystems V and includes such modules as a Meeting Manager, Electronic (i.e., networked) Brainstorming, Policy Review, and even Group Write. The anonymity this system offers apparently serves to bring out more participation. See also David Kirkpatrick, "Here Comes the Payoff from PCs," *Fortune*, March 23, 1992.

4. Thomas Teal, "Service Comes First: an Interview with USAA's Robert F. McDermott," *Harvard Business Review*, September–October 1991, 116–127, and "USAA Premium Treatment," special edition of *Business Week*, October 1991, 124. USAA also insures grown dependents of its policyholders through a wholly owned subsidiary. It is the fifth largest auto insurer in the United States and the fourth largest home insurer. Its banks, however, are open to all customers. As for the low recognition level, USAA readily admitted this is a recent edition of its magazine *Aide*, October 1992, 11–14. McDermott retired in 1993 after twenty-five years with USAA.

5. The general rule is that tax on the gain of the former home is postponed if a new residence is purchased at a price higher than the adjusted sales price of the former, and provided that the new home goes to settlement within two years, plus or minus, from the date of settlement on the former home. Taxpayers can also take a one-time exemption of the tax on the gain (up to $125,000) if they are over fifty-five years of age and lived in the house at issue as their primary residence for three of the immediately preceding five years.

6. Solicitation number IRS-91-001. The length of this solicitation was nearly a thousand pages, and more than nine hundred questions were raised. The IRS conducted a pilot study that ran for nearly eight years and published a "lessons learned" document that was highly critical of its own mistakes. The estimate of the eventual cost can be found in U.S. General Accounting Office pamphlet GAO/OCG-93-24TR *Internal Revenue Service Issues*, December 1992, 8.

7. Ulrich Sieber, *The International Handbook on Computer Crime* (New York: John Wiley & Sons, 1987), 4.

8. The amount for the companies would probably be less because the Postal Service offers discounts on postage for mass mailings that meet certain presorted criteria.

9. This proposition is open to question. During World War II, some momentous decisions were made by parties conferring thousands of miles apart. For example, the counterinvasion of the Philippines was moved up by two months based on a message sent from Admiral Halsey (upon discovering less Japanese force than earlier presumed) to MacArthur, who then radioed the Joint Chiefs of Staff, who were attending the second Quebec Conference at the time. Approval was forthcoming within an hour.

10. *The New York Times*, May 7, 1993, D7. The business of distributing information electronically is already a $10 billion a year business.

11. For example, see "Use of An Artificial Neural Network for the Diagnosis of Myocardial Infarction," *Annals of Internal Medicine*, December 1991, 843–848. The system was developed by Dr. William Baxt at the University of California, San Diego. Without it, emergency room doctors detected heart attacks about 78 percent of the time. With the system, the rate increased to 97 percent.

12. Five of the best known packages are *Turbo Tax* (ChipSoft), *Tax Cut* (Meca Software), *J. K. Lasser's Your Income Tax* (Simon & Schuster), *Personal Tax Preparer* (Parsons Technology), and *MacInTax* (Softview). The list prices range from $49 to $99, and the packages often sell at a discount.

13. *Arizona Daily Star*, June 18, 1993, A4. This program subsequently received a major grant from the Ford Foundation for expansion throughout the state of Arizona.

14. At one time, Barnes and Noble advertised the unit for a lease fee of $11.95 per month.

CHAPTER 6

1. For example, see "A Confederation of Glitches," *Newsweek*, September 21, 1992, 70–72.

2. The models had to be submitted on what is sometimes called a three-dimensional spreadsheet (Solicitation No. IRS-91-001, J-IV-1 through J-IV-8, and J-XV-1 through J-XV-7).

3. The students were all adult learners with ten to fifteen year's work experience. Almost without exception, the reactions were lively and sometimes livid. The model presented was essentially as depicted here, although a different illustration was used. Only a few believed that anything could be done to more than slow the

rate by which such a system would be implemented. This was not formal research, and even if it were, the results would still be merely opinion. Yet the near total resignation to the idea indicates just how compliant the population will likely be with respect to the increasing pervasiveness of automation.

4. *St. Louis Post-Dispatch*, January 11, 1993, BP3; and a telephone conversation between Mr. Bloy and the author on January 25, 1993. The name of the company is Infomax. The service is called "Find People Fast." It is located at 4600 Chippewa, Suite 244, St. Louis, Missouri 63116. The telephone number for customer service is 1-800-829-1807. The Salvation Army offers a similar service for a fee of $10, and it will conduct research in depth if necessary. However, it will release the information only if the person sought (if alive) consents to it.

5. For details, see note 2 in chapter 13. Before 1994, the tax credit came in three parts: (a) the basic benefit for all individuals that met income and dependents criteria; (b) a supplementary allowance for health insurance, payable if the individual in fact pays for health insurance; and (c) a special one-time benefit for a dependent child born during the tax year (in addition to the added exemption). The new singular credit roughly equals the sum of these three former credits (adjusted for inflation).

6. Robert J. Samuelson, "Nationalize Health Care," *Newsweek*, October 26, 1992, 56. In dollar terms, the federal government directly paid $282.2 billion of the $666.2 billion dollar health care bill (42.4 percent) in 1990, according to National Center for Health Statistics, *Health United States, 1991* (Hyattsville, Maryland, Public Health Service, 1992), 274 (table 120).

7. George D. Lundberg, "National Health Care Reform: The Aura of Inevitability Intensifies," *Journal of the American Medical Association*, May 13, 1992, 2521–2524.

8. *Health United States, 1991*, 221, 229, 235.

9. Geoffrey H. Wood and Robert F. Shriver, *Computer Crime: Techniques, Prevention* (Rolling Meadows, Illinois: Bankers Publishing Company, 1989).

10. "Report Cites U.S. Inaction on Bank Cases," *The Washington Post*, October 19, 1992, A7. Also see the four-part series on insurance fraud prepared by the Associated Press and printed in many papers, circa April 1992.

11. General Accounting Office Special Report GAO/HR-93-13, *Internal Revenue Service Receivables*, December 1992. The figure cited in this publication is $111 billion (for 1991). The IRS estimate for 1994 is $127 billion.

12. "The FBI is Shifting 50 Agents to Health Care Fraud Duties in 12 Cities," *The Washington Post*, March 24, 1992, *Health Magazine*, 5. Although some estimates of health care fraud exceed $50 billion, it is not all concentrated in Medicare and Medicaid. The majority of it still occurs with private insurers. But if the government enacts a single-payer health care funding system, then the entire lot would fall to the government.

13. IRS Publication 17, 320.

14. "Inspector General Under Fire," *Modern Maturity*, April–May 1991, 7. The American Medical Association tried unsuccessfully to get then President Bush to fire Kusserow.

15. Carol J. Loomis, "An Annual Report for the Federal Government," *Fortune*, May 1973, 193–199, 322, 324.

16. When a few widowed Civil War veterans reached the age of ninety or so, they often remarried a very young family friend for the purpose of providing her with a lifetime pension. In turn, a few of these child welfare-brides have lived into *their* nineties and as such are still entitled to pensions. Interestingly, when General Omar Bradley assumed the directorship of the Veteran's Administration in 1945, he was surprised to learn that pensions were still being paid to widows from the War of 1812.

17. If 85 percent of the benefit is taxed at the 28 percent rate, it means that the entire benefit is being taxed at 23.8 percent. This would result in a net additional benefit of roughly five or six dollars a month in return for additional lifetime contributions of roughly $150,000 (including the employer's share).

18. Draft Commission Findings, Bipartisan Committee on Entitlement and Tax Reform (Senator J. Robert Kerrey [D-Nebraska] chairman), July 12, 1994. The crucial statement was that "unless benefit growth is reduced or taxes raised, by 2012, projected outlays for entitlements and interest on the national debt will consume all government revenues."

CHAPTER 7

1. For an overview of chaos, see James Gleick, *Chaos: the Making of a New Science* (New York: Viking Press, 1987).

2. Because the separate computers would not be aware of interactions, a separate scanner would be necessary to identify those interactions, compute the results of the interaction, and feed the information back into the affected elemental computers.

3. Bill Moyers, *A World of Ideas II* [interview with Murray Gell-Mann] (New York: Doubleday, 1991), 189.

4. Physics is currently enshrouded in a number of "principles" that claim, among other things, that at the lowest level nature operates on a statistical basis (indeterminacy), and that nothing of the roots of nature can be known with absolute assurance because it is impossible to measure and observe all aspects at the same time (complementarity) due to limitations in the instrumentation itself. Einstein, among others, refused to accept these self-imposed limitations ("God does not play dice with the universe"), but even if nature at root is wishy-washy, a model can be programmed to mimic any statistical function.

5. For example, see Gregg Easterbrook, "A House of Cards," *Newsweek*, June 1, 1992, 24–33, and "Under the Sun—Is our World Warming?" *National Geographic*, October 1990, 66–99, especially 82–83.

6. For a good reference on a wide variety of decision support programs in this field, see Richard E. Pratt, *Knowledge-Based Systems in Agriculture* (New York: McGraw-Hill, 1991).

7. "The Electronic Goddess—Computerizing Bali's Ancient Irrigation Rites," *Newsweek*, March 6, 1989, 50. Stephen Lansing, an anthropologist, and James Kremer, an ecologist (University of Southern California), solve the problem.

8. For example, see Stephen S. Hall, "James Watson and the Search for Biology's 'Holy Grail,'" *Smithsonian*, February 1990, 40–49.

9. "Penicillin From a Screen?" *Newsweek*, September 14, 1992, 58–59.

10. One of the most promising models is being developed at the Federal Reserve Bank in Minneapolis by its Director of Research, Arthur Rodnick, and is funded in part by a grant from the National Science Foundation (Mike Meyers, "Economists Play 3-Year Supercomputer Game," as reported in the *Minneapolis-St. Paul Star Tribune*, June 22, 1989, and reprinted in a large number of other papers at various dates).

11. Almost thirty years ago, Norbert Wiener observed that econometricians were attempting to replicate the mathematical physics of 1850, that is, without questioning the data or how it was obtained (*God and Golem, Inc.*, Cambridge: MIT Press, 1964, 89–91.) This would support the point that money per se is not a primary factor but rather more of an effect.

12. If one assumes that a gross national product that is equal to or less than $500 (or its equivalent) per person per year makes for a penurious economy, then the balance of the world's wealth is indeed concentrated in a few nations. The author calculated this data for a five year period (1986–1990) and published it in *Geopolitics and the Decline of Empire* (Jefferson, NC: McFarland, 1990).

13. These factors were delineated by Alfred Thayer Mahan in the opening treatise within *The Influence of Sea Power Upon History 1660–1783* (Boston: Little, Brown, 1890), 22–88.

CHAPTER 8

1. As discussed in note 9, chapter 4. a large percentage of office visits are medically unnecessary.

2. Hershel Jick, "Drugs—Remarkably Nontoxic," *New England Journal of Medicine*, October 17, 1974, 824–828. Whether the import of this paper still holds after twenty years of new drugs is unknown, but it is not likely. Whatever the flaws of the Federal Drug Administration may be, it adheres to high standards on drug testing. As the Jack article points out, toxicity results primarily from sustained use or abuse, not chemistry per se.

3. For example, see D. I. Bainbridge, "Computer Aided Diagnosis and Negligence," *Medicine, Science, and the Law*, April 30, 1991, 127–136. Bainbridge readily admits that at the moment, the few malpractice claims associated with decision support programs focus on inadequacies in them. Yet as these programs improve and proliferate, the emphasis in malpractice will probably shift to a failure to use them. The logic behind this is that while a doctor is not expected to have a working knowledge of state-of-the-art research, the opposite is true when that art becomes common practice.

4. Earl Ubell, "How Computers are Helping Doctors Treat You Better," *Parade Magazine*, March 13, 1988, 3–7. More scholarly references are available, but the fact that such stories are carried in popular magazines is in itself significant.

5. Nancy Imperiale, "Call Up the Computer; the Doctor's In," *Orlando Sentinel*, January 2, 1992. The program is now available commercially and in all probability it will have been updated and expanded by the time this book is published. See also "On-line Medicine," *U.S. News & World Report*, October 5, 1992, 87.

6. For example, see Morton Wagman, *Computer Psychotherapy Systems. Theory and Research Foundations* (New York: Gordon and Breach Science Publishers, 1988).

7. Ibid., 105–129.

8. For example, see "UA [University of Arizona] Defends Its Low Rate of Graduation," *Arizona Daily Star*, November 18, 1992, A1–A2, based on a survey of twenty-two colleges and universities in the western part of the United States. Graduation rates were correlated directly with average Scholastic Aptitude Test (SAT) scores. Many other sources depict an even grimmer picture.

9. *Outlook 2000*, U.S. Department of Labor, Bureau of Labor Statistics Bulletin 2352, April 1990, 70 (table 3).

10. Leonard S. Cahen and Nikola N. Filby, "The Class Size/Achievement Issue," *Phi Delta Kappan*, March 1979, 492–495, 538ff. The researchers used a meta-analysis technique to alloy the findings from more than a hundred different research papers.

11. "Saving Our Schools," *Business Week*, September 14, 1992, 70–85. The Edison Project is due to open its first set of model schools in 1996, seed-funded by the Whittle Communications Project in the amount of $60 million, with the intent of funding the larger balance by private investment. However, a subsequent lack of anticipated investment funds has caused the Edison project to be scaled back.

12. See "Wired for Learning," *U.S. News & World Report*, October 28, 1991, 76–79.

13. For example, see Arthur Whimbey, *Intelligence Can be Taught* (New York: E. P. Dutton, 1975). This book was based on extensive research, but with rare exceptions the only significant gains made were in early childhood years and were based on developing concentration and logical reasoning skills.

14. Part of this proliferation of knowledge is due to the expansion of colleges with concurrent expansion of faculties. Given the well-known "publish-or-perish" syndrome, exacerbated by the increased emphasis on grantsmanship, these expanded faculties are compelled to add to the pile. Unfortunately, there seems to be a limit to just how far the frontiers of knowledge can be pushed back in a finite period of time. Accordingly, some of this additional "knowledge" has only marginal value at best. Does anybody really need to know the value of π carried out to three million decimal places?

15. The photograph that accompanies this section depicts the library and stadium at the University of Arizona in Tucson. Since 1980, this library dropped from twelfth to twenty-eighth place among all academic/university libraries due primarily to reduced funding (*Arizona Daily Star*, May 10, 1993, A10). Given that the magnanimously funded libraries at Harvard, Stanford, MIT, and the like crowd the top ten, this means that UA's status fell from virtually the top of the heap of the balance by eighteen notches while its stadium gained expensive private "sky boxes" clearly in evidence in the photograph.

16. *Datamation*, November 1, 1988, 122. The Patent Office processes about 125,000 applications a year, with each one requiring reference to an average of 1,600 pages drawn from 27,000,000 pages on file (and rising).

CHAPTER 9

1. *The New York Times*, January 23, 1993, A10. The school was Irving Junior High School. *Time* magazine carried a one-page article that lamented the declining ethics and public indifference (Jon D. Hull, "The Knife in the Book Bag," February 8, 1993, 37). Few other publications did so.

2. Will Durant, *Our Oriental Heritage* (New York: Simon & Schuster, 1935), 48.

3. James Paterson and Peter Kim, *The Day America Told the Truth* (New York: Plume, 1992).

4. Stanley Milgram, *Obedience to Authority: An Experimental View* (New York: Harper Colophon Books [Harper & Row], 1974). The original experiments were reported in *Journal of Abnormal Psychology*, 1963, vol. 67, 317-378.

5. Buck BloomBecker, *Spectacular Computer Crimes* (Homewood, Illinois: Dow Jones-Irwin, 1990), 161-169.

6. Alfred T. Mahan, *Naval Strategy* (Boston: Little, Brown & Company, 1918), 289.

CHAPTER 10

1. For example, see Bruce Sterling, *The Hacker Crackdown* (New York, Bantam, 1992).

2. Wanton negligence is reckless or heedless disregard for the rights of others with a high probability of inflicting damage or loss consequent to one's actions or decisions. Driving at 67 miles per hour (assuming a 65 miles-per-hour speed limit) on an interstate highway on a clear day in light traffic may be speeding but hardly reckless driving. By contrast, driving at 90 miles per hour, under any circumstances, can be so construed, even if no one is injured or no property damage occurs. See *Craig v. Stagner*, 159 Tenn. 511, 19 S.W.2d 234, 236.

3. Geoffrey H. Wood and Robert F. Shriver, *Computer Crime: Techniques, Prevention* (Rolling Meadows, Illinois: Bankers Publishing Company, 1989), 5. However, the loss *per incident* is much higher in damage cases than with theft. The average money theft (in 1988) was about $10,500; the average program theft, $55,200; and the average systems damage, $93,600.

4. Ibid., 1-3.

5. *Black's Law Dictionary* defines fraud as "an intentional perversion of truth for the purpose of inducing another in reliance upon it to part with some valuable thing belonging to him or to surrender a legal right" (*Brainerd Dispatch Newspaper Co. v. Crow Wing County*, 196 Minn. 194, 264 N.W. 779, 780). The definition of embezzlement is stated as "the fraudulent appropriation of property by a person to whom it has been intrusted or to whose hands it has lawfully come." In short, the only difference is that the Big Bad Wolf was fraudulent in deceiving Little Red Riding Hood as to his true character, whereas had he been appointed her guardian before eating her up, it would have been embezzlement.

6. Ulrich Sieber, *The International Handbook on Computer Crime* (New York: John Wiley & Sons, 1988), 11.

7. See Clifford Stoll, *The Cuckoo's Egg* (New York: Doubleday, 1989). The investigation culminated with the arrest of a computer programmer in West Germany on charges of espionage.

8. The author knows of at least one such company from personal experience. The credit card company rectified the matter by immediately crediting the account and then back-billing the company. An aside from the staffer indicated that this was not the first instance with that company. That company did not contest the matter.

9. Ken Wasch, "Don't Copy that Floppy," *Syllabus*, November–December 1992, 11–12. Wasch is the executive director of Software Publishers Association.

10. See Sieber, *The International Handbook on Computer Crime*, 12–15; also Wood and Shriver, *Computer Crime: Techniques, Prevention*, 4–5.

11. Meta-analysis means "the logical integration of data and findings from separate but related research in order to infer more generalized findings." These meta-findings seldom constitute rigorous scientific proof, but to the extent that they consistently explain the mass of specific but diverse findings, they come to be regarded as significant and as new directions for further research. The findings on teaching effectiveness versus class size (Chapter 8, Figure 18) are a case in point.

12. For example, during World War II, a team of Australian commandoes (in civilian clothes) were caught within Japanese lines and sentenced to death in a military court (essentially as the British spy Major André was during the American Revolutionary War). At the trial, the prosecutor said "With such fine determination they infiltrated into the Japanese area. We do not hesitate to call them real heroes. The valorous spirit of these men reminds us of the daring enterprise of our own men of the Naval Special Attack Corps. The respect the Australian people showed them we must return to those in our presence. When the deed is so heroic, its sublime spirit must be respected and its success or failure becomes a secondary matter" (James Ladd, *Commandoes and Rangers of World War II*, New York: St. Martin's Press, 1978, 228). This was a wartime situation, but practitioners of civil disobedience believe themselves to be fighting a war, and some of them are willing to lay down their life for the cause in which they believe.

13. Buck BloomBecker, *Spectacular Computer Crimes* (Homewood, Illinois: Dow-Jones-Irwin), 1990, 210–220.

14. A virus is a segment of operating system programming that overrides other operating software and either erases data (or software) or overwrites it with meaningless characters.

15. For example, see National Research Council Committee on Law and Justice, *Understanding and Preventing Violence* (Washington, D.C.: National Academy Press, 1992).

16. Again see Sieber, *The International Handbook on Computer Crime*, 29–31; and Wood and Shriver, *Computer Crime: Techniques, Prevention*, 1–10.

CHAPTER 11

1. For example, see Stephen L. Magnum, "Impending Skill Shortages: Where is the Crisis?" *Challenge: The Magazine of Economic Affairs*, September–October 1990, 46–52. The difference between new and replacement jobs is that new jobs are

those added to the labor market, while replacement jobs are those vacated by individuals who retire, change jobs, or die. To the individual seeking work, this difference is moot. To an economist surveying the labor market, it is important. A high replacement-to-new job ratio means that field of work is stagnating and will only grow worse in the long run.

2. Published by Andrews and McMeel (Kansas City), 1992.

3. Published by Norton, 1993. The draft of *Age of Automation* was written before Peterson's book was published.

4. Robert Naylor, Jr., "Reich says the U.S. is spawning new 'anxious class' of workers," *The Washington Post*, August 31, 1994, F1. Reich said that the bulk of the labor pool, actual or potential, was subdividing into three classes: (a) the overclass, (b) the anxious class fearful for their jobs, and (c) the familiar, inner-city underclass. The overclass corresponds with the technocrats; the anxious class, the workers; and the underclass, the absorbers. For obvious reasons, Reich did not dwell on the other two classes—namely, the well-to-do and the retirees.

5. *The Forbes 400*, 1994.

6. Despite tax liability on up to 85 percent of the Social Security benefit, the vast majority of recipients have sufficiently moderate incomes that they pay little if any such tax. Furthermore, virtually all beneficiaries are entitled to a higher standard deduction.

7. The first Social Security recipient (Ida M. Fuller) paid in about $20 and received approximately $22,000 in benefits. Others, especially centenarians, have received a benefit ratio a hundred times their contribution. On the other hand, the estate of an individual who dies just before reaching retirement age, leaving no survivors, will receive nothing except having had a small amount of insurance in force for total disability. In general, current retirees have received considerably more than they contributed, but the vast increases in the FICA tax are changing this picture rapidly.

8. *The New York Times*, March 14, 1993, A18. Additionally, many articles have appeared in recent journals that address the problem of permanent unemployment and the fact that it is cheaper to provide permanent welfare than to create "artificial" jobs. See also the two Steven Prokesch articles in the April 18, 1993 edition of *The New York Times* (A22 and I1); "All Work and No Play," *The Wall Street Journal*, June 4, 1990, supplement, 17; and "Is Europe's Social-Welfare State Headed for the Deathbed?" *Newsweek*, August 23, 1992, 37.

9. Bureau of the Census, *Statistical Abstract of the United States: 1992*, 112th edition, 315 (table 491). Earlier editions provide data prior to 1945.

CHAPTER 12

1. Cornelius E. Gallagher, "Computing Power in Real Time," in Alan F. Westin, editor, *Information Technology in a Democracy* (Cambridge: Harvard University Press, 1971), 220.

2. Ibid., 221.

3. Jane Healy, *Endangered Minds, Why Our Children Don't Think* (New York: Simon & Schuster, 1991). The 20 percent decrease in creativity corresponds, for

example, almost exactly with the decline in Scholastic Aptitude Test (SAT) scores. Also see Larry Woiwode, "Television: The Cyclops That Eats Books," *Imprimis*, February 1992, 1–3. Woiwode's paper has been republished in many newspapers. Also see the George Will column "We'll Never Combat the Epidemic of Violence that Television Engenders," circa April 1993. In it, he mentioned that seven different U.S. and Canadian studies clearly demonstrated the ill effects of prolonged exposure to television.

4. The specific policy advertised is named *Teachers Life Preferred*. Admittedly, the rates for this term insurance are probably the lowest in the country from among companies that consistently earn high ratings for financial stability.

5. As of December 31, 1993, annual statements report $67,483,167,923 for TIAA and $53,618,239,096 for CREF, for a total of $121,101,407,019. Source: *The Participant*, April 1994.

6. "One-stop Shopping for Credit Reports," *Consumer Reports*, December 1992, 745. The company is Credco Inc., which has been selling credit information to business since 1961. All one gets for the $24 is a consolidated report, albeit printed in plain English. If there are any errors, they can only be rectified by writing the bureau(s) directly.

7. Roy P. Basler, ed., *The Collected Works of Abraham Lincoln*, vol. 2 (New Brunswick: Rutgers University Press, 1953), 405–406 [*emphasis in the original*].

8. As described in Anthony Lewis's *Gideon's Trumpet* (Random House, 1964), the defendant was found guilty of burglary but did not have the benefit of a public defender at his trial. He petitioned the Supreme Court on handwritten legal paper. The Court granted the motion and appointed Abe Fortas (later a Supreme Court justice himself for a brief period) as his attorney. As a result, Gideon was acquitted, and the requirement for the state to provide competent defense counsel for the indigent is now well established, although not always carried out in practice.

9. For example, see Joan Schwartz, "How Did They Get My Name," *Newsweek*, June 3, 1991, 40–42. In a 1990 Harris Poll conducted for Equifax (one of the major credit bureaus), 79 percent of the respondents were concerned with threats to privacy, up from 47 percent in 1977.

10. For a commentary on this, see Karen Nussbaum, "Computer Monitoring—A Threat to the Right to Privacy," in Roy Dejoie et al., editors, *Ethical Issues in Information Systems* (Boston: Boyd & Fraser Publishing Co., 1991), 134 –139. An organization known as Computer Professionals for Social Responsibility has done much to publicize the excess of automation, and another organization (9-to-5, located in Cleveland, Ohio), focuses on micromanagement excess.

11. See William Barnhill, "Privacy Invaders," *AARP Bulletin* [American Association of Retired Persons], May 1992, 1. AARP uses information brokers to obtain addresses of individuals turning fifty in order to send them an invitation to join.

12. When an individual is denied credit based on a bad credit report, he or she is entitled to a free copy of that report.

13. *The New York Times*, May 8, 1993, A17.

14. "Vulnerable on All Counts," *Ethical Issues in Information Systems*, 155–166.

15. Kenneth C. Laudon, "Data Quality and Due Process in Large Interorganizational Record Systems," ibid., 140–154.

16. Ibid., 147, 150.

17. For example, see "Data Bank: Public Safeguard or Black List?" *Medical World News*, November 1991, 22–23. Several hundred articles and papers have been published on this matter.

18. Arthur S. Link, editor, *The Papers of Woodrow Wilson*, vol. 21 (Princeton: Princeton University Press, 1976), 70. The speech was given in Chattanooga, Tennessee, on August 31, 1910, before the local chapter of the American Bar Association.

19. Jean Seligmann, "Software for Hard Issues," *Newsweek*, April 27, 1992, 55. See also *The New York Times*, January 1, 1992, A8. The *Apache* program had an accuracy rate of 95 percent, and that was before it was revised.

CHAPTER 13

1. See note 11 for chapter 6, specifically General Accounting Office Special Report HR93-13, *Internal Revenue Service Receivables*.

2. For details, see IRS Publication *1994 1040 Forms and Instructions*, 27–31. The earned income tax is a credit against tax liability that in most cases exceeds that liability more than enough to compensate for the employee's share of the Social Security (FICA) tax and leave some left over. For the 1994 tax year, the taxpayer (single or married) must have at least one dependent child and not have an income more than $23,755 ($25,295 for two or more dependents). Single taxpayers between the ages of twenty-five and sixty-five, with incomes less than $9,000, are entitled to a much smaller credit. Up through an income of $7,750, the credit is 26.3 percent of that income (32.6 percent for more than one dependent child). From $7,750 to $12,000, it is a flat amount: $2,038 ($2,528 for two or more children). From $12,000 to $23,755 ($25,295 for two or more dependents), the credit declines as a linear inverse function to $0. Furthermore, income received from Aid to Families with Dependent Children (AFDC), Medicaid, Social Security, food stamps, low-income housing, and most other welfare programs is not included when calculating total income. Finally, eligible individuals may fill out form W-5 and obtain advanced periodic payments of this credit (up to 60 percent of it). A similar credit exists for elderly citizens (and the totally disabled) who fall within certain income caps, except that Social Security benefits must also fall within a certain level.

3. Dale R. Detlefs and Robert J. Myers, *1992 Guide to Social Security* (Louisville, Kentucky: William M. Mercer, Inc., 1992), 10. Myers was a former Deputy Commissioner of the Social Security Administration and before that its chief actuary for twenty-three years. The government itself goes out of its way to avoid distributing payment/benefit tables, although an individual may submit Form SSA-7004-PC to receive an estimate of benefits.

4. As cited in note 6, chapter 6, specifically: National Center for Health Statistics, *Health United States, 1991* (Hyattsville, Maryland: Public Health Service, 1992), 274.

CHAPTER 14

1. Jerome S. Bruner, "*The Process of Education* Revisited," *Phi Delta Kappan*, September 1971, 18–21. Bruner's original book was intensely academically oriented and made some idealistic assumptions about the goals and aspirations of students. The article cited is, in part, a reappraisal of some of those assumptions.

2. For example, see David L. Clark, Linda S. Lotto, and Martha M. McCarthy, "Factors Associated with Success in Urban Elementary Schools," *Phi Delta Kappan*, March 1980, 467–470. This was a meta-analysis that drew on some 1,200 studies. Many factors beyond the structure of curriculum contributed to success, but of the twelve factors cited, four of them were in this area.

3. The number of employees who are subject to this kind of micromanagement has been estimated at twenty million. In 1993, a law was proposed in Congress (The Privacy for Consumers and Workers Act) to regulate this situation, but it had few teeth in it. It would have only required that employers inform their employees in advance of monitoring and, in the event, the law was not passed. Thus, had the law been passed, it would have meant that the recording apparatus could be left on at all times at negligible expense, regardless of how much information was actually reviewed by managers.

4. Jerome Lawrence and Robert E. Lee, *Inherit the Wind* (New York: Random House, 1955), 83.

5. Asimov included the key points in another nonfiction book entitled *The Complete Robot* (London: Grafton Books, 1983). Both books are frequently cited.

6. For a good survey of the psychoanalytic process, see Karl Menninger, *Theory of Psychoanalytic Technique* (New York: Basic Books, 1958). Harper & Row brought a paperback edition several years later that is still in print.

7. Karen Horney, *Our Inner Conflicts* (New York: W. W. Norton & Company, Inc., 1945), 240 (in the paperback reprint).

8. Interestingly, *Webster's New World Dictionary of the American Language* (New York: World Publishing Company, 1972, 491) defines *existentialism* as being "based on the doctrine that existence takes precedence over essence, and holds that man is totally free and responsible for his acts, and that this responsibility is the source of the dread and anguish that encompass him."

9. For example, see Lucia Solorzano, "What Makes Great Schools Great," *U.S. News & World Report*, August 27, 1984, and Barbara Kantrowitz, "What Kids Need to Know," *Newsweek*, November 2, 1992, 80. The latter describes many of the positive gains made as a result of E. D. Hirsch's book *Cultural Literacy*.

10. A harbinger of this trend occurred in Baltimore when the School Board privatized nine of its 159 schools. A Minneapolis firm, Educational Alternatives, Inc., spent 26.7 million dollars and used 1,100 computers, hiring and training its own interns as teaching aides but in reality as de facto teachers (ostensibly to bypass teaching certification requirements). The results were good enough for the Board to continue with the second year of a five-year contract. See *The Washington Post*, June 20, 1993, C1.

11. Sir William Osler, *A Way of Life and Other Selected Writings* (New York: Dover Publications, 1951), 246.

Index

A. M. Best Company, 155, 170
abortion, 42
accuracy (of data), 195
adding (in a computer), 21
Affymax Research Institute, 98
Aid to Families with Dependent Children (AFDC), 62, 95
AIDS, 60
Alamogordo (New Mexico), 10
Alcott, Louisa May, 68
Alexander, Franz (quoted), 45
algorithm, 190
Allen, Robert, 73
Allen, Woody, 46, 115
Allied Forces (World War II), 100
America: What Went Wrong? (Barlett and Steele), 140
American Association of Retired Persons, 148
American Express Company, 55
American Medical Association, 95, 106
Americans With Disabilities Act of 1991, 60
amniocentesis, 42
amoeba, 11
amyotrophic lateral sclerosis, 25
analytical engine (Babbage), 4, 44
anaphylactic reaction, 125
androids, 6, 15, 41, 178
Animal House (film), 181

Annapolis, Maryland, 181
anti-submarine warfare, 58
anti-trust legislation, 149, 173
Apache (software), 161
Apple Computers, 69, 108
Ars Magna (Lull), 3
articulation (robotics), 191
artificial intelligence, 37, 190
artificial life, 12
Asia, 10, 101
Asian Development Bank, 96
Asimov, Isaac, 42, 178
assembler (programming language), 34, 196
assembly lines, 24, 141
asteroids, 51
Atlas Shrugged (Rand), 59
Attending (software), 106
audit trails, 16, 72
Augusta, Ada (Countess of Lovelace), 4, 44, 104
Austerlitz (battle), 126
automated mail carts, 24
automated teller machines, 131
automation, 2, 46, 48, 52, 56, 63, 74, 86, 117, 125, 130, 161, 164, 185, 188, 190; amelioration of problems, 7; and corporate integrations, 173; and jobs, 5, 7, 139; and obedience to authority, 125; and socioeconomic classes,

About the Author

GEORGE M. HALL teaches Computer Science and Sociology at Pima Community College. He is the author of more than ten books, six on the subject of computer technology, including *Systems, Strategy, and Integration* (1990) and *Image Processing* (1991). His book, *The Fifth Star* was published by Praeger in 1994.

ISBN 0-275-95194-4

90000>

EAN

9 780275 951948

HARDCOVER BAR CODE